SEX ROLES IN TRANSITION

The Changing Dialogues between
Men and Women

SEX ROLES IN TRANSITION

The Changing Dialogues between Men and Women

Fakir M. Sahoo

KALPAZ PUBLICATIONS

DELHI - 110052

SEX ROLES IN TRANSITION

The Changing Dialogues between
Men and Women

Rs. 840

ISBN: 81-7835-244-3

Published in 2004 in India by
Kalpaz Publications
C–30, Satyawati Nagar
Delhi–110 052
E-mail: Kalpaz@hotmail.com

Lasertypesetting by: Varsha Graphics, Delhi
Printed at: Mehra Offset Printers, Delhi

To
F.M. Sahoo's Wife, Reeta
&
S. Sinha's Husband, Abhimanyu

Contents

List of Tables

Preface

Human adaptation and growth is a complex process. The complexity of such process is further increased by the rapidity with which changes are taking place all over the world. The globalization has not only opened up new opportunities, it has also posed challenges for adjustment. In such a scenario, the study of changing sex roles offers immense possibilities.

The present title "Sex Roles in Transition" is our attempt to share behavioural perspectives with readers. Although the review encompasses psychological literature and the investigation pertains to behavioural measures, the major implications are directed to scholars of different persuasions. It is asserted that the broad spectrum of sex role research requires collaborative works that crosscut various disciplines such as political science, sociology, anthropology, management, education, and women studies. The mutual interactions and exchanges at these levels are likely to generate definitive knowledge. The work is intended as a source-book for this purpose.

It is also important to recognize that India is a plural society. The observations and findings may require validation in other parts of India. Such a possibility is more a matter of academic exploration than limitation.

Finally, we hope that the book would be helpful for understanding a very important aspect of our personal life—the search for identity. The continuing exploration of our identity and adaptation would be a worthwhile concern.

Fakir M. Sahoo

Part I
Domains of Divergence

1
Issues of Gender

Gender studies have received research attention from the beginning of the last century. Although there are various forms of differences, gender inequality is considered fundamental in almost all societies. Prior to significant amount of psychological research, developmentalists took lead in this direction and contributed substantially towards the growth of the field.

There is an interesting aspect of this line of research. This is a field where scholars of different persuasions have met and exchanged ideas. This is also an area where theoretical and applied interests have been blended. In addition, the active exploration of this area by feminist groups and individuals has attached social and political significance to the enterprise. Before answering specific questions, it is pertinent to identify fundamental issues.

Framing the Issues

Issues of gender require well-articulated explication. In the past, the only focus was on sex difference. A substantial content of conceptual as well as empirical research has been evinced since Maccoby and Jacklin published their classical book *The Psychology of Sex Difference* in 1974. Although a wealthful body of information is presented in this work, the contemporary changes in the structure of society and human relationship demand a fresh reexamination. Gender issues can appropriately be comprehended within three basic inquiry: the epistemological concerns, question of sex difference, and origin of difference.

The Epistemological Concerns. As indicated earlier, psychological interest in gender issues has varied over time. In the earliest days of publication of journals by the American Psychological Association, there was some interest in gender, but it did not become a widely used variable in psychological research until the mid-1960s. Developmentalists have had a more continuous interest in gender issues than have psychologists working in other areas. There were two reasons for this. First, developmentalists were historically more likely than other researchers to use both male and female subjects in their studies. Second, more women were in child-development-related employment.

However, gender studies have grown in volume in recent years. At the same time, there has been epistemological concern. Is sex differences a myth or a reality? A fundamental question is raised.

The recent postmodernism movements (constructivism and deconstruction) challenge the idea of a single meaning of reality and concern themselves with the way meaning is represented (Hare-Mustin and Marecek, 1988). Constructivism posits that we do not discover reality, we invent it. Our experience does not directly reflect what is "out there" but is an ordering and organizing it. Knowing it is a search for "fitting" ways of behaving and thinking. Rather than passively observing reality, we actively construct the meanings that frame and organize our perceptions and experiences. Thus, our understanding of reality is a representation, that is, a "re-presentation" not a replica of what is "out there". Representations of reality are shared meanings that derive from language, history and culture. Accordingly the idea of accurate representation is a compliment we pay to those beliefs that are successful in helping us to do what we want to do.

Constructivism challenges the scientific tradition of positivism, which holds that reality is fixed and can be observed directly, uninfluenced by the observer. As Heisenberg (1952) has pointed out, a truly objective world, devoid of all subjectivity, would be unobservable. Constructivism also challenges the positivist assumption that it is possible to distinguish facts and values. For constructivists, values and attitudes determine what is taken to be facts. It is not that psychological laws are wrong or useless. Yet, they are explanations based on a set of social conventions (Kuhn, 1962). Thus, positivism seeks facts whereas constructivism identifies assumptions.

Constructivism as a postmodernism development has influenced psychological research. Drawing inspiration from symbolic anthropology, ethnomethodology, and related movements in sociology, constructivist views have also influenced social psychology. From constructivist standpoint, theories of gender take a different flavour.

Constructivism focuses our attention on representation of gender, rather than on gender itself. According to constructivist position, the "real" nature of males and females can not be determined. The very term *gender* illustrates the power of language categories to determine what we know of the world. The use of gender in context other than discussions of grammar is quite recent. Gender was appropriated by American feminist to refer to the social quality of distinctions between the sexes. Gender is used in contrast to terms like sex and sexual differences for the explicit purpose of creating a space in which socially mediated differences can be examined apart from biological differences. We still lack an adequate term for each gender. Male-female has the advantage of including entire life span but it includes biological differences and fails to distinguish humans from other species. Men-women refers to humans, but the term is restrictive to adults. Thus male-female and men-women couplets are used interchangeably to denote the entire life span.

What constitutes a difference is not a simple question. Research that focuses on mean differences may produce one conclusion whereas studies emphasizing range and overlap may produce another conclusion. The size and direction of gender difference in specific behaviours such as aggression and helping behaviour would vary depending on the norms and expectations held for men and women in that society. The very criterion for deciding difference vis-à-vis similarity is a perplexing task.

A stream of psychological research on gender de-emphasizes differences. Most differences between male and females are seen as culturally and historically fluid. Hyde's (1981) meta-analysis of cognitive difference is one such example.

Another source of influence in the task of judging male-female difference has involved feminist psychodynamic theories (Chodorow, 1979). Although these theorists provide varying theories of the origin of sex-differences, they all stress deep-seated and enduring differences between women and men in "core self-structure", identity and relational capacity. Gender differences in psychic structure give rise to cognitive differences (for example, differences in moral reasoning and in organizing knowledge). All these theorists represent differences between men and women as essential, enduring and highly dichotomized.

These two lines of inquiry have led to two widely held but incompatible representation of gender, one that sees few differences between males and females and another that sees profound differences. Both groups of theorists have provided empirical support for their respective positions.

From the standpoint of constructivisim, theories of gender are representation based on social conventions. Such theories embody one or the other of two contrasting biases, *alpha bias* and *beta bias* (Hare-Mustin, 1987). Alpha bias is the tendency to exaggerate differences; beta bias is the tendency to minimize or ignore differences. The alpha-beta distinction is akin to errors in hypothesis testing. In hypothesis testing, alpha or Type 1 error involves reporting a significant difference when it does not exist. Beta or Type II error involves overlooking a significant difference when it does exist. Here the term bias refers not to the probability of "error", but rather to a systematic inclination to emphasize certain aspects of experience and overlook other aspects. This formulation of bias refers to the idea that all knowledge is influenced by the standpoint of the knower.

Alpha Bias versus Beta Bias. Alpha bias is the exaggeration of differences. The view of male and female as different and opposite and thus as having mutually exclusive qualities is shared pan-culturally. Throughout history women have been depicted as the reposition of non-masculine traits, as "otherness". In Bacon's model of science, nature was cast in the image of the female to be studied.

In psychology, alpha bias can be seen most readily in psychoanalytic theories. Freudian theory takes masculinity and male anatomy as the human standard. Femininity and female anatomy are deviations from the standard. The Jungian idea of the animus and anima places the masculine and the feminine in opposition. More recent psychodynamic theories also depict female experience as simply divergent from male experience. For example, Erikson (1964) holds that female identity is predicted on "inner space", a somatic design that "harbours......a biological, psychological and ethical commitment to take care of human infancy" (p.586) and a sensitive indwelling. Male identity is associated with "outer space", which involves intrusiveness, excitement and mobility leading to achievement, political domination and adventure-seeking.

Parson's sex-role theory which dominated the social theories of the 1950s and 1960s also exaggerates male-female difference (Parson & Bales, 1955). The very language of sex role theory powerfully conveys the sense that roles are fixed but dichotomous. It was asserted that men were instrumental and women were expressive; men were task-oriented and women were relationship-oriented. Men's nature suited then for paid work and public life, women were credited with "goodness" for making their own needs secondary to those of the family. Parson believed that separate spheres for men and women were functional in reducing family conflict and in increasing harmony. The role definition Parson put forward became a criterion for distinguishing normal individuals and families from pathological and pathogenic ones.

Alpha inclination to stress difference can also be seen in feminist psychodynamic theories (Chodorow, 1979). Their emphasis on women's special nature and the richness of women's inner experience has been an important resource for cultural feminism. Cultural feminism is a movement within feminism that encourages women's culture, celebrates the special qualities of women and values relation among women as a way to escape sexism of the larger society.

According to Chodorow (1979), boys and girls undergo contrasting experiences of identity formation during their early years under the social arrangement in which women are the exclusive caretakers of infants. She argues that girls' identity is based on similarity and attachment to their mothers. Boys' identity is predicted on difference, separateness and independence. These experiences are thought to result in broad-ranging gender differences in personality structure and psychic needs in adulthood. Women develop a deep-seated motivation to have children, men develop the capacity to participate in the work structure. Although Chodorow bases her psychodynamic theory of personality development on western societies and situations, her observations are considered transcultural features. Her work is taken to assert essential differences between women and men and to view these differences rather than the social structure as the basis for gender roles.

More recently, some critics Glick & Fiske (2001) have pointed out that mass empirical research have identified sexism only with hostility towards women, ignoring the corresponding tendency to place (atleast some) women on a pedestal. These critics term this tendency as *benevolent sexism* and claim that benevolent sexism is a subtle from of prejudice. Both hostile and benevolent sexism are presumed to be "legitimizing ideologies", beliefs that help to justify and maintain gender inequality.

Beta bias, the inclination to ignore or minimize differences, has been prominent in psychological theory. Prior to the 1970s, most generalizations that psychologists made about human behaviour were based on observation of males. The male was the norm against which human behaviour was assumed to represent all experience. Generalizations about human development based only on the male life course represent a partial view of the humanity.

Women and men typically have different access to economic and social resources, and their actions have different social meanings and consequences. Both bias can be seen in recent social policy and legislation that try to provide equal benefits for men and women. Beta bias can also be seen in educational and therapeutic programmes that ignore aspects of the social context. They groom women for personal or professional success by providing training in what are deemed "male" behaviour or skills such as assertiveness, authoritative speech pattern or "male" management styles. Such programmes are based on the assumption that a certain manner of speaking or acting will elicit the same reactions regardless of the sex of the actor.

Beta bias occurs in system approaches to family therapy. The four primary axes along which hierarchies are established in all societies are class, ethno-cultural group membership, gender, and age. Within families, class and group ethno-cultural memberships are constant, but gender and age vary. However, family system theories disregard gender and view generation (that is age) as the central organizing principle in the family. In so doing, they ignore the fact that mothers and fathers, though they may be of same generation, do not necessarily hold comparable power and resource in the family. System theories put forward a neutered representation of family life.

As pointed out earlier, the correctness of alpha position vis-a-vis beta position is difficult to be established. Constructivism plays down such debate. However, it is possible to identify the utility factor. What are the consequences of such positions with respect to representation of gender?

Alpha bias has been the prevailing representation of gender. It has effects on our understanding of gender. The idea of gender as male-female difference has cast masculinity and femininity as opposite poles of continuum of personality. The Terman-Miles M-F personality scale (Terman & Miles, 1936), the femininity scale of the California Personality Inventory (Gough, 1957) and other measures are indicative of this utility. An explicit consequence of alpha bias is the disregard for variability in social position of man vis-à-vis woman. Many differences between men and women are product of their differences in social positions. Men's tendency to reason may stem from the fact that the principles were formulated to protect men's interest. Women's concern with relationship can be understood as the need to please others that arises from a lack of power. Typically those in power advocate rules, discipline, control and rationality, whereas those without power expose relatedness and compassion. Thus, in husband-wife conflicts, husbands call on rules and logic, while wives call on caring. When women are in dominant position, as in parent-child conflicts, they emphasize rules whereas children appeal for sympathy and understanding. Such an observation suggests that these differences can be accounted for by an individual's power position in the social hierarchy rather than by gender.

Feminist psychodynamic theorists assert male-female difference through out life. Critics have challenged that a brief period in early life is responsible for broad-ranging changes in men's and women's lives. Further questions have been raised as to whether patterns in infant care giving are strong enough to influence social transformation. Feminist psychodynamic theory seems to overlook economic condition, social role conditioning and historical change.

Another consequence of alpha bias is the tendency to view men and women as embodying opposite and mutually exclusive traits. Such a dichotomy does not fit with human experience. For example, an overemphasis on male autonomy in home and workplace does not recognize women's contribution. Similarly, women's exclusive role in child rearing ignores the contribution of males.

An important positive consequence of alpha bias in focussing on differences between women and men is that it has allowed some theorists to assert the worth of some "feminine" qualities. This has the positive effect of countering the cultural deviation of women and fostering a valued sense of identity in them. The focus on women's special qualities by some feminists has also prompted such revolution.

Beta bias or minimizing the differences also has consequences for understanding gender. Equal treatment under the law has enabled women to gain greater access to educational and occupational opportunities. It also draws attention away from women's special needs and from differences in power and resources.

In therapy, treating men and women as if they are equal is not always equitable. In marital and family therapy, equal treatment may overlook structural inequality between husband and wife. When the social status and economic resources of the husband exceed those of the wife, one to one bargaining as a strategy to resolve conflicts between partners will not lead to equitable results. "sex-fair" or "gender-neutral" intervention that advocates nonpreferential and nondifferential treatment of women and men to achieve formal equality may inadvertently foster inequality.

Thus, it seems that alpha bias and beta bias have generated some paradoxes. This is understandable in view of the fact that postmodernism accepts randomness, indeterminacy and paradoxes. Constructing gender is a process, not an answer. With this perspective, we have discussed respective empirical extensions and predictable consequences. Since alpha bias is more prominent in contemporary research, it is pertinent to examine psychological research relating to the origin of sex difference.

The Origin of Sex Difference

The study of the origin of sex difference has stimulated a broad spectrum of research traditions. However, the specific origin theories can be grouped into two broad rubrics: evolved disposition versus social roles.

According to evolutionary psychologists, the critical causal path is evolutionary adaptation to psychological differences. Women and men possess sex-specific mechanisms; they differ psychologically and tend to occupy different social roles. On the contrary, the critical causal path, according to social role origin theory, starts from social structure to sex differences. Men and women tend to occupy different social roles and they become psychologically different.

Both of these theories recognize the value of adaptation, both of them convey functionalistic approach. However, evolutionary theory emphasizes the past and early experiences, whereas social role theory stresses proximal and contemporary experiences. A brief description of these theories brings out some salient features.

The Evolved Disposition View. From the standpoint of evolutionary psychology, human sex difference reflects adaptations to the pressure of the differing physical and social environment that impinged on males and females during primeval times (Buss, 1995). The evolutionary psychologists believe that the primitive stage was hunting-gathering status. Males and females faced different adaptive problems as they evolved. The two sexes developed different strategies to cope with survival and growth.

The aspect of evolutionary theory that has been applied most extensively to sex difference is the theory of sexual selection initially proposed by Darwin. In the evolutionary context, it is proposed that sex-typed feature of humans evolved, through male competition and female choice of males. Women constituted the sex that devoted greater efforts to parental investment. They were limited reproductive resources to men. Women were restricted to the number of children, they could propagate during their life time. Men therefore competed for access to women. Women chose their mates from among the available men. Women were selected for their wisdom in choosing males who could provide resources to support parenting efforts. Women's preferences for such men, in turn, produced sexual selection pressures on men to satisfy these criteria.

The concept of sexual selection posits that sex difference in parental investment favoured different strategies for reproductive success for men and women. It also established different adaptive mechanisms governing mating behaviour. It was to the males' advantage to devote a large portion of their time to short-term mating. Women, in contrast, benefitted from devoting a smaller portion of time to short-term mating and a larger portion of their time to long-term mating. It is also argued that men did not have full freedom of knowing paternity owing to concealed fertilization on the part of women. Men appeared to adapt to paternity uncertainty by exerting sexual control over women and developing sexual jealousies and a motive to control women's sexuality.

According to this position, sex difference as psychological disposition arose from differing fitness-related goals of women and men that followed from their contrasting sexual strategies. Men competed with other men for sexual access to women. Men's evolved disposition favoured violence, competition and risk-taking. Women, in contrast, developed inclination for long-term relation with a male who could support family. As a result, men strove to acquire more resources than other men in order to attract women. Women developed preferences for successful and ambitious men who could provide resources.

Evolutionary psychologists assume that ancestral humans had a hunting-gathering socio-economic system. The idea of division of labour in which men hunted and women gathered suggested sex-differentiated pressure linked to survival and reproduction. Such an arrangement favoured men, who were psychologically specialized for hunting and women who were specialized in gathering. This led to differential cognitive skills. Men developed superior spatial skill that followed from hunting activities and women developed superior spatial location memory that followed from gathering.

The evolutionary theory implies the role of various mediating mechanisms. It is assumed that sex-differentiated psychological mechanisms and developmental programmes are "genetic", hereditary or inherited. Their structure design has its characteristics form because of the information in our DNA. Some evolutionary accounts also emphasize that genetic factors trigger biochemical processes that mediate psychological sex differences, especially by means of sex differences in hormone production. Besides, sex-typed evolved mechanisms are translated into behavioural sex differences by various cognitive and affective processes.

Social Structures Theory. A competing origin theory to explain sex difference recognizes the role of social structure in the scheme. It is based on the germinal thesis that women have less power and status than men and control fewer resources. This feature of social structure is indicative of gender hierarchy. In feminist language, it is patriarchy. In addition, women perform more domestic work than men and spend fewer hours in paid employment. Although more and more women are now entering the work force, women are thinly represented in the higher level of organization hierarchies.

The determinants of distribution of men and women into social roles are many and include the biological endowment of men and women. The sex-differentiated physical attributes that influence role occupancy include men's greater size and strength. The greater physical strength gives advantage to men in the context of jobs that demand strenuous physical activity. However, these attributes of men may be less important in post-industrial societies where many jobs are mechanized and less dependent on physical strength. Another physical attribute influencing role distribution is the childbearing and child-rearing activities of women. The obligation of child-care ncecessitates continued absence from work. Although this is not so problematic in countries where there is less birth rate and availability of non-maternal care, stereotypic belief system works against the interest of women.

In general, physical sex difference influences the roles held by men and women. This is further illustrated when men and women are joined in cooperative relationship and establish clear division of labour. The particular character of the activity each sex performs determines its placement in social structure. Historians have indicated that men specialized in activities such as warfare and herding; this brought greater status, power and wealth to men. Women specialized in activities such as housekeeping, child-rearing and sharing; this brought loving appreciation for women. Thus, when sex differences emerged, it clearly favoured men.

The differing distribution of men and women into social roles forms the basis of a social structural meta-theory of sex difference. The first meta-theoretical principle derives from the greater power and status that tends to be associated with male dominated roles. Men's accommodation to roles with greater power and status produces more dominant behaviour; women's accommodation to roles with lesser power and status produces more subordinate behaviour. Dominant behaviour is controlling, assertive, relatively directive and autocratic and may involve sexual control. Subordinate behaviour is more compliant to social pressures less aggressive, more cooperative, and may involve a lack of social autonomy.

The second principle follows from the differing balance of activities associated with the typical roles of each sex. Women and men tend to adjust sex-typical roles by accepting the specific skills and resources linked to successful role performance. A variety of sex specific skills and beliefs arise from typical family and economic roles of men and women. For example, women learned domestic skills such as cooking, men learned skills in market economy. The psychological attributes and social behaviours developed accordingly. Women's accommodation to domestic roles favoured a pattern of interpersonally facilitative and friendly behaviour called communal orientation. Women's acceptance and continuation with child-rearing activities stimulated the growth of nurturance. From a broader perspective, women's association with nurturing role facilitated the acquisiton of interpersonal skills and ability to communicate nonverbally. In contrast, men's association with paid employment facilitated a pattern of assertive and independent behaviours termed as instrumental or agentic orientation.

In social structure theories (Eagley, 1987), differential role occupancy affects behaviour through a variety of mediating process. In social role theory, an important mediating process is the formation of gender roles by which people of each sex are expected to have characteristics that equip them for the tasks that they typically carry out. These expectations contain the preferred or desirable attributes of men and women. Gender roles are emergent from the productive work of the sexes. The characteristics that are required to perform sex typical tasks become stereotypic of women or men. To the extent that women more than men occupy roles that demand communal behaviour, domestic behaviour or subordinate behaviour for successful performance, such tendencies become stereotypic of women and are incorporated into a female gender role. To the extent men more than women occupy roles that demand agentic behaviours, resource acquisition behaviour or dominant behaviour for the successful role performance, such tendencies become stereotypic of men and are incorporated into a male gender role. Gender roles facilitate the activities typically carried out by people of each sex. For example, the expectation that women be group-oriented and compassionate facilitates their nurturing activities.

People communicate gender stereotypic expectation in social interaction and can directly induce these expectations. Gender-stereotypic expectations can also affect behaviour by becoming internalized as a part of individual self-concept and personality. Under such circumstances, gender roles affect behaviour through self-regulation process. The principle that underlies these processes involves the maximization of utilities. People perceive these utilities from the reward and cost experience in social interaction.

Gender roles evolve with specific roles based on factors such as family relationship and occupation. These specific social roles contribute directly to sex-differentiated behaviour when women and men are differently distributed into them. For instance, women go into homemaker role and men into the producer role. In contrast, when men and women occupy the same specific social roles, sex differences tend to diminish.

The social structural perspective provides a broad theoretical framework within which many social scientific theories of sex difference can be placed. These theories emphasize different aspects of the process by which societies produce sex-difference. For example, developmental psychologists have studied socializations in the family, school, and peer group. Social psychologists have investigated the impact of gender self-schemas, social expectations, and pattern of social interaction. Sociologists have implicated organizational factors such as employment practices.

Thus, social structural position views that women and men are differentially distributed into social roles and these differing role assignment is a source of a sexual division of labour and gender hierarchy. The division of labour compeled with gender hierarchy leads to sex differentiated behaviours by triggering social and psychological processes by which men and women seek somewhat different expectations to maximize their outcomes. Sex difference in behaviour is a reflection of prevailing social conditions.

It is important to recognize that both evolution theory and social structure theory stress functionalistic adaptations. The basic difference lies in the direction of causal influences. Although proponents of each theory have reported empirical studies to support their respective positions, the acid test lies in the future. All over the world, social conditions and structures are changing; floor-crossing is increasing. Women are entering paid employment in large numbers. In such a transforming social scenario, future studies will generate definitive answers.

Box 1

Recapitulation at a Glance
What are the major issues?

Basic Issues

1. Maccoby and Jacklin published their classical book 'The Psychology of Sex Difference' in the year 1974. This comprehensive review identified sex differences in several areas of human functioning. But what is the present status of such differences?

Elements of Bias

2. Psychologists with *alpha bias* have tended to exaggerate sex differences.
3. Psychologists with *beta bias* have tended to overlook sex differences.
4. What are the areas of *real* sex differences?

The Origin of Sex Difference

5. The origin theories can be grouped into two broad rubrics: evolved disposition versus social role theories.
6. The evolved disposition theory explains sex difference from an evolutionary standpoint.
7. The social roles theory explains difference in terms of sex-linked tasks, roles, and power.
8. The basic issue is to examine the strength of each of these theories in the light of emerging research data.

2
Spatial and Motor Activity Level

The examination of sex difference in a specific domain of human functioning need not be construed as an attempt to prove superiority of one sex vis-à-vis other sex. Rather the analysis of difference and related factors explicates the role of mediating mechanism. As pointed earlier, social structural theorists highlighted the role of sexual division of labour during pre-historic times and its resultants in contemporary life functioning. They argued that hunter's role of men equipped them with superior spatial ability whereas gatherers' role of women gave them the benefit of spatial location memory. The difference was also reflected at the level of motor activity.

The contribution of division of labour argues in favour of males' higher spatial and motor abilities. In recent years, the role of other critical factors has been identified in addition to gross sex difference in this area.

Spatial Ability

The spatial ability is an essential component of everyday adaptation. Locating places and persons, driving, drawing, jumping and dressmaking require spatial ability. The bulk of research has clearly shown that males have distinct advantage over females in this area. However, fine-grained studies in this area have addressed to the issue of delineating critical factors.

There has been three fundamental issues that have been addressed: (a) What is the magnitude of sex difference in spatial ability? (b) On which aspect of spatial ability are sex differences found? and (c) When in the life span are sex differences in spatial ability first detected?

Spatial ability generally refers to skills in representing, transforming, generating and recalling symbolic, non-linguistic information. A considerable dispute surrounds the identification of specific spatial abilities and the characterization of the processes used to solve spatial items. The psychometric perspective yields categories that depend on the tests used for the investigations. This approach may not yield agreement across investigations. In contrast, the cognitive perspective identifies processes used to solve the tasks. A classification of spatial abilities may be suggested on this basis.

Categories of Spatial Ability

The cognitive perspective identifies three categories of spatial ability: spatial perception, mental rotation, and spatial visualization.

In spatial perception test, subjects are required to determine spatial relationship with respect to the orientation of their own bodies, inspite of distracting information. One example is the Rod-and-Frame Test (RFT) in which subjects must place a rod vertically while viewing a frame oriented at 22°.

Another is Piaget's water-level test. The apparatus has two pairs. There is a cylindrical glass bottle (the real bottle) half-filled with liquid and mounted on an axis to permit rotation. There is also a similar bottle cut in half lengthwise (the pretend bottle) attached to a cardboard disc and mounted on an axis. A circular disc, half of which is coloured red to represent the water in the pretend bottle, is mounted on an axis behind the pretend bottle and is visible through the pretend bottle. On each trial, the subject is asked to predict the orientation of the water surface in the real bottle (which is covered) by adjusting the pretend water disk within the pretend bottle.

There is also a paper-and-pencil version of the water level task. On the first page of the test materials, a sample bottle in the upright position is presented with the water level drawn incorrectly. Each of the following pages contains onę bottle without a waterline (test bottle). Each of the test bottles is rotated (say 25 degree) from the upright. Subjects are asked to draw the water level line on each of the pictures of test bottle. On the water level task the deviations in degrees from the horizontal of the line drawings are measured. Responses within five degrees of horizontal are considered correct.

Some process analyses of spatial perception tasks suggest that subjects use the gravitational vertical to locate the correct orientation. Respondents rely on kinesthetic cues for locating the gravitational horizontal or vertical. For example, respondents to the RFT report relying on whether the position "feels" upright. Respondents to water level tasks report relying on whether the water "feel" level. The other feature of spatial perception tasks is to focus on disenbedding or overcoming distracting cues. Respondents can either ignore or correct for the possibly misleading cues from tilted objects in their visual field. Reliance on kinesthetic cues may accompany a decision to ignore the distractor cues in the situation.

Mental rotation test is the other variety. Shepard and his colleagues have studied the ability to rotate a two or three-dimensional figure rapidly and accurately. They devised indirectly administered tasks to measure the speed of response to different amount of rotation. Subsequently, Vanderberg and Kuse (1978) modified Shepard-Metzler Mental Rotation Test for group administration. Other potential measures of this variety are Flags and Curds from the French Kit (French, Ekstrom & Price, 1963) and Primary Mental Abilities (PMA) space (Thurstone & Thurstone, 1941.)

Some investigations have used mental rotation card variety. Mental rotation is assessed using the Card Rotation Test (CRT). For each row in the test, subjects must decide which of eight two-dimensional figures is the same or different from a Standard. Some figures differ only in their orientation on the page, while different figures are mirror-image reversals.

It is hypothesized that during a mental rotation, the respondent's internal cognitive processes have a one-to-one correspondence with the external rotation of the object. Thus, a gestalt-like process governs the rotation of objects.

The third category of spatial ability is labeled spatial visualization. These tasks involve complicated multistage manipulation of visually presented information. These tasks may involve the processes required for spatial perception and mental rotation but are distinguished by the possibility of multiple solution strategy. Spatial visualization tasks include Embedded Figures Test (EFT), Hidden-Figures Test (HFT) and paper folding and a few other tests. Successful performance on spatial visualization involves flexibility in selecting the optimal strategy for each item.

Meta-Analytic Results

In contemporary research, meta-analysis is preferred as a research tool to draw valid inferences from empirical studies. The meta-analytic methods are preferable to previously used "eyeball analysis" or "vote-counting" method. In the meta-analysis, researchers synthesize effect sizes or standardized mean differences between groups on a variable.

Linn and Peterson (1985) provided such mean effect sizes between males and females on spatial ability tasks. They identified 172 studies for meta-analysis and portioned the effect sizes using the three spatial ability categories indicated earlier.

The 62 spatial perception effect size yielded a magnitude of 0.44 favouring males. The effect size for subjects under 13 years of age as well as for subjects within the age group of 13 to 18 was found to be 0.37. In contrast, the mean effect size for individuals above 18 years of age was 0.64. This implies that one third of a standard deviation (favouring males) for those 18 and under and two-third of a standard deviation for those above 18 years of age.

The mean effect size of sex difference in mental rotation was higher; it was 0.73 favouring males. Males tended to outperform females on mental rotation at any age. The sex difference was postulated to result from differential rate of rotation, differential efficiencies in strategy applications, differential use of analytic processes or differential caution.

In the meta-analysis of the 81 effect estimates for spatial visualization, it was found that effects were small (d=0.13). For most of the studies, no significant difference between males and females was found. Furthermore, the magnitude remained relatively unchanged across the life span.

The meta-analytic results contradicted the assertion that sex difference in spatial ability is first detected in adolescence. For spatial perception, differences are detected in individuals at about age 8.

Many hypothesize that sex differences in spatial ability result from hormonal changes at puberty. Since meta-analysis showed no change in the magnitude of spatial ability sex differences in early adolescence, a pubertal mechanism for sex difference seems unlikely. Others indicate a relationship between spatial ability and the timing of pubertal maturation. It is suggested that later maturers would be better spatial visualizers than earlier maturers because of the effects of maturational timing on the development of hemispheric specialization in the brain. The hypothesis that the brain functioning of late maturers becomes more laterally specialized for spatial ability would explain sex difference in spatial ability since boys mature 1-2 years later than girls on the average.

Genetic factors constitute the other major biological mechanism used to explain difference in spatial ability. The primary plausible mechanism is that a spatial gene is carried on the X-chromosome. However, the total body of research examining the X-linked hypothesis has not been uncontroversial. Additional studies are needed to draw definitive conclusions.

The role of social and structural variables can not be ruled out. It appears logical to infer about the role of social factors by examining the relationship between androgyny and spatial ability.

In a different tradition, Jamison and Signurella (1980) examined the association between masculinity and success on Piaget's water level task. The investigators considered both the variables of sex as well as role orientation. As described earlier, Piaget's water level task involving real bottle and pretend bottles were presented. Both men and women were subjects. The performance of male sex-typed, female-sex typed and androgynous individuals as measured by the Bem's Sex Role Inventory was also examined.

The results supported previous finding that male exhibit greater spatial ability than do females. In addition, the results also showed that subjects with masculine sex role orientation performed better on the water level task than those with feminine sex role orientation. While the association between water level performance and sex-role orientation points to a relationship between socialization and cognitive performance, the correlation does not support any causal influences about the effects of sex role orientation on individual differences. It is not known whether the correlation results from the tendency of those with ability on cognitive spatial tasks to develop other characteristics associated with masculinity or from the fact that those who are socialized to be more masculine are also encouraged to master spatial ability.

Signurella, Tamisa and Krupa (in press) carried out a similar study of causal influences in spatial ability tasks. The specific objective was to find out whether the self-concept held by people with masculinity or the activity preferences shown by individuals with masculine orientation predict water-level task performance. Participants were both men and women with masculinity and femininity orientations as measured by the Bem's Sex Role Inventory. In addition, subjects were given spatial activity perception measure. The questionnaire consisted of 10 masculine, 10 feminine and 10 neutral activities. Subjects were asked to indicate how often they participated in such activity by using the 7-point scale at the top of the page. The scale was anchored by "never participated in the activity" (1) and "participated in the activity more than once a week" (7). Subjects were also told that seasonal activities should be given a 7 if the subjects participated in these activities more than a week during the session.

For the measurement of spatial ability, subjects were given paper-and-pencil format of water-level task. They were given a booklet and told to look at the drawing of the sample bottle on the first page, described as one-half full of water. The subjects were told that for the remaining bottles they were to draw the water line on the bottle, imagining that the bottle was one-half full of water and that the bottle cap was on tightly. The investigators used four pictures of test bottles. Accordingly the score on the water level task was the number of correct bottles (total possible score=4). The investigators also used Card Rotation Test (earlier) as a measure of spatial ability.

Signurella et al (in press) used causal analysis procedures to determine the possible predictors of spatial ability. They were testing two possible hypotheses. Bem's gender schema theory leads to the prediction that individuals perform in ways that are consistent with their sex-role congruent self-concepts. In other words, people with masculinity sex-role orientation would behave in masculine way; people with feminine role orientation would behave in feminine ways, and androgynous individual would behave in balanced ways. In contrast, the other view stresses activity preference. It posits that a person's preferred activity would determine performance in various domains.

Signurella et al (in press) found supportive evidence for the role of activity preference. Self-concept and spatial activities both had significant direct effect on spatial performance, but self-concept had no significant indirect effect on spatial performance through spatial activities. It implies that both self-concept and spatial activities make direct significant contribution to the prediction of spatial performance. The findings were explained in terms of Spence's theory of gender identity.

Spence argues that as children mature, the role of gender identity in guiding the gender-congruent attributes and behaviours minimizes and the result is considerable diversity within each sex in the particular constellations of gender-congruent and gender-incongruent characteristics and behaviours that individuals exhibit. Thus, Spence's theory posits that by adolescence self-concept measures such as BSRI and spatial activity measures would be independently related to spatial performance. This is what Signorella et al (in press) found in their study. The development of sex difference in spatial performance was viewed to be direct result of sex differences in self-concept and activity performance.

Motor Activity Level

Activity level is a dimension of individual difference that appears as a primary component in a wide variety of skills. In view of its linkage with human development, psychologists have devised various tools to scale activity level (AL) at various stages of growth such as infancy, pre-school stage, childhood, adolescence and so on. Although it is widely believed that males have higher motor AL than females, the question of AL sex difference has required several scientific clarifications. What are the acceptable measures of activity level? When does it originate? What are the moderating variables? If there is a sex difference in AL, does it influence caregiver's behaviour towards a boy vis-à-vis girl? These questions and related issues need to be solved through systematic investigations.

Instead of examining specific studies, it is useful to discuss the generalizations obtained from a recent meta-analysis. Eaton and Enns (1986) present a meta-analysis encompassing 127 sex-difference contrasts. Sample size ranged from 2 to 25,000 with a median of 65. The mean chronological age of the samples ranged from 2 months before birth to 30 years with a median of 55.5 months. A variety of research strategies were represented with 25 per cent of all comparisons done in home setting, 25 per cent in pre-school setting, 10 per cent in laboratories, 9 per cent in school classrooms, and 30 per cent in a variety of other settings.

Activity level has been operationalized and measured in a number of ways. The meta-analysis discussed here used diverse measures. Activity level refers to customary level of energy expenditure through movement. Movement, frequency, duration, amplitude and type may all affect the expenditure of energy. In general, large, frequent, long-duration or expansive movement requires more energy than fine, infrequent, short-duration and restricted ones. So analysis included studies using measures of movement type, frequency duration, and specific limb movement as well as whole body actions.

The estimation of the size of sex effects and conclusions were derived by the use of appropriate statistical analysis. Apart from indicating men's greater activity level as compared with women's, a number of interesting findings were obtained.

Developmental Factors

Maccoby and Jacklin (1974) suggested that sex difference in motor activity is age-specific. They concluded that there was no evidence for sex difference in children under 12 months, more consistent sex differences emerged during pre-school years. On this basis, one would predict a positive correlation between age and activity level; one may also expect to come across greater sex difference in AL as men and women become older.

However, the analysis of Eaton and Enns (1986) presented somewhat different picture, though not a contrasting one. They found that AL sex difference was present during infancy. The mean effect size for pre-natal studies was non-significant but there was a significant AL sex difference during infancy. For pre-school and older subjects, data pointed to a clear AL sex difference.

Although AL sex difference was noted during infancy and pre-school years, a note of caution needs to be sounded. A bulk of the studies considered (approximately 90 per cent of the studies) were of samples with mean age 15 years or less. So the relation between AL sex difference magnitude and age is applicable from infancy to middle adolescence. It would not be safe to stretch the finding beyond adolescence.

Some theorist opines that age correlates with sexual differences. They argued that social influences take time and consequently some sex difference do not emerge till adolescence. In Eaton and Enns' (1986) meta-analysis, AL sex difference was present before adolescence. The early appearance of AL sex difference brings an important implication. It suggests that social influences may magnify the existing differences but they are unlikely to create those differences.

Situational Factors

Activity level sex difference is found to be situation-specific. Maccoby and Jacklin (1974) hypothesized that girls freeze under stress, where boys remain relatively normal. Consequently, boys are likely to be more active than girls under conditions of stress. However, there is no impressive evidence suggesting a greater reduction of activity level of girls vis-à-vis boys under condition of stress. Some investigators have induced stress among young children by having the youngster's mother leave the room. In such conditions, boys and girls report comparable reduction of activity.

The meta-analysis under discussion does not show greater AL sex difference under condition of high stress. In contrast, greater effect size is found in low rather than in high stress situations. Similarly, greater difference is found in familiar situations than in novel situations.

Previous assumptions were different. Novel and unfamiliar situations were thought to have a specific kind of influence. It was assumed that boys in comparison with girls were likely to explore the environmental novelty. Similarly it was thought that boys would be more active in natural and unstructured setting such as playground. The presence of same sex peers would stimulate higher activity level in boys than in girls. Such a sex-relation "contagion" was a well known tendency in children to select same sex peers as playmates. Boys choosing other boys as playmates were considered to be more active than girls choosing other girls as playmates. However, the overall pattern of results derived from the meta-analysis suggested that AL sex difference is explicitly expressed in a familiar non-threatening, unrestricted social setting.

Measurement Factors

The AL measures fall into three general categories. Instruments designed to measure motor activity do not depend on human judges and are the most objective of the three types of measures. Measures based on observational system (for example, counting the squares of a floor grid into which a child enters) are probably more susceptible to bias than instruments because observers have to make coding decisions within a social context. The gender of subject is known and might influence coding decisions. Rating measures, which have typically required parents caregivers or other persons to rate a focal individual AL could be influenced by social stereotypes. To the extent AL sex differences are a product of social stereotypes, measurement biases are likely to creep into the assessment of activities.

Eaton and Enns (1986) considered specific measures of arms movement as well as general measures such as body movement. Activity level sex difference emerged irrespective of measurement type.

In general, males were found to be more active than females. Eatons and Enns note that attaching a descriptive statistics to the overall mean difference is a difficult job, but it is possible to compare the findings with others in the literature. In the context of other sex differences meta-analysis, a difference of one-half standard deviation is large for a behavioural variable. In the case of AL sex difference, it is roughly one-half a standard deviation, a difference that accounts less than 5 per cent of the variance in the AL distribution. Indeed, a 5 per cent of explained variance in a specific social and cognitive variable is an upper boundary for sex differences. Differences of this boundary magnitude and their mean effect size include: spatial activity, 0.45, aggression, 0.50; mathematical reasoning, 0.44; and proportional reasoning, 0.48. Within this context, it can be concluded that sex difference in AL is a stable difference.

The finding was also resistant to a number of other social influences. Although it was anticipated that raters, under the influence of social stereotypes, would overestimate sex differences, male raters were comparable to female raters. Similarly the percentage of male authors provided useful information that sex differences were not limited only to those looking for them, not only to the past, or only to investigators of a particular gender. Of course a limiting condition was the lack of adequate prenatal studies. Whether or not additional prenatal studies in future will show AL sex differences remains to be seen.

Box 2

Recaptulation at a Glance

Spatial Ability

1. Sex differences favouring males arise on some types of spatial ability tests, but not others.
2. Large differences are found only on measures of mental rotation.
3. Smaller sex differences are found on measures of spatial perception.
4. When sex differences are found, they can be detected across the life span.

Motor Activity Level

5. In general, males are more active than females.
6. The maximum sex difference in activity level is found in situations that offer a good deal of latitude for the expression of individual difference: a familiar, non-threatening, unrestricted social situation.
7. Age emerges as an important mediating variable. The relation between activity level sex difference and age is primarily applicable from infancy to middle adolescence and it would be hazardous to extrapolate beyond adolescence.

3

Cognitive Performance

Cognitive functions of humans have special characteristics. In fact humans are basically "cognizing" beings; they map their external reality through internal representation. They attend to sensory inputs, they organize and codify the received inputs; they retrieve the stored materials at appropriate time. The use of codes and symbols at various stages of their function gives a unique character to human activity.

Although there are many forms of cognitive activity, a few of cognitive functions have been well-studied. These include spatial perception, verbal ability and mathematical ability. These areas have also received research attention in the context of gender difference. The issue of spatial ability has been discussed in the last chapter. It would be interesting to examine sex differences in verbal and mathematical ability prior to explicating possible causes of such differences.

Verbal Ability

Sex difference in verbal ability is one of the prominent areas of psychological research. The existence of gender difference in favour of girls and women has taken the status of established fact. The classical authors such as Anastasi and Tayler recognized female superiority in the area of verbal skills. Maccoby (1966) concluded:

> Through the preschool years and in the early school years, girls exceed boys in most aspects of verbal performance. They say their first word sooner, articulate more clearly and at an early age, use longer sentences, and are more fluent. By the beginning of school, however, there are no longer any consistent differences in vocabulary. Girls learn

> to read sooner, and there are more boys than girls' who require special training in remedial reading program, but by approximately the age of ten, a number of studies show that boys have caught up in their reading skills. Throughout the school years, girls do better on tests of grammar, spelling, and word fluency. (P. 26).

In the major classical review of psychological sex difference, Maccoby and Jacklin (1974) located 85 studies reporting an analysis of sex difference. They concluded:

> It is probably true that girl's verbal abilities mature somewhat more rapidly in early life, although there are a number of recent studies in which no sex difference has been found. During the period from preschool to early adolescence, the sexes are very much similar in their verbal ability. At about age 11, the sexes begin to diverge, with female superiority increasing through high school and possibly beyond. Girls score higher on tasks involving both receptive and productive language, and on "high level" verbal tasks (analogies, comprehension of difficult written material, creative writing) as well as "lower-level" measures (fluency). The magnitude of female advantage varies, being most commonly about one-quarter of a standard deviation. (P.351).

A number of investigators have also concluded that females were superior in verbal ability, having a slight advantage in the preschool year, with difference becoming stronger and more reliable after age 10 or 11.

Despite the consensus on the existence of sex differences in verbal ability, there are disagreements with respect to the nature of sex difference. There are two fundamental questions in this respect. First, details are needed to know which types of verbal ability show difference and which do not. Second, it is important to ascertain the developmental timing of the appearance or disappearance of the difference. Anastasi argued that gender differences are found for simple verbal tasks, whereas Maccoby and Jacklin concluded that female superiority was found in both high-level and low-level tasks. Anastasi and Maccoby also agreed that females were superior to males in vocabulary in the preschool years, whereas Maccoby and Jacklin (1974) observed that sexes were similar in verbal ability in the preschool and elementary school years, with female superiority emerging around age 11 and increasing through high school and possibly beyond.

Scientific information is needed beyond the global statement that females have superior verbal ability to males. With a view to understanding the detailed nature of female superiority and the developmental timing, it is better to count on meta-analysis than on isolated studies.

The Meta-Analysis

The traditional reviews of psychological gender differences (e.g., Maccoby, 1966) used the method of *narrative review*. The reviewers located as many studies of gender differences as possible, organized them in some fashion, and reported his or her conclusion in narrative form. The narrative review, however, is subject to some serious criticism. It is non-quantitative, unsystematic, and subjective, and the task of reviewing 100 or more studies simply exceed the information-processing capacity of the human mind.

The Maccoby and Jacklin (1974) review represented a considerable advance over previous ones. It included far more studies than had been done before. It also permitted systematic use of *vote counting*. The reviewers provided listing of studies that permitted the count of studies favouring females, the count of studies favouring males, and the count of studies reporting no difference.

General criticisms of the method of vote counting have also been raised. Statisticians have pointed out that vote counting can lead to false conclusions; If there is a true effect in the population, but the studies reviewed have poor statistical power (perhaps because of small sample size) and only a minority of studies will find a significant effect.

Meta-analysis has been defined as the application of quantitative methods to combining evidence from different studies. Meta-analysis commenced in the 1960s to make important contribution to the literature in psychological gender difference. Of course, Maccoby and Jacklin (1974) had earlier estimated effect size for a few studies on sex difference. They concluded that the magnitude of sex difference in the verbal ability was about one-quarter of a standard deviation (i.e., $d = 0.25$). Hyde (1981) performed a meta-analysis on the 27 studies of verbal ability of subjects 11 or older (corresponding to the age at which Maccoby and Jacklin concluded that the sexes begin to diverge in verbal ability) in the Maccoby and Jacklin sample of studies. Her finding of a median value of $d = 0.24$ confirmed Maccoby and Jacklin's estimate.

Since the time of the Hyde (1981) review, statistical methods in meta-analysis have advanced considerably. Most relevant is the development of heterogeneity statistics. These statistical methods allow one to determine whether a group of studies are uniform in their outcomes. Applied to the present problem, these methods allow one to determine whether the magnitude of sex difference varies according to the type of verbal tasks and whether the magnitude of sex difference varies with age.

Hyde and Linn (1988) performed a meta-analysis of studies reporting statistics in gender differences in verbal ability. In addition to studies included in the Maccoby and Jacklin review, recent studies were also considered. The objective was not only to assess the magnitude of sex difference, the purpose was also to determine whether the magnitude of difference is declining over decades. The analysis was directed to find out sex difference across various types of verbal tasks such as vocabulary, analogies and essay writing.

The meta-analysis included studies from three different sources. The studies listed in the Maccoby and Jacklin (1974) analysis were included. The studies abstracted by the American Psychological Association were considered and those dealing with sex difference in verbal ability were selected. In addition, a large number of journals published in the year 1986 were surveyed and pertinent studies were identified and selected. The process resulted in initial pool of 176 studies reporting at least some usable information on gender difference in verbal ability.

Since the purpose of the research was to shed light on the nature of gender difference in general population, studies of various defects in verbal performance (e.g., stuttering, and dyslexia) were excluded. Such studies typically find a preponderance of male subjects with the problem and are used as evidence of female verbal superiority. Studies dealing with early language learning by children in the age range of 18 months to 3 years were also excluded. There have been claims that girls are verbally gifted compared with boys. Evidence is cited that girls learn to talk earlier and produce longer utterance at earlier age than boys do. Again, such distinct classes of studies were excluded.

The meta-analysis coded maximum possible information including the mean and standard deviation of sex difference, number of males and females used as subjects, mean age of the subjects, the type of verbal tests used, year of publication, and sex of the first author of the article. The effect size computed for each study was defined as the mean for females minus the mean for males, divided by the pooled within-sex standard deviation. The positive value of d represent superior female performance and negative value represents superior male performance.

The Magnitude of Difference

The unweighted mean value of *d* averaged over 120 available values was small and positive, indicating that overall, females outperformed males. The studies that represented the testing of 1, 418, 899 subjects yielded a mean value of *d* to be +0.11. A gender difference of one-tenth of a standard deviation is surely a small difference.

There has been some debate over the interpretation of effect sizes. Cohen considered a *d* of 0.20 small, a *d* of 0.50 medium, and a *d* of 0.80 large. Thus the effect size of 0.11 obtained from meta-analysis is very small. However, several other analysts have argued that many effect sizes that appear to be small are actually large in terms of their practical significance. For example, an effect reported as a correlation of 0.20, when measuring the success of a treatment for cancer, translates into increasing the cure rate from 40 per cent to 60 per cent, something that surely has practical significance. On the other hand, using the approximation formula $d = \sqrt{2}r$, the effect size of 0.11 translates to an *r* of 0.055 which yields only a 5 per cent increase in "success rate" i.e. from 47.5 to 52.5 per cent). While an effect size of 0.11 might have some practical significance, if the topic is cancer, it has almost no significance for understanding the nature of difference between male and female verbal ability.

The effect size for the gender difference in verbal ability can be compared with gender differences of other domains. For gender differences involving mental rotation, studies have reported mean effect size, $d = 0.73$. Hyde (1981) has reported mean effect size of $d = 0.43$ for gender differences in mathematical performance. For gender difference in aggression involving subjects of all ages, the mean effect size is $d = 0.50$. For social psychological studies of aggression by adult subjects effect size is found to be, $d = 0.40$. Gender difference in helping behaviour is found to be $d = 0.13$. Thus, the magnitude of gender difference in verbal ability is one of the smallest of the gender differences.

Another interesting feature of the meta-analysis was the finding with respect to change over decades. Studies were grouped into two categories: those published in 1973 or earlier (corresponding to Maccoby and Jacklin's sample of studies) and those published in 1974 or later. It was found that for pre-1973 studies, the mean effect size was $d = 0.23$ whereas for post-1973 studies the effect size was $d = 0.10$. Homogeneity test indicated that the group mean was significant. Thus, the gender difference is smaller in recent years.

Two theories have been proposed to explain cognitive gender difference on the basis of the notion that lateralization of functions occurs somewhat differently in male and female brains. The Buffery and Gray hypothesis (1972) is that left hemisphere dominance for verbal functions is attained earlier in girls. This is consistent with girls' superior verbal ability. It does not permit spatial processing to be as bilateral in girls as it is in boys. Consequently it gives advantage to boys in spatial ability.

The second one is the Levy hypothesis. It states that females, like left handed males, are more likely to be bilateral in verbal functions. This, in turn, inhibits spatial processing capabilities, which will develop best with great lateralization of functions. Levy also argues that bilateral verbal processing is advantageous.

Developmental Consideration

Studies were grouped according to the average age of subjects as follows: 5 years and younger, 6 to 10 years, 11 to 18 years, 19 to 25 years, and 26 and older. These groupings were chosen because of certain conditions. The 5 years and younger group (preschoolers) attends to the issue of whether there is an early advantage for girls in the development of verbal ability. The 6-to-10 year old group encompasses the elementary school years. The 11-to-18 year old group (adolescence) addresses Maccoby and Jacklin's (1974) assertion that sexes begin to diverge around age 11 in verbal ability with female superiority increasing through the high school years and possibly beyond. The 19 to 25 year old groups represents college students and other young adults. The 26 years and older group represent adults.

It is found that when effect sizes are averaged over all tests, the effect sizes are small and positive (favouring females) for all age groups and do not show impressive variation. Vocabulary measures yield similar results, with the exception of a negative effect size (favouring males) for the 6 to 10 age groups. Reading comprehension tests show values close to zero for all age groups, with exception of the 5 year and younger age group. Here findings favour males.

Meta-analysis is capable of showing age trends in the magnitude of sex difference. Hyde (1984) found that gender differences in aggression were twice as large for preadolescents (d =.54) compared to college students (d =.27). The meta-analysis of Hyde and Linn (1988) found little evidence of age trends in the magnitude of sex difference. This finding was obtained when combining all measures of verbal ability as well as considering an oft-used test separately. The majority of the effect sizes were 0.11 or less. Thus, Maccoby and Jacklin's observation of clear superiority of females to males around age 11 was not supported. It is plausible that the difference has been minimized in recent years.

Varieties of Measures and Other Factors

Although a very small gender difference is revealed, an important question concerns the specificity of measurement. It is possible that the effect is sensitive to the method of measurement. In order to answer this question, specific measures were considered separately. However, the generalization is not changed substantially. The only exceptions are modest gender difference of 0.20 standard deviation, favouring females on measures of general verbal ability. A difference of similar magnitude was found to favour females on anagrams. A difference of approximately one-third of a standard deviation favoured females on the quality of speech production

As pointed out earlier, the year of publication of a study is linked with the gender difference finding. The meta-analysis showed a declining trend in gender difference. Hyde (1984) found similar trend in gender difference in aggression in more recent studies. Linn and Peterson (1985) recorded some decline in gender differences in spatial ability in recent years. Chapman, Brush and Wilson (1985) reported decline in gender differences in mathematical performances. Thus, the findings on verbal ability are consistent with trends in other domains.

Several explanations of the recent smaller differences in verbal ability can be offered. It is unclear whether it results from an increase in male performance or a decline in female performance. These possibilities can not be sorted out because there is no common matrice! across studies. Possibly greater amounts of cross-sex behaviour of boys and girls have enriched their experiences in the "other" domains.

The trend over time also helps to reconcile the present conclusion and Maccoby and Jacklin's observation. Maccoby and Jacklin completed a few effect sizes for gender difference in verbal ability and found that the effect size was typically $d = 25$. They concluded that gender difference in verbal ability was well-established. It was smaller than the gender difference in quantitative ability or spatial ability. Hyde's (1981) analysis yielded a d of 0.24. Hyde and Linn's (1988) pre-1973 studies yielded a d of 0.23. Thus, all these studies are consistent. The new information comes from the post–1973 studies many of them are based on large sample sizes, which yield a d of 0.10

In the past, some investigations have found significant sex difference in effect sizes depending on the sex of the researchers. Hyde and Linn (1988) found a significant difference in effect size in those studies whose first author was male compared with those whose first author was female. Female authors reported greater sex differences favoring females. However, both effect sizes were so small that the difference may not be taken seriously.

While Hyde and Linn's (1988) meta-analysis has provided refined generalizations, there is another method of cross-validating the results. It has been recently suggested that the most valid way to assess gender differences is to examine the norms to standardized psychological tests. There are several reasons for such consideration. First, such norms are based on large representative samples. Second, publication bias is eliminated because of the availability of results of statistical significance. Third, experimented bias is minimized because examinees in normative groups are tested in large numbers. The examination of sex difference in the sets of normative data provides wealthful information.

Differential Aptitude Tests (DAT)

Differential Aptitude Test is a battery of eight reliable group administered paper and pencil tests. Three DAT scales assess verbal ability: verbal reasoning (analogies test) and spelling and language (two tests of English skills). The other scales include perceptual speed (clerical speed and accuracy), three-dimensional spatial visualization (space relations, arithmetic and numerical ability), mechanical aptitudes (mechanical reasoning), figural reasoning (abstract reasoning).

Each DAT aptitude is measured by a single type of item, and item types have remained constant over the standardization of the DAT conducted in 1947, 1962, 1972 and 1980, although new forms were administered to each normative session. The DAT standardization period spans a 33-year period, means and standard deviations of test scores of boys and girls for grades 8 to 12 are available. Consequently, the DAT norms provide an excellent database for the investigation of sex difference.

A total of 193, 844 students (95, 462 boys and 98, 382 girls) were examined for the DAT standardization. The sample sizes, by year, were 21, 994 (1947), 48,450 (1962), 62,900 (1972) and 60,500 (1980). By grade, sample sizes were 39,307 (8th grade) 43,345 (9th grade), 42,381 (10th grade) 36,603 (11th grade) and 32,208 (12th grade). Gender differences were compared by grade and eight DAT aptitudes. The effect sizes were obtained for each ability. Negative signs were assigned to *ds* when female performance was higher than male performance.

Examination of gender difference with respect to first three scales of DAT showed that girls scored higher than boys on spelling, language and clerical speed and accuracy tests. This was true for all grades and all normative years. Year of DAT standardization had an effect on gender difference for all three tests. Year means indicated constant decrease in effect magnitude from 1947 to 1980.

Thus, the findings obtained from the DAT analysis are consistent with Hyde and Linn's (1988) conclusion. Further, the DAT analysis also provided information regarding abilities other than verbal ability. For all grades and year, male students scored higher than their female peers on mechanical reasoning and on space relation. There were no notable mean gender differences on three DAT tests: verbal reasoning, abstract reasoning, and numerical ability.

Scholastic Aptitude Test

As with DAT, the Scholastic Aptitude Test (SAT) can be regarded as a database to draw inferences regarding gender differences in verbal ability. The Preliminary Scholastic Aptitude Test (PSAT) and Scholastic Aptitude Test (SAT) of the American College Entrance Examination Board each consists of two tests: a verbal scale (PSAT- Verbal, SAT-Verbal) and a quantitative scale (PSAT-Mathematical, SAT-Mathematical). The PSAT-verbal and SAT-verbal each contains anagram, analogy, sentence completion and reading comprehension items. The PSAT-Mathematical and SAT-Mathematical each contains a roughly equal number of arithmetic, elementary algebra and plane geometric problems. The types have remained largely unchanged since the first norming of the PSAT in 1960.

A total of 99,654 high school juniors and seniors (49,326 boys and 50,328 girls) were examined for PSAT. Norms were completed in the year 1960, 1966, 1974 and 1983. The normative data for SAT were examined for juniors and seniors for the same years in which the PSAT was formed. The sample size for the SAT was over 170,000 for each cell in the Sex X Grade X Year matrix.

Gender differences, *ds*, were completed by grade, year and tests (Fiengold, 1988). There was a slight gender difference in PSAT-verbal favouring girls (*d* = – 0.12) among high school juniors in 1960, but it had faded completely by 1974, There was no gender difference on the PSAT-verbal in 1966 or 1974.

The gender differences found on SAT–Verbal were small for both grades for all years. A small trend for boys to be improving relative to girls on SAT-verbal from 1960 to 1983 was observed.

Thus, gender differences based on DAT and SAT standardization data point to similar conclusions. These instruments were formed in 1947 and 1960, respectively. Girls scored higher on these DAT tests (spelling, language, and clerical speed and accuracy) and (for high school juniors) on the PSAT-Verbal. The examination of the norms for SAT-Verbal revealed a small gender difference in favour of boys. Beginning from 1972, the traditional gender difference favouring females on the SAT-Varbal has been reversed. One possibility is that the content of the material, either vocabulary words or reading passages that measure comprehension, has become more technical in recent years. For example, if it is material covered in physics or chemistry classes to which females have had less exposure, then females would be at a disadvantage in performing on the test.

Taken together, meta-analytic studies and standardization norms present a coherent picture. It is shown that females had an edge over males with respect to verbal ability. The difference is considered small in view of the empirically derived sex difference indicators in other domains. The most interesting aspect of the analysis is the decline of the magnitude of sex difference. It is correct to maintain that sex difference in verbal ability has disappeared. Prior to explicating possible causal explanations, it is useful to discuss sex difference in mathematical performance.

Mathematical Achievement

In recent decades, there has been much concern about women and mathematics. Mathematics has been identified as the "critical filter" that prevents many women from having access to higher paying, prestigious occupations. Within the fields of psychology and education, gender differences in mathematics performance have been studied intensively. Anastasi, in her classic differential psychology test, stated that although difference in numerical aptitude favoured boys, these differences did not appear until well into the elementary school. Moreover, she maintained that if sex difference in computation did appear, they favoured females. In contrast, males surpassed females on tests of mathematical reasoning. Maccoby and Jacklin (1974) expressed similar views. They concluded that one of four sex differences that "were fairly well-established" was that "boys excel in mathematical ability" (p. 352). They also observed that there were few sex differences until about ages 12-13, when boys' mathematical skills increase faster than girls (p. 352).

The literature on education has reported similar conclusions. Fennema (1974) reviewed published studies and concluded:

> No significant differences between boys' and girls' mathematics achievement were found before boys and girls entered elementary school or during early elementary and

> early high school years, significant differences were not always apparent. However, when significant differences did appear, they were more apt to be in the boys' favour when higher level cognitive tasks were being measured and in the girls' favour when lower- level cognitive tests were being measured. (pp. 136-137)

Stage, Kreinberg, Eccles, and Becker (1985) reviewed major studies that have been reported upto 1985. They concluded that:

> The following results are fairly consistent across studies using a variety of achievement tests: (1) high school boys perform a little better than high school girls on tests of mathematical reasoning primarily solving word problems; (2) boys and girls perform similarly on tests of algebra and basic mathematical knowledge and (3) girls occasionally outperform boys on tests of computational skills. .... Among normal population, achievement differences favouring boys do not emerge with any consistency prior to the 10th grade, are not typically very large, and are not universally found even in advanced high school populations. There is some evidence, however, that the general pattern of sex differences may emerge some what earlier among gifted and talented students. (P 240)

There is a consensus that, overall, gender differences in mathematics performance has existed in the past and continue in the present. It is concluded that the overall differences in mathematics performance are not apparent in early childhood, they appear in early adolescence and usually favour boys in tasks involving high cognitive complexity (problem solving) and favour girls in tests involving less complexity (computation).

Despite such global conclusions a number of fundamental questions remain unanswered. First, different studies report different magnitudes of sex difference. Second, although some indications have been given with respect to the role of the level of cognitive complexity of the tasks involved, no fine-grained analysis of task contents has been attempted. Third, an important question concerns the age at which gender differences appear and disappear. Fourth, the examination of sex difference across ethno-cultural groups has been neglected. Finally, the possible explanations of gender differences require empirical testing.

The Meta-analytic Solution

As pointed out earlier, meta-analytic studies are considered suitable to answer a broad spectrum of questions. Hyde (1981) performed a meta-analysis on 16 studies of quantitative ability of subjects aged 12 or older that were included in Maccoby and Jacklin's (1974) review (12 being the age at which Maccoby and Jacklin concluded that the sexes begin to diverge in mathematics performance). Hyde found a medium effect size of 0.43 and noted that the difference was not as large as one might have expected given the widely held view that the difference is well-established.

The Hyde (1981) meta-analysis included only studies reported through 1973. There is a need to update it with recent research. In addition, statistical methods have advanced considerably in recent years. In view of these developments, a more refined meta-analytic study of sex difference in mathematics performance was conducted by Hyde, Fennema and Lamore (1990).

The sample of studies came from various sources. The authors used computerized data base prepared by the American Psychological Association and other professional associations. The studies reported on the Maccoby and Jacklin (1974) review were included. Furthermore, relevant studies published in the pertinent journals were included.

Large sample normative data were also obtained from American College Testing Programme Test (ACT), Graduate Management Admission Test (GMAT), Scholastic Aptitude Test (SAT), SAT Mathematics Level 1 and Level 2, Differential Aptitude Test (DAT), Graduate Record Examination (GRE), and a few other similar programmes.

The result was 100 usable sources yielding 259 independent effect sizes. This represents the testing of 3,985,682, subjects (1,968,846 males and 2,016,836 females). For each study, the following parameters were considered and coded: (a) statistical parameters such as mean, median and standard deviation, (b) number of male and female subjects, (c) the cognitive level of the measure (computation, concepts, problem-solving, and general or mixed), (d) the mathematics content of the test (arithmetic, algebra, geometry, calculus, and mixed), (e) age(s) of the subject, (f) the ethnicity of the sample, and (g) the selectivity of the sample (general sample, national sample, college students etc.). The effect size computed was *d*, defined as the mean for males minus the mean for females, divided by the mean within sexes standard deviation. Thus, positive values of *d* represent superior male performance and negative values represent superior female performance.

The Pattern of Difference

Averaged over 259 studies, the weighted mean effect size was 0.20. When data from SAT were excluded, the remaining 254 effect sizes yielded a weighted mean *d* of 0.15. On both cases, the small positive value indicates that overall, males out-performed females by a small amount. When samples of general population was considered, *d* was –0.05, it reflected superiority of females, but in a negligible magnitude.

When effect sizes were considered in the context of the cognitive level of the task, the overall effect sizes were also small. Yet, there was a slight female superiority in computation, and slight male superiority in problem-solving.

The analysis according to the mathematics content of the test indicated that there was no gender difference in arithmetic or algebra performance. The only male superiority in geometry was small and the tests with mixed content showed the largest gender difference.

The analysis for the magnitude of gender difference showed some interesting features. The gender difference was close to zero in general samples, a large difference favouring males was found for each successive level of selection for higher ability. The gender difference was moderate to large for highly selected samples ($d = 0.54$) and for samples selected for extreme precocity ($d=0.41$).

Studies were divided into two categories depending on the year of publication: those published in 1973 or earlier and those published after 1973. This division was made in view of the landmark study of Maccoby and Jacklin in the year 1974. For studies published in 1973 and earlier, *d* was 0.31 based on 57 effect sizes; For articles published in 1974 or later, *d* was 0.14 based on 217 effect sizes. Thus, the data showed both the increase in research on gender difference and a substantial trend for decline in gender difference in recent years.

In the American context, it was shown that there was no gender difference for Blacks, Hispanics and Asian Americans. The slight difference for Asian Americans favoured females. Only for white Americans, was there evidence of superior male performance. However, the difference was still small in this case.

In the meta-analysis, the Scholastic Aptitude Test (SAT) data were analyzed separately. It yielded discrepant results. The overall effect size excluding the SAT was 0.16. Yet, the 1985 SAT data yielded the mean effect size 0.40. The SAT produced a considerably larger gender difference than overall meta-analysis. However, the difference in findings is explainable. The SAT data are based on a moderately selected sample, those who are college bound. As indicated earlier, selectivity of the sample tends to give an upward push to the gender difference in favour of males. A close examination of demographic features of subjects sampled for SAT reveals that a large number of females take SAT. Males appear to be somewhat more advantaged in terms of parental income, father's education and attendance in private schools. In short, the male SAT sample may be more selective than the female sample.

Age Trends

The ages were divided into five subgroups: (a) 5- to 10-year olds, (b) 11- to 14-year olds, (c) 15- to 18-year olds, (d) 19- to 25-year olds, and (e) those 26 and older. These age groups were chosen for two reasons. First, they represent roughly the elementary school, middle or junior high school, high school, college, and adulthood. Second, some authors have asserted that there is no gender difference until the age of 12, when it begins to emerge.

The analysis with respect to age categories showed that there was small female superiority in the elementary and middle school years. There was a more substantive male superiority in the high school years, the college years and beyond, although the last finding is based on a few effect sizes.

The results of the analysis of Age X Cognitive level were also considered. Females were superior in computation in elementary schools and middle school, although the differences were small. There was essentially no difference at any age level in understanding mathematical concepts. Problem solving however, presented a different picture. There was a slight female superiority or no gender difference for the elementary and middle school groups, but a moderate gender difference favoured males in high school and college years. These are precisely the years when students are permitted to select their own courses and female elect somewhat fewer mathematics courses than do males. Differences in course selection appear for some but not all of the gender differences in performance on standardized tests in the high school and college years.

The interpretation of the magnitude of effect site has been detailed. Some idea of the magnitude of the overall effect size of –0.05 for general population or the effect size of 0.29 for problem solving in high school students can also be gained by comparing these effect sizes found in other meta-analyses. The meta-analyses of gender difference in verbal ability reported earlier stated *d* to be 0.11. The authors concluded that the value was so small as to indicate no difference (Hyde & Linn, 1988). A meta-analysis of gender differences in the magnitude of difference depended on the type of spatial ability tested (Linn & Peterson, 1985). For measures of spatial perception (e.g. the rod-and-frame test) *d* was 0.44. For measures of spatial visualization (e.g. hidden figures test) *d* was .13. For measures of spatial relation (e.g. PMA space on the Vandenberg) *d* was 0.73. In all cases, differences favoured males. Linn and Peterson concluded that the only substantial gender difference was in measure of spatial rotation.

Thus, the overall effects size of 0.15 (or - 0.05 for samples of only general population) for gender difference in mathematics performance can surely be called small. The largest effect sizes obtained were 0.29 and 0.32 for high school and college years respectively. These are minor differences comparable to gender difference in aggressive behaviour.

While gender difference in mathematics performance is concluded to be small for the general population, the difference is admitted at certain levels such as high school and college years. There are several explanations advanced for this difference.

Theoretical Models

A number of theoretical models have been proposed. At one end of the spectrum, Benbow and Stanley (1980), based on their research with mathematically precocious students, argued that boys have more natural mathematics ability and that there must be a biological basis for this gender difference. A secondary report of the results in *Newsweek* (December 15, 1980) featured the headline: "Do Males Have a Math Gene", emphasizing possible biological basis. Others have proposed biological theories that stress brain lateralization. The lateralization hypothesis states that the left hemisphere of the brain is concerned with logical mathematical thinking whereas right hemisphere is concerned with emotional-intuitive functions. Because of left hemispheric dominance in men and right-hemispheric dominance in women, males indicate greater mathematical ability than do females.

In contrast, Eccles and her colleagues argue that the critical factor is not innate ability, but rather course selection (Eccles, 1987). She has constructed an Expectancy Factor X Value model of achievement motivation. It is posited that course choice and occupational choice are a function of expectations for success and the subjective value of the task. These, in turn, are a function of such factors as gender role socialization, self-schemes, and anticipated demands of the task or role. According to the model, the child's perception of important socializers (e.g. parents, teachers), beliefs and attitudes, the child's self-concept of his or her own mathematics ability or the child's causal attributions for success or failure in mathematics and the child's affective memories are all related to expectation of success and the subjective value of the task (Eccles, 1987). Thus, the Eccles model emphasizes socialization as well as cognition and affect.

Siegel, Galassi, and Ware (1985) contrasted a social learning theory of mathematics performance with a mathematics aptitude and anxiety model. According to the social learning model, skills, incentives, efficacy, expectations should be the critical factors in mathematics performance. The aptitude-anxiety model posits that mathematics performance is a function of math aptitude, math anxiety and gender-role identity. Empirical data indicated that social learning variables predicted more of the variance in mathematics performance than the mathematics aptitude-anxiety variables.

Fennema and Peterson (1985) proposed an Autonomous Learning Behaviour model. It postulates that failure to participate in independent learning experience in mathematics contributes to the development of gender differences in mathematics performance. According to this model, internal influences (beliefs about oneself and mathematics) and external influences (parents' expectation, teachers' expectation, and societal stereotyping of mathematics) partially determine what learning experiences students have in schools. These learning experiences, in turn, determine what mathematics is learned. In order to learn high cognitive level mathematics, it is necessary to participate in independent learning activities. Thus, if teachers have lower expectations for females in mathematics and if females have more negative affect and attitude about themselves and mathematics, they will participate in fewer autonomous learning activities and thus learn less mathematics than males do.

The Eccles, Siegel et al, and Fennema-Peterson models all emphasize affective and attitudinal variables as contributing to the gender gap in mathematics performance. In addition, there has been much popular theorizing on the importance of affect. For example, the popularized and highly publicized concept of math anxiety has been postulated to account for at least a part of the gender difference in mathematics performance.

Underlying the work dealing with gender difference in mathematics is the assumption that there are gender differences in mathematics affect and mathematics attitude and that these gender differences, in turn, influence performance in mathematics tests, selection of courses, and selection of careers. For example, if females experience higher level of math anxiety then males, this may interfere with their learning of mathematics and their, performance on mathematics tests and discourage them from taking elective mathematics courses. Since this assumption regarding the role of affect and attitude is implicated in a number of explanation models, it is important to examine the veracity in empirical terms.

Mathematics Attitudes and Affect

While a number of studies deal with mathematics attitudes and affects, a comprehensive treatment of the subject matter is possible through meta-analysis. Hyde, Fennema, Ryan, Frost and Hopp (1990) provide such a meta-analysis. The authors implicitly made a distinction between attitude and affect. There is some controversy amongst social psychologists about such distinction. Many subscribe to a three-component model in which attitudes consist of cognition (beliefs), affect, and behaviour. Others criticize this model and recommend a reformulation in which attitude is defined as an evaluation of a stimulus object (e.g., mathematics) based on three general classes of information: (a) cognitive information,(b) affective information, and (c) information about past behaviour. The authors choose the latter model to make a distinction between attitude and affect. They argued that they were examining a spectrum of variables that have varying mixtures of cognitive and affective components, For example, math anxiety is mostly affective in nature, where as stereotyping math as a male domain stresses beliefs or cognition.

Hyde et al's (1990) meta-analysis was geared to examine the role of attitudes and affects in gender difference in mathematics performance. They observed that there are two major scales that have been used to measure attitude and affect in the context of mathematics. The most prominent is the Fennema-Sherman Scales (Fennema & Sherman, 1976). The scales are as follows: confidence in learning mathematics, mathematics anxiety, usefulness of mathematics, mathematics as a male domain, attitude towards success in mathematics, effectance motivation in mathematics, mothers' attitude, fathers' attitude, and teachers' attitude.

The other important scale in this area is the Mathematics Anxiety Rating Scale (MARS, Richardson & Suinn, 1972). It is a 98-item scale that taps math anxiety in both everyday situations and academic situations.

The meta-analysis used studies that dealt with attitude and affects towards mathematics in general and such assessment by the Fennema-Sherman and MARS in particular. A large number of studies sampled from computerized data bases were employed. The search process generated 70 usable articles yielding 126 separate samples. This represented the testing of 63,229 subjects (31,116 males and 32,113 females).

For each study, following information was coded: (a) all statistics on gender difference in mathematics, (b) the number of females and males tested, (c) the mathematics attitude-affect variables measured Fennema-Sherman (F-S) scale confidence, F-S anxiety, F-S attitude towards math success, F-S effectance motivation, F-S attitude of mother, F-S attitude of father, and F-S attitude of teacher, (d) the age of subjects, (e) ethnicity of subjects, and (f) publication year of the article.

As described earlier, the mean effect size in meta-analysis is expressed in terms of *ds*. The *d* is defined as the mean for males minus the mean for females divided by the mean with-in sex standard deviation. Thus, positive values of *d* represent higher scores for males. On the Fennema-Sherman scale, all measures are scored so that higher scores mean attitudes more favorable towards mathematics performance. For example, a higher score on self-confidence means greater self-confidence, a higher score on anxiety scale means less anxiety. Therefore, positive values of *d* mean that males have more favorable attitude towards mathematics. When measures other than the Fennema-Sherman scales were used, the direction of the difference was reversed, if necessary to be consistent with the Fennema- Sherman scales. For example, on the MARS scale of math anxiety, higher scores indicate higher anxiety. Accordingly the sign for the *d* values was reversed for the MARS.

The analysis yielded effect size for the Fennema-Sherman scale. When all age groups were pooled, almost all effect sizes were small, and 3 of the 9 effect sizes were 1/10 standard deviation or less. The only exception was the scale that measured stereotyping of mathematics as a male domain which produced a large effect size ($d = -0.90$) This indicated that males stereotype mathematics as masculine significantly more than females do. It was also noted that the largest effect size for mother's attitude, father's attitude, and teacher's attitude occurred in the high school years. This was indicative of the fact that during high school boys reported more favorable attitude towards their mathematics performance than girls. The peak of the gender difference in stereotyping mathematics as a male domain also occurred in the high school years. The obtained analysis of effect size for measures of mathematics attitudes and affect for scales other than the Fannema-Sherman scale including the MARS presents similar pattern of results. There were few large gender differences. There were significant differences among age groups. The age trend for general attitude towards mathematics was in the direction of increasing gender differences (male having more positive attitudes) with increasing age. The same was true of math self-concept or confidence. Age trends in math anxiety was not significant. It was also noted that the large effect size ($d = +0.26$) for math self-confidence occurs during high school years.

The role of sample selectivity was considered. The effect size was smallest for highly selected samples. That is, among students selected for excellent performance, the gender difference in math anxiety was essentially zero. At the other end of the spectrum, the effect was largest ($d = +0.30$) for remedial samples, such as students in math anxiety classes or remedial mathematics classes.

Thus, the meta-analysis indicated that gender difference in most aspect is small. The one exception is the stereotyping of mathematics as a male domain. The effect size (– 0.90) for the Fennema-Sherman math-as-a-male-domain scale is large; effect size of this magnitude is rather unusual in meta-analytic literature on sex difference. The only effect size that exceeds this value is the meta-analysis of gender difference for certain motor performance. Gender difference for throwing distance and throwing velocity is 2.0 and greater for some age groups. The effect size for speed in the 100-metre dash exceeds 1.0 beginning around puberty. The direction of the effect size the Hyde et al. (1990) study indicates that males stereotype math as a male domain considerably more than females.

One explanation for the lesser presence of females in advanced mathematics courses and mathematics-related careers considers stereotyping to be a critical factor, but the focus is on females. That is, argument is made that girls and women hold stereotyped views of mathematics as being a male domain, these stereotyped view defers them from pursuing courses or careers. The meta-analysis makes it clear that it is male who stereotypes mathematics more than female. It is worth-noting that means for females as well as males fall in that portion of the scale. It indicates a rejection of stereotypes. Yet, the means for males in the direction of stereotyping is greater than for females.

With the exception of math as a male domain, all other measures of attitude and affect yielded small effect sizes. In general, gender differences in mathematics attitudes and affects are close to zero. So these variables are not good explanations for gender differences in mathematics performance. Interestingly the gender difference in mathematics self-confidences is about the same as the magnitude of gender difference in mathematics performance. The larger effect sizes were for complex problem solving among high school students ($d = +0.29$) and college students ($d = 0.32$). The gender difference for mathematics self-confidence is somewhat large ($d = 0.26$) in the high school years and is of approximately the same magnitude as the gender differences in mathematics performance.

It has been argued that math anxiety is a gender issue. This argument is based on the belief that females experience more math anxiety than do males and that anxiety prevents females from mathematics courses and, mathematics-related careers. However, the meta-analysis does not indicate sex difference in math anxiety. The largest gender difference in math anxiety is observed for remedial samples. This finding may indicate that there are more females with very high levels of math anxiety, and perhaps, those are the levels that prevent one from taking an optional mathematics course. However, this finding for extreme groups should not be generalized to samples of the general population, for which gender difference in math anxiety is small.

From a broader perspective, some analysts have advanced a different explanation to account for cognitive performance. Nash has argued that individuals will perform better on cognitive tasks when their self-concepts match with the gender stereotyping of the task. For example, an individual considering mathematics as a male domain will show good performance in mathematics if he or she regards himself or herself masculine. It does not matter whether the individual is male or female.

There is an interesting proposition and this requires empirical testing. Signurella and Jamison (1990) provided such an empirical testing. They carried out a meta-analytic study dealing with gender difference in spatial, verbal and mathematical ability. The meta-analytic studies in the areas of spatial and mathematical skills have indicated small to moderate degree of gender difference in favour of males; the authors considered masculinity (Masculinity score minus Femininity score or M-F score) as a critical factor for spatial and mathematics performance. Similarly, meta-analytic studies have indicated small gender difference in verbal ability in favour of female. Accordingly, femininity was considered critical in this context. It is important to recognize that masculinity or femininity is indicative of gender linked self-concept of an individual. On the basis of Nash's argument, the authors predicted that masculinity would be significantly related to performance in spatial and mathematical ability, femininity would be significantly associated with verbal ability.

The results of Signurell and Jamison (1990) largely supported Nash's (1979) postulates. It was shown that higher masculine and lower feminine self-concept scores were associated with better performance in spatial and mathematical tasks. These results were more consistent for females than for males.

For boys and men, there was a weaker although significant relation between M-F and spatial perception. The average correlation between M-

F and spatial perception was 0.29 and the test of the combined probability was significant. Similarly, there was an average correlation of 0.10 with spatial visualization performance for both sexes, and combined probability was significant. For the M-F measures the association between better performance on mental rotation (a higher form of spatial skills) and more masculine M-F scores was 0.16 for boys and men and 0.10 girls and women. In both cases the combined probabilities were significant. Thus, the positive relation was shown.

With respect to mathematics performance, it was shown that there is significant association between better mathematics performance and higher M-F scores. The results from the mathematical tasks were similar to the spatial perception results. However, no significant association emerged between better verbal performance and higher feminine scores. Thus, Nash's 1979 hypothesis, though not supported for verbal tasks, was accepted in the context of spatial and mathematics performance. Although a significant explanation for sex difference on cognitive performance has not yet emerged, it appears plausible that masculinity and femininity in self-concept, either alone or interacting with biological factors, demand further attention as mechanisms in the development of sex difference.

Implications

The empirical studies reviewed in the context of cognitive performance offer several major implications:

The meta-analytic studies provide little support for the global conclusions that boys excel in spatial and mathematics abilities and girls excel in verbal ability, the overall gender difference is small at most. Furthermore, a general statement about gender difference is misleading because it masks complexity of the pattern. For example, females are superior in computations, there are no gender differences in understanding of mathematical concepts, and gender difference favouring males in problem solving does not emerge until the high school years.

It is important to examine the role of critical factors in areas where gender differences do exist. It is known that females begin high school to perform less well than males on mathematics problem-solving tasks, Problem-solving is critical for success in many mathematics-related fields such as physics and engineering. In this sense, mathematics skills may continue to be a critical filter. The curriculum in mathematics, beginning well before high school, should emphasize problem solving for all students. The school must take responsibility in the teaching of problem solving, both because it is an important area of mathematics and because it is an issue of gender equity.

Boys may have more access to problem solving experiences out side the mathematics classroom than do girls, creating boy's pattern of better performance. The proportion of boys and girls in the classrooms of physics and chemistry may provide useful information in this respect.

Apart from examining role of external mediating factors such as sex discrimination in education and in employment, internal factors such as internalized belief systems may more thoroughly be examined. Hyde et al. (1990) in their meta-analysis looked into the role of confidence, math-anxiety and similar factors. No stable predictor of gender difference in cognitive performance has been identified. Although there are competing theories such as social learning and autonomous learning behaviour model, there is no critical study to compare and evaluate them at an empirical level. The role of attribution (subjects explanation of success or failure in cognitive performance) has been indicated (Hyde et al., 1990) but specific elements of explaining success or failure have not been investigated.

It is important at this stage to delineate possible mediating mechanisms (such as self-concept, attribution, stereotypes, etc.) and examine their roles in the causal network. The exploration of the gender-linked cognitions, affect and behavioural exposure (both imposed and derived etics) will provide answers to many questions on gender differences.

Box 3

Cognitive Performance Highlights

Spatial Ability

1. There is a small amount of gender difference favouring males.
2. The magnitude of gender difference in spatial ability is dependent on the type of spatial tasks. The difference is higher in complex task, such as mental rotation compared to tasks of spatial perception.
3. The magnitude of difference is declining over decades.

Verbal Skills

4. There is slight female superiority in verbal performance.
5. There is also trend for the decline in sex difference in recent years; the view of no difference may be accepted for all practical purposes.

Mathematics Performance

6. There is a small amount of gender difference in mathematics performance; this difference does not emerge before high school years.
7. The difference is a function of the level of complexity of cognitive tasks. Females are superior to males with respect to computation while males are superior to females on problem solving. There is no sex difference on understanding mathematical concepts.
8. Over the decades, the gender difference in mathematics performance is declining.
9. Males more significantly than females consider mathematics as a male domain.
10. There is no sex difference on math anxiety.
11. There seems to be some support for the association between self-concept and cognitive performance; yet, this needs further research.

4

Motivational Antecedents

The transition from empirical findings to explanatory concepts is a complex process. While identifying sex difference at an empirical level, some possible mediating variables have also been hinted. Yet, the comprehensive understanding of sex difference in cognitive performance requires further cognitive analysis. More specifically, the role of specific internal factors (belief system and cognition of subjects) need explication.

The consideration of internal factors stresses the significance of human needs and motives. Apart from their possible linkage with cognitive performance, the sex difference in the areas of human motives is also an important area of scientific concern. Such motives are identified for detailed review. These include achievement motivation, affiliation motivation, aggressive behaviour, and helping behaviour.

Achievement Motivation

Two areas of cognitive functioning reveal fairly consistent pattern of sex difference although the Magnitude of sex difference is declining over recent decades. Males demonstrate superior performance on spatial tasks, especially on complex forms of spatial task (mental rotation) than do females. Furthermore, males also show superior mathematics performance involving problem solving than do females during high school and college years. Since superior spatial-visual ability underlies restructuring skills and better mathematics performance is linked with a wide variety of achievement situations, it is important to delineate the mediating mechanisms for superior cognitive performance. It may be indicated here that the need pattern of males and females seem to be different. In a study (Ojha, 1995), it was shown that achievement, domination and heterosexuality, and aggressiveness were masculine needs, whereas deference, order, affiliation, and nurturance were feminine needs.

In this context, a number of possible explanatory models have been suggested. Four of them need detailed explication. These include attribution model, learned haplessness model, self-concept model, and value-expectancy model.

Attribution Model

Wiener and his colleagues have proposed attribution theory to account for a wide range of human behaviour (Weiner, 1972). More specifically, the model posits as to how people explain their success and failure and thereby form expectations about future outcomes. These expectations, in turn, influence individuals' future action. Attributions implying that success is likely and that failure is surmountable have the most positive effect on both affect and subsequent achievement behaviour.

Sex differences in achievement pattern may be mediated by sex difference in causal attribution. It is generally argued that males tend to attribute their success to internal, stable causes and their failure to external and unstable causes, whereas females tend to reverse this pattern taking personal responsibility for their failures but not for their success. Because sex differences in attributional patterns may be most marked for sex-typed achievement tasks and because mathematics and English are typically sex-stereotyped, more consistent findings are expected in studies dealing with mathematics and verbal performance. Studies focussing on mathematics have shown that females rate lack of ability and/or skill as a slightly more important cause of their math failures than males. Males also appear to rate slightly more important cause of success in mathematics than do females. Consequently sex difference in cognitive performance might be mediated by sex difference in attributional pattern. Prior to examining its empirical testing, other models may briefly be discussed.

The Model of Learned Helplessness

The model of learned helplessness is another construct that has been applied to achievement situations. Extending the work of Seligman (1978) and his colleagues into achievement situations, Dweck and her associates have studied achievement behaviour and cognitions of "learned-helpless" and "mastery-oriented" children (Dweck & Repucci, 1973). Seligman (1975) originally postulated that a prolonged exposure to uncontrollable (bad) situations induces a state of helplessness. Once induced, helplessness generates cognitive, affective and motivational deficits in an organism. Dweck in her studies found that learned-helpless children readily give up or show a steady decline in the effectiveness of their problem-solving strategies when confronted with failure. Mastery-oriented children, on the other hand, show increased persistence or improved performance in the face of failure.

Many studies have examined possible attributional differences underlying learned helplessness. In each of these studies, the attribution of failure to external, stable factors or to lack of ability has been associated with increased helplessness. In contrast, attribution to variable, situational factors, controllable internal factors such as task difficulty or lack of effort have been associated with mastery-orientation. These studies point to the significance of attributional processes (explanatory styles as mediators of learned helplessness).

The sex difference in attribution styles suggests that females may be more prone to a learned helplessness response especially for tasks involving mathematics. If this is the case, then sex difference in math and English achievement may be mediated by sex difference in learned helplessness. The weight of the argument is dependent on whether on not there is sex difference in learned helplessness.

However, learned helplessness has rarely been studied for subject areas that are sex-typed. Boys and girls may vary in the frequency of learned helpless behaviours depending on the subject domain under consideration. Girls may be more likely to exhibit learned helplessness in a male-stereotyped subject such as mathematics, whereas boys may be more likely to exhibit learned helpless behaviour in a female stereotyped subject such as language.

Learned helplessness has been operationalized in a variety of ways. In order to test the prediction based on learned helplessness model, it is appropriate to look into these four parameters: (a) attributing failure to stable, internal cause (b) attributing both success and failure to uncontrollable causes, (c) exhibiting a debilitating behavioural response to failure, and (d) teacher's behaviour check list.

Self-Concept Theories

The significance of self-concept of ability has been discussed extensively in achievement literature. Ability perceptions influence a variety of achievement behaviour including academic performance, and task choice. People with positive perception of their ability approach achievement task with confidence and high expectation for success and consequently perform well on these tasks (Bandura, 1997). That males and females have different perception of their competence has also been documented. Compared with males, females tend to have lower estimates of their abilities, performance, and expectations for future success in some achievement situations, even when they actually perform as well if not better than males. It is not entirely clear, however, whether these sex differences reflect a generalized low-self-concept/low-expectancy pattern in females. Several critics suggest that the male sex-typing of experimental tasks typically used in research may account for the apparent consistency of these sex differences. When the sex appropriateness of the experimental task is manipulated, females expect to do less well than males on male-typed tasks, females expect to do at least as well as males on feminine and neutral tasks.

These results suggest that sex difference in ability ratings and expectations are task-specific. Both males and females may hold higher expectations for their performance on these tasks perceived as more appropriate for their sex. If this is case, then sex differences in the pattern of ability estimates could mediate the sex difference in achievement. Both children and adolescents tend to sex-type math and language. Mathematics, when it is sex-typed, is viewed as a male domain. In contrast, reading and language are stereotyped as female domains. Therefore, sex difference in the ability estimates and expectancy ratings of students should vary across these subject domains. Boys should evidence higher confidence than girls for mathematics, whereas girls should evidence higher confidence than boys for verbal tasks. In addition, girls should be more confident of their verbal abilities than their mathematical abilities. On the contrary, boys should be more confident of their mathematical abilities than verbal abilities. Before we examine the testing of these predictions at an empirical level, the fourth-theory, expectancy-value theory, needs to be explicated.

Expectancy Value Theory

Eccles and her colleagues have proposed that sex difference in achievement can be best understood if a more complex model of choice behaviour is employed rather than models primarily based on expectancies and causal attributions. Building on expectancy-value theory, Eccles (1983) has elaborated a model linking achievement choices to expectancies or incentive value of the task.

Inherent in expectancy-value model of behaviour is the assumption that task value influences behavioural choices. Task value can be operationalized in a variety of ways. Atkinson linked the value of engaging in a task to the degree of difficulty or challenge inherent in the task. Success at hard task was assumed to have greater value than success at easy task. Several theorists have broadened Atkinson's concept of task-value. According to these theorists, the value of a task is determined both by the characteristics of the task and by the needs, goals and values of the person. The degree to which a particular task is able to fulfil needs, to facilitate reaching goals, or to affirm personal values influences the value a person attaches to engaging in that task.

Eccles and her associates have suggested that task value be conceptualized in terms of four major components: attainment value, intrinsic value or interest, utility value, and cost. Attainment value represents the importance of doing well on a task. Intrinsic or interest value is the inherent enjoyment or pleasure one gets in engaging in an activity. Utility value is the value a task acquires because it is instrumental in reaching a variety of long and short-range goals. Finally cost is what is lost, given up, or suffered as a consequence of engaging in a particular activity. For example, a person's perception of the amount of effort needed for success can influence the perceived cost of various achievement activities. Career decisions are not made in a vacuum and in many cases students must choose among several equally attractive alternatives. The perception of the amount of effort needed to do well in any given career will have a significant effect on career decisions. To the extent that the amount of efforts needed to do well exceeds the perceived worth of the outcome, the value of engaging in the activity should decrease. Similarly, to the extent the amount of effort needed to succeed in a career is perceived to interfere with other salient adult roles (e.g., parenting), the perceived cost of pursuing such a career should increase. Perceived cost of engaging in an activity can also be influenced by psychological factors such as fear of failure, test anxiety, and conditioned affect.

Individual differences on subjective task value are created by differential past experiences, by social stereotypes, and by differential information from parents, teachers and peers about the importance of and/or the difficulty involved in doing well at any particular activity. Because males and females have quite different socialization experiences regarding the relative importance of various achievement activities, sex differences in achievement may result from sex differences in subjective values attached to various activities. If this hypothesis is correct, we should obtain sex X subject area interaction on measures of subjective task value.

The predictions as expected with each of the four theoretical perspectives require testing. An empirical study carried out by Eccles, Adler and Meece (1984) provided an empirical testing of these alternate theories.

Test of Alternate Theories

Eccles et al. (1984) carried out two interrelated studies to examine the specific predictions that emerge from each of the four theories described earlier. The studies evaluated the comparative utility of these theories in explaining sex differences in academic achievement patterns. It was assumed in each of the four perspectives outlined above that sex differences in proposed mediation variables contribute to sex difference in achievement choices and behaviour. Eccles argues that subjective task value is a more powerful predictor of sex differences in academic achievement plans and actual course enrolment than are the variables associated with expectancies and self-concepts. By assessing all of the constructs associated with each theory, Eccles et al. (1984) tested the Eccles (expectancy-value) theory as well as the link of each proposed mediator in actual achievement situation.

Study I was designed to test the predictions associated with the attribution and the learned helplessness theories, Subjects were given a number of anagrams and number sequences of increasing difficulty to solve. Their attributions, expectancies for future success and behavioural responses to failure ware assessed. Self-concept of ability was also assessed for each domain.

In general, there was very little consistent evidence of sex difference on either indicators of learned helplessness or on attribution pattern believed to underlie this phenomenon for either math or verbal tests. By and large the sexes did not differ on the majority of measures commonly associated with learned helplessness, especially the behavioural indexes. The support that emerged was limited to a few measures of social cognition: attributions for success and failure in math to ability, and expectancies during the failure trials for both the math and verbal tasks None of these differences, however, translated into a sex difference in actual behaviour.

The only support for the learned helplessness perspective was provided by the two ability attribution variables. Low expectancy females in the success-failure math group rated lack of ability as a more important cause of their failures than did anyone else. Similarly, they rated ability as a less important cause of their math success than did any other groups.

Thus, there was very little support for learned helplessness model of sex difference in achievement motivation. There was some evidence of sex difference in ability attribution that was consistent with expectancy/ self-concept perspective, but these differences occurred only in low-expectancy subjects.

Study 2 (Eccles et al., 1984) was designed to test the hypothesis concerning expectancy x value model. The emphasis was on task value. Subjects completed a questionnaire designed to measure their attitudes towards their math and language courses. Sex differences in ability expectation and value ratings were assessed, and the hypotheses associated with these measures were also tested. Study 2 was also designed to test Eccles' major prediction that the subjective task value is the most powerful predictor of sex difference in achievement performance.

As predicted, subjective task value emerged as the most powerful predictor of students' educational plans and as the significant mediator of sex difference in both subjective educational plans and actual course enrollment. Furthermore, the significant Sex X Content Area interaction on subjective task value yielded the predicted pattern of sex difference. Females had a more positive attitude towards language and a less positive attitude towards math than did males. Comparable results did not emerge for measures reflecting expectancies for success and confidence in either one's math or language ability. Finally, as predicted by Eccles, there were sex differences in actual choices but not in the grades students attained while the students were enrolled in the courses.

This is not to say that variables associated with confidence in one's academic abilities do not influence achievement behaviour. The findings of Eccles et al. (1984) indicated that self-concept of ability had a significant positive longitudinal effect on course grades in both math and languages, but subjective task value had a stronger effect than confidence in one's academic ability on students' plans and decisions regarding enrolment in both math and language courses.

These results suggest that performance and choices are influenced most directly by different motivational constructs. Atkinson has argued that achievement motivation is aroused once one is in an achievement situation. In addition, self-concept of ability has been suggested as the motivational construct most closely linked to the arousal component of achievement motivation. High self-concepts elicit high arousal and low self-concepts elicit low arousal. Thus, it is expected that variables related to expectancies and self-concept of ability would have their most direct impact on performance measures in situations involving little opportunity for escape situations likely to arouse the achievement motive system. In contrast, variables related to subjective task value may have their largest impact on the decision to place oneself in a particular achievement setting and perhaps on performance when there is a viable option. If this is the case, then subjective task value should play more important role in mediating achievement-related decisions like whether to enroll in a math course, what to major in, and what occupation to select. Certainly confidence in one's ability to proceed is an important factor. Yet, subjective task value appears to be a major influence on which particular achievement task an individual selects.

The findings of Eccles et al. (1984) does not rule out the possibility that sex differences in confidence in one's ability, when they are present, contribute to sex difference in some achievement behaviour. Their data however, as well as other studies suggest that sex difference in the variables traditionally associated with self-concept of ability are not as large nor as consistent as once believed. Sex differences appear to be more consistent on measures of subjective task value. If males and females attach different values to various achievement tasks, then it seems likely that this sex difference is the more important influence on sex differences in achievement-related choices such as course and career selection.

Apart from motivational antecedents of achievement behaviour, the other parallel process that has engaged much research attention involves affiliative orientation. In fact, the pertinent literature on sex stereotypes leads to a form of popular belief that women have greater affiliation motives than do males. What is the magnitude of its empirical support? What are the experiential determinants of affiliative orientation? These are some of the basic questions that need careful analysis.

Affiliative Orientation

Affiliative orientation is one of the fundamental human motives. It refers to the tendency to form friendship and association to greet, join and live with others, to cooperate and converse socially with others and to love to form groups, etc. This tendency is reflected both at the level of thought and behaviour. It is an indication to enjoy being with friends and people in general. Recently, the construct has been conceived as having four components: social comparison, emotional support, positive stimulation, and attention.

Both projective techniques and questionnaires have been used to operationalize affiliation. The Thematic Apperception Test (TAT) is an oft-used measure of affiliative orientation. In addition, personality questionnaires such as Jackson's Personality Research Form (PRF) and Edward's Personality Preference Schedule (EPPS) are also used to tap affiliative orientation.

A number of studies have shown correlates of affiliative motivation. It is indicated that highly affiliated people more often seek social contact with others, communicate more often with colleagues, and visit friends more frequently than less affiliative people. Although these and other behavioural correlates of affiliation motivation have been identified, there is not much information to explain as to how affiliation energizes people to think, feel and act in different settings. It appears plausible that the role of gender and analysis of daily experiences would clarify some of the fundamental issues.

The Role of Gender

The empirical studies do not provide converging evidence on affiliative motives of women. In a study of married couples, wives showed higher affiliative scores than husbands on the Psychological Screening Inventory. McAdams and Constantian (1983) found no significant sex difference in the level of affiliation and intimacy motivation. However, they reported interesting differences in the thoughts and behaviours of highly affiliative men and women. Moreover, women in the study were two times more likely than men to think about people or interpersonal relationships. Hill (1987) using his newly developed Interpersonal Orientation scales observed small but significant sex difference in two of four components (emotional support and positive stimulation of affiliation). Some studies using projective measures reported higher affiliation motivation among females (Agrawal & Upadhyay 1983). Stewart and Chester (1982), after extensively reviewing affiliative motives using the TAT, argued that there was no conclusive evidence regarding sex difference in the strength of the affiliation motive. However, in a review of gender difference in affiliative orientation, Minton and Schnicider (1980) concluded that women scored higher both on projective and questionnaire measures of affiliation. Schroth (1985) also found significantly higher affiliative scores on both the TAT and the EPPS for female subjects. Another study found that among a sample of over 1,500 college students, women had significantly higher intimacy motivation than did men.

At behavioural level, many investigators have observed sex difference in establishing close relationship. For instance, compared with men, women stressed emotional sharing in their friendship, but men emphasized common activities. Women seemed to develop earlier competence for establishing intimate relationship. They also appeared to be more capable of experiencing intimacy in their relationship than did men. When compared with men, women's same-sex interaction appeared to be more pleasant, satisfying, meaningful and involved, and there were more disclosures by either partner.

Despite such tilt towards the prediction of affiliative orientation of women, the analysis of sex difference in affiliation and related-behaviours needs further scrutiny. A comprehensive approach to the study of sex difference would involve the analysis of social meaning of affiliativeness. In this context, the linkage between daily experiences and affiliative behaviour needs to be examined.

Experiential Correlates

Considering the significance of relationship between affiliation motivation and day-to-day experiences, Wong and Csikszentmihalyi (1991) carried out an empirical study to examine the role of gender as well as daily experiences in affiliation motivation. They focussed on five elements of daily functioning: expressed wishes, thoughts, activities, companions, and feeling in different situations.

Affiliation was measured by the Personality Research Form (PRF), a well-established personality measure. Affiliation was defined as a tendency to enjoy being with friends and people in general, accept people readily, make efforts to win friendship and maintain association with others. Sixteen questions sought information about affiliativeness. These were embedded in the questionnaire that measured other characteristics. Subjects were asked to indicate "True" to statements in PRF that described their characteristics and "false" to those that did not. A score was given to each question related to affiliation. An individual's total score varied from 0 to 16.

The bulk of the data was collected by Experience Sampling Method (ESM). The method requires repeated measurement of subjects' everyday activities, thoughts, and experiences in the natural setting. Subjects' expressed wishes were obtained by the question, "If you had a choice, who would you be with"? Their companions were indicated by the question, "Who were you with?" Subjects' thoughts and activities were measured by the question" What was the main thing you were doing? Responses from these open-ended questions were first coded in a large number of specific categories.

In the case of wishes and companions, responses were collapsed into two categories: friends and alone. In the case of thoughts and activities, unstructured informal social activities were grouped into one category and all other responses were grouped into another category. Apart from the measures, information about subjects' self-image was provided by the administration of a self-image questionnaire.

Analyses were geared to examine the role of both gender and the affiliative orientation. The comparison of affiliative scores indicated significant sex difference. Though small in magnitude, females showed significantly higher affiliation scores than did males. With respect to the dimension of expressed wishes, it was seen that highly affiliative subjects more often wished to be with friends and less often wished to be alone than less affiliative subjects. Males and females did not differ on expressed wishes. However, the analysis on the percentage of responses indicating that they were with friends (or alone) revealed sex difference. Women spent more time with friends than did males.

In percentage of activities in which respondents indicated that they engaged in social interaction, talking, parties, going out with friends were considered. Females indicated a greater degree of social interaction then did males. People with greater affiliative motives showed higher interaction compared with less affiliative subjects. There was also an interesting interaction effect. Highly affiliative females more often reported engaging in social interaction with others than did less affiliative females. However, the difference between highly affiliative males and less affiliative males was much smaller and was in opposite direction. Highly affiliative males actually reported slightly smaller percentage of social information episodes than less affiliative males.

The percentage of episodes in which subjects reported interpersonal thoughts concerning friends and social interactions was also examined. Highly affiliative subjects more often thought about friends than did less affiliative ones. Female respondents reported more interpersonal thoughts than did male subjects.

In general, affiliation motivation seems to have the strongest relationship with expressed wishes for being with others, whereas gender appears to influence what actually happens in everyday life, the time one spends with different companions and the time one engages in different social activities.

The experiential variables (happiness, alertness, concentration, unselfconsciousness, feeling good about oneself, motivation, involvement, and control) were aggregated within each person to obtain average scores for two conditions: when they were accompanied by friends and when they were alone. The analysis was directed to determine how gender and affiliative orientation are linked to the quality of experience. The situation effect was significant for all variables. Subjects reported feeling better when they were with friends than when they were alone. The Sex X Affiliation seemed to affect the male and female subjects quite differently. Highly affiliative females reported most positive experiences than did less affiliative women while they were with friends. However, the experience of highly affiliative males and less affiliative males did not differ significantly when males were with their friends. When they were alone, highly affiliative males and females again had quite different experiences. Whereas the former felt worse than other males, the latter actually had better experiences than other females. In general, affiliative females seemed to feel better than less affiliative females in both friends and alone situations. The reverse was true for males, although there were fewer differences between affiliative and less affiliative subjects when compared with the female group.

Wong and Csikszentmihalyi (1991) explain this interaction effect by conjecturing about mediating mechanisms. If male and female subjects do indeed differ in how successful they are in developing friendship and in how much they enjoy them, the nature of their affiliation motive and their ability to enjoy relationship may also be different. Their hypothesis is that males' affiliation motive may be described as a fear of rejection, a strong desire to interact with others triggered by unfulfilled wishes and yet a lack of skill to enjoy the interactions. Females' affiliation motive would be better described as a positive enjoyment: a strong desire to interact with others resulting from positive experiences and an ability to enjoy the interactions. Some studies seem to support this conjecture. Women indicate more intense friendship and they disclose more personal information to their friends. Moreover, women generally score higher than men on the TAT measure of intimacy motivation, which is designed to avoid themes of fear of rejection and to capture the more affirmative aspects of the need for establishing social relationships.

Furthermore, it seems plausible that an optimal experience depends on the successful negotiation between the person and the environment. People may face problems if their personality does not match the gender stereotypes of their society. From such a standpoint, affiliative men may have to overcome the mismatch. The study of opportunities for motive satisfaction that are available in the social environment may clarify this issue. Since social stereotypes affect one's choice of actions and experiences and the opportunities for affiliation are perceived differently by different groups within the same society, a careful examination of the motive in a broader social perspective is needed.

Just as affiliation has been recognized as a primary motive linked with human adaptation, similar status has been accorded to the aggression motives in the process of human adjustment. A fundamental aspect has concerned gender differences in aggression.

The Tendency to Aggress

The social psychological literature has extensively reported sex difference in aggressive behaviour. While such literature has generally indicated that men are more aggressive than women, the recent emphasis has gravitated to the analysis of conditions under which women and men differ.

Several considerations prompt such a reorientation. First, sex differences reviewed in the literature have focussed primarily on children's aggressive behaviour. Yet the tendency for males to be aggressive than females is larger among children than adults. Moreover, the methods used to study aggression are quite different in the child and adult literature. Therefore, reviews containing substantial amounts of child studies provide larger estimate of sex differences in aggression than are valid for adults.

Second, the survey of pertinent literature shows that researchers have operationalized aggression as behaviour intended to inflict harm or injury. Its operationalization has not been uniform. In the laboratory-experimental tradition, there has been heavy reliance on a "teacher-learner" paradigm in which college student subjects take the role of a teacher who must deliver electric shocks or other aversive stimulus to punish a learner for apparent errors. Within the field-experimental tradition, aggression has been elicited by exposing people to a mildly frustrating event such as some one cutting into line in front of them or a driver not moving when a traffic light turns green.

Such contextual variations pose questions relating to the generality of findings. In addition, a systematic comparison of conditions (through comparative analysis of studies) is needed to test alternate theories of aggression. It is useful to consider the conclusions derived from a meta-analysis in this context.

Gender and Aggression

In order to examine the relationship between gender and aggressive behaviour, a meta-analysis over other forms of informative source has been pointed out earlier. In the context of aggressive behaviour, Eagly and Steffen (1986) provided such a meta-analytic review. The authors limited their sample of studies with behavioural measures. They omitted studies that assessed aggressiveness by means of projective and other self-report measures. They also excluded from consideration numerous applied literatures on aggressive behaviour such as research on violent crime. Although research on violent crimes adds to our understanding of gender-related aspects of aggression, such behaviours reflect many factors in addition to the tendency to aggress. For instance, crime reflects access to opportunities for participating in criminal activity.

Eagly and Stiffen (1986) sampled studies from computerized database. The resulting sample of 63 studies yielded 81 sex-of-subject reports. The following information was coded for each report: (a) date of publication (b) source of publication, (c) percentage of male authors, (d) sex of the first author (e) sample size (male, female and total) (f) numbers of behaviours or responses aggregated in the aggression measure, (h) setting (laboratory, field) (i) type of aggressive behaviour (shocking, delivering noxious stimuli, hitting, psychological injury including verbal, nonverbal and written), (j) surveillance of aggressive act (private/ public), (k) freedom of choice to aggress (aggression required, free choice), (l) amount of provocation, and (m) sex of target of aggression.

The effect size used in the Eagly and Steffen's (1986) study was *d:* the difference between the means of two groups, divided by the pooled (within sex) standard deviation. The analysis of the sex-of-subject effect size showed that there was an overall sex difference in aggression based on available reports. The mean effect size (d = 0.26) indicated greater aggression by men than by women. The conclusion that men aggressed more than women was supported by counting test results demonstrating that.89 proportion of reports indicating a sex difference in favour of the male direction. (disregarding significance) departed significantly from 0.50, the proportion expected under null hypothesis. Greater aggression by men than by women was also consistent with a second counting test, which demonstrated that 0.34 the proportion of reports indicating a significant sex difference in the male direction departed significantly from 0.025, the proportion expected under the null hypothesis.

The analysis of coded variables showed many interesting features. Significant between-class effects showed that the tendency for men to aggress more than women was greater in laboratory than field setting and for physical versus psychological aggression. Consistent with the significant between-class surveillance effects, post-hoc comparisons among the mean effect sizes for the three classes showed that sex difference in semiprivate contexts (target and/or experimenter present) was larger than the sex differences in public contexts (additional onlookers present). Furthermore, the tendency for men to aggress more than women was significantly large when aggression was required rather than freely chosen.

With respect to the sex-of target differences, it was concluded that subjects aggressed more against men than against women. This tendency to aggress was greater (a) in laboratory than in field setting, (b) for physical than psychological aggression (c) in semiprivate (target and/or experimenter present) than in public contexts (additional onlookers present), (d) when aggression was required than freely chosen, and (e) with greater-than-minimal versus minimal provocation.

Thus, men delivered and received more aggression than women. The mean weighted sex-of- subject effect size based on the known effect size was 0.29 less than one-third of a standard deviation in the direction of greater aggression by men than women. Similarly, the weighted mean sex-of-target effect size of 0.13 only one-eighth of a standard deviation in the direction of greater aggression against men than women should be regarded as an upper bound of this aggregated sex difference.

Although this mean sex-of-subject effect size is smaller than the mean of 0.50 reported by Hyde (1986), the preponderance of studies with child subjects in Hyde's review probably accounts for this discrepancy. According to Hall's (1984) survey of all sex-of-subject meta-analysis, the magnitude obtained for aggression sex difference is smaller than that reported for many other sex differences in social behaviour and psychological attitudes. Aggression sex differences are apparently not especially large on the average among adult subjects, compared with sex differences in other social behaviours such as helping and honourable behaviour. Although Maccoby and Jacklin (1974) concluded that aggression is the only social behaviour for which there is a clear-cut evidence of a sex difference, contemporary review of the social psychological literature suggests that aggression is not one of the larger sex differences among adult research subjects.

Interpretation of Sex Difference

Despite the variation in magnitude of aggression sex difference across children and adult groups, explanation of sex differences demands research attention. Although biological approach to the issue has employed the evidence of hormonal differences between men and women to account for aggressiveness in men, the weight of evidence emerging from the analysis of conditions. (as reported in contemporary meta-analytic studies) favours a structural approach. The structural approach emphasizes social-role-interpretation of sex difference. Like other social behaviours, aggression is viewed as a role behaviour and therefore as regulated by the social norms that apply to people. In the context of sex difference in aggression, it is posited that aggression is sustained or inhibited by the social roles occupied mainly or exclusively by persons of each sex.

Gender role is an important class of social role in this connection. The male gender role includes norms encouraging many forms of aggression. Psychologists and popular writers have claimed that men are expected to be tough, violent, and aggressive. Similarity, research on gender stereotypes has shown that men are rated as more aggressive than women and as more extreme on related-qualities such as assertiveness and competitiveness (Brovermen et al., 1972). Gender stereotype-research has also established that such qualities are considered more desirable in men than women. Koteswaraiah and Rani (1996) studied impact of gender and gender role orientation on expression of aggression. The results indicated that both gender and gender-role orientation had effects on the expression of aggression. Females and persons with masculine orientation had greater expression of aggression than males and persons with feminine orientation. Jahan (1996) found that males were prone to aggression and females were more prone to regression while dealing with frustration.

The traditional female gender role places little emphasis on aggressiveness. The role emphasizes caring and other communal qualities. In addition, female gender role emphasizes avoiding physical harm to oneself. In particular, rules of coalition and avoidance of strangers are intended to lessen the possibility that girls and women become victims of sexual assaults.

Apart from gender roles, there are other forms of social roles. The military roles of men and homemaker roles of women may underlie sex difference in aggression. Military roles foster a numbers of traditionally masculine attributes. Aggressiveness is central among these attributes. Military indoctrination may transmit an ideology that legitimizes a wide range of aggressive behaviour.

Similarly, participation in competitive sports may promote aggressive behaviour. Men are more likely than women to have gained experience in competitive sports. The behaviour and the values fostered by athletic role affect more men than women. Like military roles, athletic roles require controlled aggression directed primarily towards opposing players and groups.

Most occupations pursued disproportionately by men may lack such clear-cut implications for aggression. Yet managerial roles in business and industry may incorporate an element of aggressiveness. Although aggressive behaviour typical of these roles is primarily directed externally towards rival competitors, a pattern of competitive (if not openly aggressive) behaviour towards fellow employees tipifies modern managers.

The social-role frame work directs attention to certain contextual features of studies of aggression. Most importantly, it predicts that sex differences are larger for aggression causing pain or physical injury in the target person than for aggression causing psychological or social harm. It is argued that the female role includes norms that discourage placing oneself in physical jeopardy and females tend to avoid physical aggression because of its greater likelihood of provoking physical retaliation. This prediction is supported in terms of larger sex differences for physical versus psychological aggression.

Eagly and Steffer's (1986) meta-analysis also examined several other situational variables as correlates of aggression sex difference. One such variable is whether subjects exercised freedom of choice about aggressions or were required to deliver an aggressive behaviour (and therefore merely chose to intensify the act). The amount of provocation or frustration that subjects faced were also examined. Strong external pressures in terms of either reduced freedom of choice or extreme provocation might out-weigh gender-related normative factors and therefore lessen any sex difference.

Studies were also classified according to whether the aggression was more likely to have been under surveillance by other people. An audience of onlooker might often increase the magnitude of sex difference in aggression, because it would make gender-role obligation salient. In contrast, the possibility that surveillance by onlookers might reduce the likelihood of retaliation by the target suggests that the sex difference may be lessened by an audience. It is true that women avoid aggression that may lead to retaliation. Furthermore, the absence of surveillance by the target could also reduce the likelihood of retaliation and thereby lessen sex difference, because a target cannot retaliate against an unknown or absent aggressor. The complexity of these considerations requires a closer look at the surveillance issue.

The contextual factors considered also included laboratory versus field setting. Finally the number of behaviours aggregated for aggression was examined. For example, a "teacher-learner" experiment in which the teacher is supposed to shock the learner for each of 36 mistakes provides an aggression measure aggregated over 36 behaviours. To the extent that measures were based on multiple observations over occasions or situations, they should yield more reliable estimates of sex difference.

Psychological Process. It is plausible that relevant psychological processes mediate the impact that social roles have on behaviour. It is likely that both skills and belief system play their parts. An analysis of aggression from the standpoint of skills suggests that people are able to behave aggressively to the extent they have acquired the relevant skill. Skills are often acquired primarily by one sex because people of this sex are more likely to occupy and anticipate occupying roles in which such skills are required. For example, skills relevant to physical aggression may be more important in men than women because their skills are imparted in both military and athletic roles.

An analysis of aggression from the standpoint of belief suggests that people behave aggressively to the extent that their beliefs about the consequences of aggression legitimize aggression. People behave unaggressively to the extent that their beliefs inhibit aggression. Emphasis on the perceived consequences of aggression follows from an expectancy-value view point, by which attitude towards a behaviour is a determinant of engaging in behaviour and is itself a function of the perceived consequences of the behaviour. In particular, the male gender role's emphasis on aggression may decrease the perceived likelihood of the negative outcomes of (a) guilt and anxiety about causing people to suffer and (b) harm to others. In contrast, the female gender role's emphasis on caring and concern for others' welfare may increase the perceived likelihood of (a) guilt and anxiety about causing people to suffer and (b) harm to others. These differing reactions may stem from other social roles as well.

Research has repeatedly demonstrated that women report more guilt and anxiety about behaving aggressively than men do. This sex difference in guilt and anxiety may underlie a sex difference in aggression.

Beliefs about harming others are considered in terms of empathy with the target of aggression. Several researchers have agreed that girls and women are generally more empathetic or sympathetic than men. Thus, the magnitude of sex difference in aggression should be positively related to the tendency for women (vs. men) to view an aggressive behaviour as causing more harm to others.

Another sex difference in belief about the consequence of aggression is the tendency for women to believe that their aggressive behaviours pose dangers to themselves. As indicated earlier, the female gender role may include norms discouraging women from placing themselves in physical jeopardy. In contrast, in various male-dominated roles, people may disregard possible harm to themselves. As consequence, the magnitude of sex difference in aggression is likely to be correlated with the tendency of women to perceive their aggressive behaviours as more dangerous to themselves than men do.

Sex differences in beliefs about the negative consequences of aggression (guilt and anxiety, harm to others, and danger to oneself) are the most likely psychological mediators of sex difference in aggression.

Apart from generating conclusions on the basis of meta-analysis, Eagly and Stiffen (1986) used a questionnaire to examine the predictions regarding perceived consequences of aggression. Sex difference in belief about the consequence of aggression was shown. As expected, male (vs. female) questionnaire respondents reported that their aggressive behaviour would cause them less guilt and anxiety about others suffering and would cause less harm to others. In addition, the guilt-anxiety and harm sex differences were substantial predictors of the aggression effects size. However, women (more than men) believed that their aggressive behaviours were likely to pose dangers to themselves, and the danger sex difference was significant predictor of the effect size.

It is noteworthy that sex difference in beliefs about the consequences of aggression emerged as most important predictor under some conditions than others. The guilt/anxiety and danger sex differences predicted sex differences in aggressive behaviour more effectively when aggressive behaviour was not required. Perhaps the optional quality of aggression in such situations favours systematic weighing of the consequences of aggression. Thus, in some circumstances, men aggress considerably more than women to the extent that women believe that an aggressive act has more negative consequences than men believe it has.

Taken together, the meta-analysis indicates that men are more aggressive than women and that this sex difference is more pronounced in physical than psychological aggression. It also shows that women and men think differently about aggression and these differing beliefs are important mediators of sex difference in aggressive behaviours. Women perceive negative consequences of aggression more often than men do. These perceptual differences are learned aspect of gender role and other social roles.

Another area of social behaviour where such social role explanations generate predictable behavioural pattern involves helping behaviour. The social role theory predicts different forms of helping behaviour in men and women. A comparative analysis of sex-linked helping behaviour and examination of contextual factors provide useful information regarding sex differences.

Helping Behaviour

The social psychological literature on helping behaviour has suggested that helping behaviour is not a unitary process. There are various forms of helping. Helping may take heroic and chivalrous forms. In heroic helping, the individual helps a target even if security of the helper in jeopardy. In chivalric helping the helper also takes the risk to protect the weak. At the other end, the helper helps his or her own group member and this involves caring and nurturant attitude. Similarly, there may be compliant helping in the sense the helper complies with the request of a target. On the other hand, assertive helping is spoken of when a helper responds willingly to the need of a target person. Since there are various forms of helping, it is important to examine the linkage between gender and helping types.

Furthermore, a bulk of researcn on helping behaviour was conducted in 1970s. This was also the decade during which experimental method was the most popular form of psychological inquiry. As such, studies of helping behaviour involved experimental manipulations either in laboratory or field setting. Consequently, this also involved the study of helping behaviour in the context of short-term relationship with strangers. Helping behaviour in term of long-term relationship was not in the focus.

In view of these considerations, it is crucial to consider a meta-analytic review that includes a broad spectrum of studies spread over several decades. Eagly and Crowley (1986) provide such a meta-analysis.

Direction of Sex Difference

Prior to the examination of mediating mechanisms, it is useful to identify the direction and magnitude of sex difference in helping behaviour. Eagly and Crowley's (1986) meta-analysis was geared to examine this in the existing social psychological literature. Like other meta-analytic reviews, the authors used computerized database. The resulting sample of 172 studies yielded 182 sex-of-subject reports. The following information was recorded from each report: (a) date of publication, (b) sources of publication, (c) sex of first author, (d) sample size (male, female, and total) (e) setting (laboratory, campus, off-campus), (f) surveillance of helping act by persons other than requester (g) availability of other potential helpers, (h) type of appeal for help, and (I) identity of requester.

In addition to the meta-analytic review, the authors used a questionnaire to elicit information from several males and females with respect to certain aspects of helping.

The mean effect sizes were computed as described earlier for other meta-analytic studies. There was significant mean size effect; men helped more than women. The mean weighted sex-of-subject effect size based on the known effect sizes was 0.34 or approximately one-third of a standard deviation in the direction of greater helping by men than women.

The conclusion that men helped more than women was supported by counting test results. It demonstrated that .62, the proportion of report indicating a sex difference in the male direction (disregarded significance) departed significantly from .50, the proportion expected under null hypothesis. It was also consistent with second counting test .15, the proportion of reports indicating a significant sex difference in the male direction departed significantly from .25, the proportion expected under null hypothesis.

It was revealed that publication year was related negatively to the magnitude of the effect size. Effects were larger (greater tendency for men to help more than women) in the studies published at earlier dates. Effect sizes also were larger to the extent that the following sex differences were obtained in questionnaire respondents' judgements of the helping behaviours. Males (compared with females) respondents (a) rated themselves more competent to help, (b) rated themselves more comfortable in helping, (c) estimated they faced less dangers from helping, and (d) judged themselves more likely to help.

Further exploration showed the sex difference in questionnaire. Respondents' ratings of competence, comfort and danger predicted the effect sizes considerably better at some levels of the categorical variables than at others. Predictions from these ratings were especially effective when the setting was off-campus, the helper was under surveillance, other helpers were available, and the appeal to the helper was the presentation of a need.

The analysis of the sex-of-victim/requester showed that women were helped more than men. Men were equally likely to receive help from women and men, whereas women were more likely to receive help from men. The weighted mean sex-of-victim/requester effect size of –0.46 or almost half of a standard deviation in the direction of grater helping received by women than men should be regarded as an upper bound of this aggregate sex difference.

The Contextual Explanation. The pattern of sex differences revealed by meta-analytic review posits the significance of social role explanations. The analysis of female gender-role argues that women are expected to place the needs of others, especially those of family members before their own. Women's consideration for others underlies their helping behaviour. In addition, women are more empathetic or sympathetic than men.

The female gender role may prescribe that women help certain people in certain ways. Women are expected to care for the personal and emotional needs of others, to deliver routine forms of personal service, and more generally, to facilitate the progress, of others towards their goals. The demand for women to serve others in these ways is especially strong within the family and applies to some extent to other close relationships, such as friendships.

Research on gender stereotype provides evidence that norms fostering this nurturant and caring helpfulness is associated with the female gender role. In stereotype studies, women have been rated more favorably then men, not only on helpfulness, but also on kindness, compassion, and the ability to devote oneself completely to others. Such attributes are considered more desirable for women than men. In close agreement with these predictions, studies have found that women, to a greater extent than men, provided their friends personal favours, emotional support, and informal counselling about personal problems.

The male gender role encourages other forms of helping. One such behaviour is heroic behaviour, especially altruistic acts of saving others from harm performed at some risk to oneself. Research on gender stereotyping provides only limited support for an association between heroism and masculinity. Attributes such as willingness to take risks, adventurousness, calmness in crises and the ability to stand up well under pressure are ascribed to men more than women. These are viewed as more desirable in men. Some support for an association between heroism and the male role comes from noting that almost all of the people who have been singled out as heroic by scholars and other writers are men. For instance, the Carnegie Hero Fund Commission of the United States has given awards to people who have risked their lives in saving the life of a fellow human being. The classification of 9,655 medallists according to their sex indicates that only 8.86% were women.

The idea that heroic forms of helping are prescribed by the male gender role suggests that men are more helpful than women under certain circumstances Because heroism implies that the helper takes risks, the amount of danger inherent in helping may affect sex difference in helping. Women may perceive many classes of situations as more dangerous than men do. For example, when helping is directed to a male stranger, women perceive greater danger than do men. In the absence of pressure to behave heroically, women may not feel as obligated as men do to bring harm to themselves in order to provide help.

The presence of an audience and the availability of other helpers may also be relevant to heroic helping. Thus, bystanders may elicit greater helping from men than women because heroic status is achieved only if there is public recognition for such heroic acts. There is no striving for glory without vivid awareness of an audience.

Related to heroism is chivalry, which is also promoted by the male gender role. Behaviours labelled chivalrous are characterized by pure and noble gallantry, heroic courtesy and designated devotion to the cause of the weak or oppressed. The helpfulness inherent in chivalry is illustrated by several of the chivalric vows taken by medieval knights: (a) to protect the weak and defenseless, (b) to respect the honour of women, (c) to live for honour and glory and (d) to fight for the general welfare of all

Thus, the helping behaviours consistent with the male gender role differ both in kind and in social contexts from those consistent with the female gender role. The helping expected of men encompasses non-routine and risky acts of rescuing others as well as behaviours that are courteous and protective of subordinates. These behaviours occur in relationships with strangers as well as in close relationship and may often be directed towards women. The helping expected of women mainly consists of caring for others, primarily in close relationships.

Apart from the gender roles, other social roles also make differential prediction for helping forms. The domestic role is a case in point. The service-oriented character of the "house-wife" role has been noted. Because this role is occupied almost exclusively by women, care giving within the family is much more commonly carried out by women than men. The view that domestic role encourages caring behaviour towards family members is consistent with women's role in close relationships. For example, studies show that women supply the major emotional support both to their husbands and to their women friends.

Other helping behaviours are prompted by occupational roles. For example, secretaries help bosses, nurses help doctors, and social workers help the distressed. Women are well represented in these occupational roles. In contrast, men are well represented in occupational roles (i.e. firefighters, law enforcement personnel, and soldiers) that require placing one's life in jeopardy.

As occupants of social roles, People-often gain skills required for helping. People also gain skills because they anticipate occupying roles that demand specific skills. For example, men are more likely to occupy roles in which they service automobiles and therefore may more likely to have gained the expertise to help people with their cars. In contrast, women are more likely to occupy roles in which they nurture young children and therefore more likely to have gained expertise to help children. Consequently, possessing appropriate skills allows men to help people with their cars and women to help children.

The analysis of the linkage between social status and helping predicts different pattern of helping on the part of men *vis-a vis* women. The classification of the sexes into higher and lower social status roles may affect helping. In general, subordinate status in hierarchical role relationship increases the likelihood that individuals could be providers of service rather than recipients. Because men tend to have higher status than women in organizations, they are more likely to receive help in attaining role-relevant goals. Women are more likely to provide such help.

The status difference between the sexes has contrasting implications for compliant versus assertive helping. Women may be less helpful than men when helping is elicited by the mere portrayal of a need. On the other hand, women may be more helpful than men when helping is elicited by a direct request and is therefore a compliant act.

The meta-analysis review of Eagly and Crowley (1986) provided empirical support for the predictions of sex differences in helping based on social role explanations. The social psychological literature has focussed on the kinds of chivalrous and heroic acts supported by the male gender role. It suggests that men should be more helpful than women to the extent (a) women perceive helping as more dangerous than men do, (b) an audience witnesses the helping act, and (c) other potential helpers are available. All these predictions were supported by Eagly and Crowley's (1986) review.

The social role theory also suggested that sex difference in helping behaviour should be influenced by sex difference in skills. Consistent with this prediction, men helped more than women to the extent that male respondents believed themselves more competent and more comfortable in helping than women respondents believed themselves to be. It is important to note that skill-related factors emerged strong predictors of effect size. The questionnaire data clearly supported this. In a study conducted in India, Jain and Bansal (1996) examined sex differences in feelings of inferiority and insecurity. They found that feeling of inferiority as well as insecurity were significantly higher among females than among males.

Eagly and Crowley's (1986) data showed that men were considerably more helpful than women when helping was elicited by the presentation of a need (and was therefore assertive) and were only slightly more helpful than women when helping was elicited by a direct request (and was therefore compliant). Men's higher status in society leads them to behave in ways that are somewhat more dominant and assertive than women. As a consequence, when helping is assertive, men are likely to help more than women.

Finally, the analysis of sex difference in helping favoured men less strongly in late publication years. The movement of societies towards greater gender equality in recent years provides possible explanation. However, there is a crucial research gap in the context of sex difference in helping behaviour. Although social-role theory has provided considerable potentials to explain sex difference in helping behaviour, social psychologists have paid little attention to the reasons why men engage in these behaviours more often than women. Future investigation may be directed towards empirical research conducted on heroism and chivalry.

Box 4

Recapitulation at a Glance

Achievement Motivation

1. Sex difference in achievement is domain specific. Males tend to edge over females with respect to analytical skills whereas females have an edge with respect to language skills.
2. The subjective task value (the importance attached to a specific domain of skills) is a strong predictor of both academic achievement plan and academic choices.
3. There is some evidence of sex difference in ability attribution (women tend to explain their success and failure in terms of their ability more often than men do).

Affiliative Orientation

1. Girls tend to show great affiliative orientation than boys do.
2. Women (and girls) spend more time with friends and less time alone than men do.
3. Females report more interpersonal thoughts than males.
4. There is a strong relationship between affiliation motive and daily experiences.

Aggressive Tendency

1. Men are more aggressive than women and this sex difference is more pronounced for physical than psychological aggression.
2. The extent of sex difference is decreasing over decades.
3. The differential beliefs regarding the consequences of aggression seem to be the cause of difference. Women report more guilt and anxiety for being aggressive.
4. Differing social roles of men and women also induce the difference in aggression.

Helping Behaviour

1. Men are more helpful than women in general.
2. Men indicate greater degree of heroic, chivalric forms and assertive forms of helping whereas women render a greater degree relationship dictated and compliant forms.
3. Social roles tend to explain gender difference in helping.

5
Personality and Social Influence

Sex differences in social behavioural domains such as aggressiveness, affiliative behaviour and helping behaviour have been discussed. The analysis not only suggests an interesting pattern of sex differences across domains, such as age groups, contexts and publication dates, the analysis also brings out possible role of mediators of sex differences. Another important area where such possible mechanisms can be investigated concerns the area of personality development and interactional patterns. In addition to interactional pattern, differences in group performances can also be examined.

Although sex-role literature provides detailed account of the sex differences in personality traits, it seems to be productive to look into the differences in personality development. It is assumed that an examination of sex differences in personality development would provide useful information regarding mediators. There are identifiable issues in connection with personality development. Almost all approaches to the study of personality development make use of the concept of stages of development; the stage concept, in turn, implies developmental milestones. Although, there exists a general impression that girls develop faster than boys, it is not known if females consistently reach developmental milestones earlier than males. It is also not known if this female advantage disappears with age or even reverses itself.

The Course of Development

In the past, research in the area of personality development was problematic in view of an unlimited number of personality dimensions and the lack of theoretical models. While measures like the California Personality Inventory (CPI) and Cattell's 16 Personality Factors provided a list of traits or attributes based on factorial studies, the divergence presented some problems. However, the emergence of well-defined models of personality development has contributed significantly towards our understanding of differences across groups. More specifically, stage theories have clarified some issues in recent years. Although a number of researchers have postulated stage theories of personality development, Loevinger's (1976) system of ego development has extensively been applied to the issue of sex differences. A critical examination of empirical studies employing Loevinger's constructs will be helpful in drawing inferences regarding sex-difference.

Loevinger's Stage Theory

Loevinger (1976) has postulated development as encompassing increasingly complex perceptions of the self and others. Conscious preoccupations move from the concrete to the abstract and time orientation shifts from the immediate to the future. The perception of other people, initially organized around simple dichotomous terms, becomes increasingly complex. In Loevinger's system, personality development proceeds through a succession of stages; each stage is characterized by a distinct developmental milestone.

The earliest stage, *impulsive stage*, is characterized by an absence of cognitive complexity and psychological insight. Perceptions of oneself and other people are organized around simple dichotomies such as good versus bad and active versus passive. Parents and peers are the constant source of labels. Individuals at this stage are oriented towards the immediate satisfaction of their needs. If these needs are frustrated, individuals resort to various forms of impulsive behaviours.

The next stage, *self-protective stage*, is characterized by the emergence of restraint in impulsive behaviour. The emergence of self-control is motivated by a desire to avoid trouble and punishment-two major concerns of this period. During this period, there is also preoccupation with issues of control. Children at this stage express greater wish to control other children than to be bossed by adults. The perception of oneself and other people continues to lack complexity. Emotions are understood with equal simplicity.

The following sequence, *conformist stage*, is characterized by a declining concern for punishment and increasing preoccupation with social acceptance and approval social interaction becomes less egocentric as individuals move towards conventional values and beliefs. The right thing is defined by social norms, which are perceived as universal and absolute.

The next stage is *self-aware level*. It represents a transition from the conformist stages. It is characterized by an emerging self-awareness and capacity for introspection. Social norms and rules are no longer viewed as universal.

The next level, *conscientious stage*, is characterized by the emergence of self-evaluated standards. Rules are followed because they are viewed as just rather than because their violation leads to punishment or social disapproval. One's personality is regarded as more complex and differentiated than at previous stages. There is recognition that other people have their own interests, problems, and opinions, making it possible for one to tolerate and appreciate alternative viewpoints.

The subsequent two stages are *individual* and *autonomous stages*. These are characterized by an increasing time perspective and increasing respect for individual difference. There is a growing appreciation of psychological causation. The individual and autonomous stages are also characterized by a preoccupation with issues of identity and emotional dependence and independence.

The Washington University Sentence Completion Test (WUSCT) is a semi-projective measure composed of 36 sentence stems. Respondents are asked to complete each stem; no additional instructions are given. The recorded responses reveal a person's characteristic way of reasoning about his actions, motivations, and personal relationships. Protocols that reveal little time perspective, impulse control, or self-effectiveness are scored at the low end of the developmental continuum. Protocols indicating a capacity for psychological insight and cognitive complexity are scored at the higher levels of the continuum. An empirically derived scoring manual is used to assign each response to a developmental level. This test has been extensively used to tap ego development.

Stereotypic Beliefs

Prior to examining inferences derived from a meta-analytic review on personality development, it is interesting to consider the backdrop against which such inferences are derived. There are several stereotypic beliefs regarding sex difference in personality. Girls are frequently portrayed as empathetic, cooperative, and socially attuned, whereas boys are depicted as impulsive, aggressive and egocentric. Even among children, girls have a reputation for greater maturity, and are perceived by their peers as more cooperative and altruistic than boys. Early studies supported the validity of these beliefs.

The sex differences in maturity that are so clearly portrayed in description of children are difficult to discern in description of adults. During adulthood, sex-stereotypic traits do not predict a clear picture of maturity of women. The depiction of bipolar personality dimensions (women's expressiveness versus men's instrumentality) provides no clues for maturity. Expressiveness is no greater hallmark of development than is instrumentality. By adulthood, males are no longer portrayed as less mature sex. Indeed, perception of maturity may undergo a change.

Another aspect of personality that demands consideration is empathy. The capacity to adopt another person's perspective is one of the distinguishing features of personality development. Because females are typically portrayed as more empathetic than males, females are judged to have greater capacity for understanding the thoughts and feeling of other people.

Hoffman (1977) reviewed the evidence for sex difference in two types of empathetic responses. The first type of empathetic response was defined as a "cognitive awareness of another person's feelings". Individuals with this ability can provide accurate description of someone else's feelings and thus display a capacity for perspective takings. The second type of empathetic response was defined as a "vicarious affective reaction to another person's situation". People with this ability can mimic the emotional response of a target person. Babies for example, might cry upon hearing the cries of another infant or adult; adults might report feelings of distress while watching a confederate receives shocks. Hoffman examined the evidence for sex difference in empathetic responses and concluded that boys and girls do not differ in their capacity for perspective taking. However, Hoffman found sex difference in the ability of new born and young children to mimic the emotional response of a target person. Thus, girls indicate greater affective empathy than do boys.

The capacity to control the expression of immediate impulses represents an important aspect of personality development. As reviewed in the preceding chapter, gender difference in aggression has been documented. As expected, males are more aggressive than females. However, there is decline of gender difference in aggression between early childhood and early adulthood. It is possible that males increase their capacity to control impulses.

In addition to self-control, the growth of moral principles is regarded as an essential aspect of personality development. Some early investigators perceived an initial female advantage, whereas other investigators perceived a male advantage.

Recent debates have primarily focussed on a possible gender bias in Kohlberg's (1984) theory and measure of moral development. Kohlberg depicted six stages in the development of moral reasoning. Moral judgement at Stage 1 and Stage 2 are characterized by concrete and egocentric concerns. Judgements of Stage 3 and 4 are characterized by a social perspective with moral decisions based on interpersonal considerations (Stage 3) and abstract societal consideration (Stage 4). Judgements at Stage 5 and 6 recognize the relative nature of many moral positions. Stage assignment is based on a person's response to a series of hypothetical moral dilemmas.

Walker (1984) reviewed the evidence for sex difference in moral reasoning in 79 studies in which Kohlberg's Moral Judgement Interview (MJI) was used. No sex difference was found. In the Indian context, Pradhan and Panda (1996) examined moral judgement of secondary school children in relation to their sex. The study reported no sex difference. Gupta (1995) also reported the absence of sex difference in moral judgement test involving Defining Issues Test (DIT).

Thoma (1986) reviewed findings of sex difference among studies in which Rest's (1979) Defining Issues Test (DIT) was used. This DIT is a paper and pencil measure of moral judgement derived from Kohlberg's (1984) theory. The DIT presents subjects with a series of moral dilemmas, followed by a list of issues that might be considered important for resolving the dilemmas. Respondents choose four issues that they judge to be most important in the resolution of each dilemma. Each choice is assigned to a developmental level according to a priori coding scheme.

Thomas (1986) analyzed findings from 54 studies in which the DIT was used. Gender differences favoured females among juniors and senior high school students, college youth and adults. Effect size did not vary significantly among age groups, suggesting that the sex difference on the DIT was small and stable. Thomas (1986) reported a continued female advantage, whereas Walker (1984) found an absence of sex difference. This gap, in addition to other issues, requires fine-grained analysis.

Sex Difference in Ego Development

As pointed out above, there were consistent findings with respect to sex differences in maturity, empathy and moral reasoning—three fundamental aspects of personality development. This gap necessitated a meta-analysis. Furthermore, a meta-analysis of studies dealing with ego development was considered primarily because, Loevinger's (1976) ego development system provides an oft-used stage model of personality development in contemporary literature.

Cohn (1991) provided such a meta-analytic review of studies employing WUSCT. Cohn's literature search yielded 134 studies derived from computerized database. The index of the effect size used in the meta-analysis was the mean difference between male and female ego scores divided by the pooled within-groups standard deviation.

The analysis of effect sizes indicated a gender difference in favour of females. Age was the most likely variable influencing the magnitude of gender difference. Gender differences were larger among adolescents than among adults. No gender difference was found among sixth graders. Junior and senior high school girls showed significantly higher scores than boys on the WUSCT. Among samples of college freshmen, gender difference declined dramatically. The mean effect size for freshmen was significantly smaller than the mean effect size for 9th graders. Although male-female difference declined by the first year of college, women still displayed slightly greater maturity in their sentence completion than did their male counterparts. After the first year in college, gender difference disappeared almost entirely. The difference disappeared among men and women in the oldest group.

To interpret the meaning of an effect size, it is necessary to return to the units of the original measure. The majority of young adolescents fell between the self-protective and conformist stages of development, with girls tending to score at least one stage higher than boys on the WUSCT. Girls appeared less egocentric and concrete in their thinking than boys and somewhat more concerned with social approval and acceptance. The majority of older adolescents fell between the conformist and self-aware levels of development. Here too, a girl tended to score at ego levels at least one level higher than boys do; it implies greater movement towards self-awareness and reflection. Male and female first-year college students tended to score between the conformist and the conscientious stages of development. There was a small tendency for young women to be more reflective than young men.

As indicated, sex differences in personality development favoured females, but the difference was neither small nor uniform across lifespan. Sex difference arose by late childhood, then present in samples of young adolescents. Among 13-year-olds, male-female differences in personality development were moderately large and this remained so for next few years. Although young boys remained bound by egocentric concerns, young girls moved towards social conformity. As boys entered a conformist period, girls approached a period of emerging self-awareness.

Sex differences in development declined among samples of older adolescents. The difference declined further among post-college adults and eventually disappeared. Sinha and Prabhat (1993) reported absence of sex difference in ego strengths of working males and females.

The dramatic decline in sex difference between high school and college sample could be due to a sampling bias. Presumably, male high school students at low, degree of ego development do not pursue college studies and would not be found among college samples. The absence of these males in college samples would automatically raise the mean ego level of men, thereby reducing the gap between males and females. Another possibility of this finding is maturational process.

Sex differences in personality developments can be attributed to one of three factors: sex difference in cognitive ability in general and verbal ability in particular, sex difference in biological maturation, and sex difference in socialization experiences.

The first explanation is not supported by available evidence. Sex difference in ego development is at least twice the magnitude of sex difference in verbal skills. Hyde and Linn's (1988) review of 165 studies revealed no sex difference in vocabulary skills or readings comprehensions - two skills that might influence the response to the WUSCT.

The second explanation of sex difference in personality development posits that girls enter puberty approximately 2 years earlier than boys, beginning around age 11. This is also the time when gender difference in ego development begins to be observed. This explanation also assumes that psychological maturity accompanies biological maturity. However, the correspondence between psychological and physiological development requires further empirical extensions.

The third explanation appears to be more likely. It posits that the roots of sex difference lie in differing socialization experiences. Lever (1978) studied the spontaneous play of 183 fifth-grade children and found that boys played in large groups with little opportunity for discussion or conversation, whereas girls played in small groups, often in dyads, in which they mimicked basic human relationships. The latter activity may encourage the growth of impulse-control and inter-personal sensitivity among girls. These two characteristics are associated with ego development.

In the context of personality development, the issue of moral development requires some analysis. Recent analysis in the area shows that there are two types of moral reasoning. Males adopt one type whereas females adopt the other. The moral judgement of males is often guided by abstract moral principles and a concern with individual right. The judgement of females is more contextual and is oriented towards satisfying competing needs of individuals in a given situation. From the standpoint of personality development, neither orientation can be viewed as more advanced than the other. Personality development may reflect the capacity to use both moral perspectives. It is likely that females use more care-oriented reasoning and males use more justice-oriented themes in moral reasoning during adolescent period. However, as females and males advance in ego levels, they make increasing use of both moral-reasoning orientations.

A transactional aspect of personality concerns influence behaviour. Individuals, while interacting with other persons, tend to influence others. A great deal of interest has been expressed with respect to the study of sex difference in social influence.

Social Influence

The classical conformity studies of Muzafer Sherif, Soloman Asch, and Stanley Milgram represent social psychological research in the areas of social influence processes. All of these studies have been geared to study the influences and the nature of influence processes. However, some of the contemporary investigators in the area have focussed sex difference in influence behaviour. Two broad issues within this specific field have been identified: the relationship between gender and social influence, gender differences in interaction style.

Influence Behaviour

The social psychological literature presents a wealth of information regarding sex differences in social influence. Maccoby and Jacklin's (1974) review of the experimental literature on conformity and persuasion found that the majority of studies reported no significant sex differences. However, among the studies in which significant differences were found, almost all of these differences indicated that females were more influencable than men.

Before statistical methods were used to aggregate research findings, the fact that most studies failed to find a significant sex difference usually would have been taken as evidence that there is no overall sex difference or that any sex difference is so small that it is generally masked by situational factors. However, use of statistical method of research integration in form of meta-analysis allows us to draw definitive conclusions.

Meta-analytic studies have established that women are more easily influenced than men (Eagly & Carli, 1981). The overall sex difference proved to be statistically significant when aggregated across a large number of studies. In addition, the magnitude of difference was assessed for each study in terms of the effect size, which was a standardized score defined as the difference between the means of the male and the female groups divided by the within-group standard deviation. Based on a sample of 148 persuasion and conformity experiments, the size of the sex difference was estimated to be between .16 and .26 in standard score units (Eagly & Carli, 1981). In terms of correlation statistics, the overall effect size corresponded to a point-biserial correlation between sex and influencability that was between .08 and .13. In other words, subjects' gender accounted for about 1% of the variation in subjects' persuability and conformity.

The meta-analytic reviews have also suggested that the tendency for women to be more easily influenced than men is somewhat stronger in experimental setting involving on-going interactions mainly in group pressure conformity experiments. In these studies, the influence induction consists of presetting subjects with other group's members who have beliefs and attitudes discrepant from subjects' own positions. These other members have surveillance over subjects' responses to their influence induction.

Although it is clear that some sex differences in influence and influencability exist in laboratory groups and other groups, it is less certain whether such difference appears in organizational context. In fact, reviews of leadership studies have questioned the presence of sex difference. They have argued that there is little difference in leadership behaviour of male and female managers or in subordinates' response to them, once factors such as type and status of jobs are controlled. More generally, apparent gender differences in the behaviours of managers and administrators are the product of the relative position of men and women in the organization.

These variations of sex differences in social influence lead Eagly (1983) to advocate social role theory to explain the difference. According to Eagly, the higher status that men ordinarily have in organizations and groups is the major cause of sex difference in influence behaviour. The higher status of men vis-à-vis women is also manifest in laboratory settings.

Eagly (1983) cites cases in our day-to-day life. It is argued that much of the impact we have on other people's behaviour occurs because they comply with our expectations about how they should behave a type of influence termed *normative social influences.* Because so many expectations that people convey about one another's behaviour stem from social roles, analysis of the impact of gender would primarily focus on normative social influence that arises in role-regulated contexts.

Each of the role relationships of everyday life, such as husband and wife, doctor and nurse, teacher and student, employer and employee, defines a set of expectations people hold about each other's behaviour. To understand how gender is implicated in role relationship, it is important to take into account their hierarchical nature. Individuals who are linked by a set of mutual role obligations are very often unequal in power, when power is understood as the capacity to influence the other person in the relationship.

The social norms associated with hierarchical roles ordinarily confer legitimacy on these inequalities of power and status. When legitimacy is established, the individual higher in the hierarchy is believed to have the right to exert influence by virtue of his or her position in the social system. The individual lower in the hierarchy is believed to have the obligation to comply with the demands that are placed on him or her.

The analysis of social influence in terms of hierarchy and legitimate authority has implication for gender issues primarily because men and women are differently distributed into social roles. Within most groups and organizations, the positions held by men tend to be higher in hierarchies in status and authority than the positions held by women. In work settings, the power differentials between men and women are clear. In settings other than work settings, power is also not equally shared. In the family, husbands generally have the power advantage for both routine decision-making and conflict resolutions, even though there are some areas of decision making in which wives have primary authority.

Because of these pervasive sex differences in the distribution of the people into social roles that are hierarchically arranged, there should be sex difference in influence and influencability, when men's and women's statuses are not equated or controlled.

There have been several controlled experiments in which the status of the communicator is manipulated in terms of high status communicator vis-à-vis low status communicator. Target persons receive communication passage in which a position discrepant from that of the target is indicated. Its impact on the target person is assessed. It is found that a communication passage received from a high status communicator produces a greater compliance than a communication received from low-status communicator.

Of course, social role analysis does not advocate an unchanged magnitude of sex difference in social influence and influencability. With social change, the difference is bound to be narrowed. In particular, it is predicted that sex difference would lessen, as women become more frequent occupants of higher status roles.

A crucial test of social status explanation concerns the study of group composition. The status explanation would predict that the gender differences would vary across mixed sex and same-sex interactions. From such a standpoint, the study of comparison of mixed-sex groups with same-sex group seems important.

Interaction Style

The study of sex differences in influence and influencability requires the investigation of the process by which this difference may occur. What are the types of behaviours people use to influence other people? What are the behaviours that are effective in inducing influence? These are some of the significant questions that demand analysis

Although stereotypical gender differences in interaction have extensively been studied, no study has directly compared mixed-sex group with same-sex group. Carli (1989) made such an attempt. She observed 128 subjects in mixed and same-sex dyads to examine effect of interaction on sex differences in influence. Subjects discussed two topics on which they disagreed. During the second discussion, one subject in each dyad was asked to influence the other member of the dyad. The observation of interaction yielded a number of interesting conclusions.

As predicted, the gender difference in interaction style was larger in same-sex than in mixed-sex groups. Second, men disagreed more with men than with women; women were more dramatic with women than with men. This revealed that both men and women showed less sex-stereotyped behaviour when interacting with those of the opposite gender. Third, there was no sex difference in influence strategy. When attempting to be influential, both men and women showed a decrease in stereotypically feminine behaviour and agreement and an increase in stereotypically masculine behaviour, task emphasis and disagreements, even though these changes were associated with reduced influence. Fourth, the gender difference in influencability was linked to differential treatment of men and women by their partners. The gender of the subject did not produce influencability. The behaviour that partners exhibited when interacting with male subjects was less influential than that they showed when interacting with female partners. These behavioural differences mediated the gender of subject effect on influencability.

It is interesting to note that subjects' ability to influence their partners is associated with their exhibiting a high amount of agreement and a low amount of disagreement. Although it has been suggested that this pattern of behaviour is particularly beneficial to women, the empirical findings show that exhibiting these stereotypically feminine behaviours benefit both sexes equally. Contrary to the prediction, the high amount of task contributions provided by subjects has no effect on how influential they are. Ordinarily an individual exhibiting high task contribution emerges as a leader. Yet, this does not occur in the process of social influence. Furthermore, it is expected that subjects would be influential to the extent they exhibit positive social behaviour in a group context. In fact, subjects like their partners when they show positive social behaviours. But one positive social behaviour–agreement is related to influence. One possible explanation is that agreement is intrinsically linked to task behaviour. When subjects express agreement, it is with each other's idea. Other positive social behaviours such as providing emotional support are unrelated to task contribution.

The examination of interaction strategy shows a picture that dispels common belief. It is believed that women would not use stereotypically feminine behaviour to induce influence. When attempting to be influential, both men and women are found to increase their use of stereotypically masculine behaviour in the form of task behaviour and disagreements and decrease their use of stereotypically feminine behaviour in the form of agreement. In addition, subjects increase their disagreements only with interacting with male partners.

Men and women actually do not differ in interaction strategy. Because the gender difference in strategy has been predicted on the power differences between men and women, the absence of gender difference makes sense in the context of the lack of sex difference in power.

It is also noted that the gender of the partner is a determinant of interaction pattern. The differential interaction shown by subjects to their male and female partners lead to the gender difference in influencability. Gender of the partner effect (the interaction between the gender of the subjects and sex composition of the dyads) is found. Subjects specifically instructed to influence their male partners disagree more than those instructed to influence their female partners. Even when subjects are not attempting to be influential, they exhibit a higher percentage of disagreements with men and agreements with women. Because influence is found to be positively associated with agreements, subjects, regardless of gender, use an interaction style that is stereotypically masculine, although less influential when interacting with men. If this pattern of behaviour occurs in real-life settings, it may contribute to the stereotype that women are more easily influenced than men.

Perhaps people entering group settings are likely to expect men to use more direct and aggressive influence strategy and may therefore be more competitive and resistant to influence themselves. In contrast, subjects expect interactions with women to be more friendly and social. Consequently, they are less inclined to be competitive and may be more open to influence. From this perspective, it is possible that the gender difference in influencability is not due to the greater receptivity of women to influence but to the greater receptivity of people interacting with women.

As indicated, one of the dominant themes in the area of interpersonal power stresses the various advantages enjoyed by the person who possesses more power than his or her partner. In a dyad, the powerful person is expected not only to optimize his or her influence, but also to be able to secure other benefits such as reward and admiration. Conversely the less power a participant possesses (or greater his or her dependence), the less he or she will be able to derive benefits.

However, in recent years, another form of social influence has surfaced in the course of research. The assumption that being highly dependent in a relationship inevitably leads to being exploited by the powerful other has been put to test. It is shown that a powerful person may respond to his or her partner's dependence with helping response; these benefit his or her partner at some cost to himself or herself. This can be termed as the influence of dependence.

The Influence of Dependence

Dependence is viewed by Berkowitz and Daniels as a cue, which arouses pervasive norm of "social responsibility" in a powerful person, who is then motivated to enact helping responses. In their studies, it has been shown that a person will work harder for a dependent person (one who may profit from the person's work output) than for a partner who is not dependent (one who will not gain from the work).

Schopler and Bateson (1965) tested the relationship between a partner's degree of dependence and the extent of help, or yielding, exhibited by the powerful person. They did not find a unitary relation between amount of yielding and the degree of dependence. Instead, when the cost of yielding was low, they found an interaction effect between sex of the subject and partner's dependence on yielding. Females yielded more to a partner who was highly dependent than to one who was less dependent. Males, on the other hand, yielded more to a low dependent partner than to one who was highly dependent. The interaction effect was interpreted as representing a difference between men and women in the kind of cues stimulating conformity to the norms of social responsibility. For females, increasing partner's dependence was thought to be a cue for arousing the norm and for the necessity to conform to it. In males, it was assumed that increasing partner's dependence also instigated cues for optimizing own outcomes because males felt their relative status advantages jeopardized by the possibility of their partner's receiving outcomes which are comparable to or better than, their own outcomes.

Later Schopler (1967) tested the interpretation of this interaction effect. Because the threat of a status disruption is enhanced when the value of the dependent partner's outcomes are similar to those of the powerful person, Schopler hypothesized that under such a condition males in the role of the powerful person will yield significantly less than females in the role of the powerful person. The results confirmed the hypothesis. There was also a second hypothesis. It was predicted that if the dependent exerts pressure for more help, thereby indicating the desire to improve the status, males would decrease their amount of yielding, while females will increase their amount of yielding. This hypothesis was also confirmed.

An important implication of the study supports the view that one of the limits on the effectiveness of dependence as an influence strategy in males occurs when their relative status advantage is threatened. If helping the partner means providing him or her with outcomes that are comparable in value to those attained by the powerful person, males will help significantly less than females.

Apart from the consideration of sex differences in specific social situations such as yielding or helping behaviour, the general questions may involve the amount of productivity in group situations. As more and more women are entering the work force all over the world, a fundamental concern has been expressed with respect to women's performance. Since work setting in modern times makes use of work groups, the examination of group performance is a crucial issue.

Group Performance

On the basis of the work with problem-solving tasks, Hoffman (1965) concluded that all-female groups do not perform as well as all-male ones. In support to the idea, female groups were found to have fewer members than male groups who could solve arithmetic problems. Female groups were also found to generate fewer creative solutions than male groups. There were also studies in which no difference was reported.

With a view to integrate the findings, a number of investigators point to the direction of task nature. They argue that most of the laboratory tasks have contents that favour males. The contents of the experimental task may tap differential ability of men and women. Women appear to outperform men on a variety of verbal tasks. Men appear to outperform women at various quantitative, visual-spatial, and field-articulation tests. Further, men demonstrate superior performance on a variety of motor activities.

In addition, the manners in which the task is phrased generate sex difference in individual and group performance. The greater accuracy of individual men at mathematical tasks appears to be highly pronounced when the problem is couched in a masculine form such as evaluation of the number of kilometers driven, but is less pronounced when presented in a feminine context such as evaluating the number of shops visited.

Similarly, some researchers have argued that sex differences in individual and group performances are a consequence of women's less favourable attitude towards problem solving tasks. From this perspective, mastery of problem and reasoning ability are aspects of the male role. Indeed, sex differences in problem solving performance have been found to be related to subjects' gender-role orientations.

While these factors could be responsible for sex differences in both individual and group performance, some other conditions may uniquely affect group processes.

Group Process

According to one model of the relation between interaction style and performance, gender should function as one input variable like group size to affect interaction. The interaction, in turn, influences group productivity. This input-process-output model assumes that there is sex difference in interaction style.

Most of the studies in which sex differences in interaction style are examined use Bale's category of active task behaviour (giving opinions and giving information) and positive social behaviour (agreeing and acting friendly). Carli's (1982) meta-analytic review, which located the largest number of studies, estimated a mean effect size (d) of 0.59 for active task behaviour, revealing greater task contribution by men than by women. The mean effect size for positive social behaviour was –0.59, revealing greater positive social activity for women. The magnitude of these sex differences in interaction appears relatively large in comparison with many psychological sex differences.

Despite such evidence, the relation between men's and women's interaction style and group performance has not been closely examined. The impact of gender on group process may take several shapes. First, men in-groups may perform better than women in-groups. This prediction is based on the possibility that men's active task behaviour may facilitate task-related activities, whereas women's positive social orientation may deflect women's attention thereby reducing women's productivity. Thus, high quality solution on the part of males is a possibility.

Alternatively women may outperform all-male groups. An important aspect of active task behaviour is that it is associated with high status in a group. Men in- groups are more likely than women to strive for high status positions. For example, men in single sex groups report a greater desire for leadership jobs than do women. If task-oriented behaviour is motivated by a desire to enhance personal status rather than by a desire for effective task performance, than men's active task orientation would interfere with task completion.

In addition, men's and women's group performance may vary with the manner in which individual contributions are combined into a final composite score. For example, men's high level of task activity might facilitate performance when members' contributions are combined, disjunctively, meaning that the group score depends on the most able member's performance. A high level of task activity would result in the most able member's contribution on the task, consequently enhancing group performance. In contrast, women's high level of social activity might facilitate performance at conjunctive tasks in which the group score is based on the least able member's contribution. If high levels of social behaviours are directed towards helping and encouraging the least able member to cooperate for task, effective performance is likely to emerge.

Finally, the effect of sex may vary with task type. Male groups might demonstrate an advantage, when task performance is maximized by a high level of task behaviour. Female groups show an advantage when tasks are maximized by a high level of positive social activity.

Towards Valid Estimate of Difference

In view of several possible determinants of group performance, it is necessary to seek for a relatively valid estimate of the magnitude of sex difference in-group performance. Wood's (1987) meta-analytic review of sex difference in-group performance is primarily directed towards this objective. The literature scan included 52 studies drawn from Hare's extensive bibliography of the pertinent literature. The sample also included relevant publications reported in the psychological abstracts and the Annual Reviews of Psychology.

Wood (1987) examined the following variables: (a) date of publication, (b) percentage of authors who were males, (c) sex of the first author, (d) sample size, (e) whether performance was for individual, dyads, triads, or four-or-more-person groups, (f) whether groups were same sex or mixed sex, (g) whether the group score represented a statistical aggregate, meaning a combination of performance scores from people who worked independently, yet believed that they were contributing to a group or an interacting group in that interaction among group members was possible, and (h) the direction of sex difference.

The 52 studies in the Wood's (1987) review yielded 19 effect size findings for individual performance and 45 effect size for same sex groups. Overall, the mean effect size for individuals was 0.38, indicating that men outperformed women when working individually. The weighted mean effect size for same-sex groups was 0.39, again indicating that men outperformed women.

For individuals, 18 of the findings were in the male direction, 3 were in the female direction, and 2 revealed no difference. It differed significantly from chance distribution. For groups, 51 of the findings were in the male direction, 28 were in the female direction and 2 revealed no difference. This result was also significantly different from chance distribution.

The examination of type of dependent measures showed that the number of solutions generated was a sensitive dependent measure. The effect size for individuals showed that men generated more solutions than did women.

The review located only 13 studies in which mixed-sex groups were examined. No significant sex difference was noted. Eight studies examined differences between mixed-sex and single-sex groups. It yielded 18 comparisons between mixed-sex and all-male groups and 16 comparisons between mixed-sex and all-female groups. Though not significant, there was a tendency for better performance on the part of mixed sex-groups.

The findings of the meta-analytic review answer several questions. Since the male advantage was observed in both the individual and group settings, it is interesting to consider what features of the setting and the tasks were responsible for superior performance of males. Perhaps there is a great deal of correspondence between the tasks men encounter in their day-to-day life and the tasks they undertake in experimental situations.

The second answer to the question whether men or women perform better in work group involves men and women's interaction style. To evaluate the impact of interaction on performance, one must isolate the effects of this factor from the effects of tasks or setting that favour one sex's abilities and interests. To this end, the sex difference at the individual level was interpreted as an indication of task or setting effect. Sex difference at the group level was compared with this value. When the estimate for group level performance differed from that for individual level performance, this was taken as evidence that group interaction was affecting performance independent of the task or setting factors that also influenced individual performance.

The importance of men and women's interaction style was evident when the type of tasks assigned was considered. Sex difference in-group performance was expected to depend on the fit between men's and women's typical interaction styles in groups and the interaction requirement of the task. Men appear to engage in more active task behaviour than do women. Women engage in more positive social activity than do men. Men and women differed in performance on tasks requiring these types of behaviour for completion. These findings concerning the interaction style have important implications for the real life work groups. Considering the differential pattern of interaction used by men vis-à-vis women, organizations and other social systems may accordingly use group compositions adaptive to their goals.

Box 5

Recapitulation at a Glance

Personality Development

1. Sex difference in ego development is moderately large among junior and senior high school students (female advantage).
2. The difference declines significantly among college-age, adults and disappears completely among older men and women.
3. Adolescent girls achieve developmental milestones earlier than boys.

4. In the area of moral reasoning, girls use care-oriented judgements and boys use justice-oriented judgements. Yet, as they advance in age, they make increasing use of both types of moral judgements.

Social Influence

5. Women are more easily influenced than are men.
6. The gender difference in interaction style is more in same-sex groups than in mixed-sex ones.
7. Men disagree more with men than with women; women are more dramatic with women than with men.
8. Men and women do not differ in influence strategy. Both men and women use masculine behaviour although agreement (not disagreement) is related to the effectiveness of influence induction.
9. Under some circumstances, the dependent also induces influence in the powerful person. Females yield more where their partners are highly dependent than where partners are less dependent. In contrast, males yield more when their partners are less dependent than when their partners are highly dependent.

Group Performance

10. Males indicate higher productivity than do females both in individual and group settings.
11. Men use active task behaviour whereas woman use positive social activity-oriented interaction style in group setting.

6

Gender and Managerial Role

The contemporary social changes constitute an inseparable entity in organizational life. In recent years, more and more women are entering work force. The swiftly changing sex-ratios in the organization bring several possibilities and challenges. It is admitted that a large number of women have now occupied top-level managerial roles. The percentage of women getting entry into the work forces is reduced at the point of promotion into managerial jobs. The proportion is further reduced when women are elevated to the status of executives. In 1984, the US Department of Commerce reported that women had 15% of entry level managerial positions, but only 5% of middle management and 1% of top management. One can easily surmise scenarios in developing countries of the world.

A fundamental issue in the area of gender-management linkage involves the perception and distribution of power in organization. Power is defined as influence by one person over others, stemming from a position in an organization, or from individual characteristics. Power can be categorized as objective or perceived. A person can have objective control over organization resources or rewards, which may or may not be perceived by self and others. The distinction is important because gender-role stereotypes lead people to perceive women as having less power than they actually have. Sex-role stereotypes may even contribute to distortion in self-perception of power among women.

Power can be derived from sources inherent in the organization: interpersonal relationship and the characteristics of the individual. A primary source of influence in an organization is derived from political power; it is linked with the individual's formal role. It includes control over resources, rewards and punishment, information, the work environment, and the work procedures.

The other source of power in a dyadic relationship is personal power or informal power, based on expertise, attractions and charisma. It involves influence through personal persuasions, faith, and personal identification. This type of power seems to gain importance in higher levels in the organizations.

Furthermore, the source of power may also be independent of the job concerns such as individual dispositions and skills. One is political skill, the ability to accurately diagnose and understand processes that underlie power. Another personal quality related to power is expert power. It is based on person's knowledge and expertise.

Because power can come from several sources, sources of power are additive in the sense that each new source adds to strength of existing power. It is also possible that some sources are redundant and add little to the existing magnitude. For example, expert power may not help someone who is very powerful by virtue of his or her referent power (power based on the process of identification).

Prior to discussing the relationship between gender and power in organization, it is necessary to understand the process of development of power. A longitudinal model of development of power envisages transition across careers. The development of power parallels the development of career, and each phase of a career presents opportunities for the accumulation of resources for power. As a result, the path of power consists of many small steps. Each step in a person's career involves opportunities and obstacles for the development of power. These factors include events under the control of recruitment, events at least partly under the control of the individual such as the decision to seek formal training and events largely beyond the control of either the individual or the organization, such as cultural rôle.

A corollary to the path-of-power hypothesis holds that the well-documented differences in power between men and women reflect differences in the factors that have influenced their development of power throughout their careers. While the occupational status of men has tended to increase over their life cycle, the status of women has tended to remain relatively constant.

Men and women may travel very different paths to power. Consistent with the view that men and women choose different paths to power, successful female and male managers have been found to differ in their choices of career strategies.

The relationship between gender and power is both longitudinal and developmental. Any observed male-female difference reflects a history of many small influences on the career developed. So it is potentially misleading to study male-female difference at a single point of time, because the groups are not comparable, Women who achieve powerful positions by way of an obstacle course may represent the hardest survivor, whereas their male counterparts may have faced fewer obstacles. If so, then at any given level of power, female managers may substantially differ from their male counterparts. As rank increases, so does potential difference.

In view of this complexity of comparisons, it is appropriate to keep track of the levels of analysis. Analysis of gender differences in power calls for four levels of analysis: social systems, organizational, interpersonal relationships, and individual level. The social system level focuses on the society at large and on roles and role expectations that develop within it. The organization level of analysis focuses on practices related to selection and promotion. The interpersonal level of analysis focuses on the relationship amongst individuals within the context of these positions in the organization. The individual level of analysis focuses upon the sources of power the individual brings to a position in an organization.

The levels represent embedded system. Because the levels are interrelated, events at any one level influence and are influenced by other levels. Inherent in each level are different sets of factors that may influence the career transitions in an individual's development of power. An understanding of the career transitions is possible when we survey the factors associated with each level.

Social System Level

The analysis of gender difference in power requires consideration of social system factors. Critical to male-female differences in the development of power are social factors in occupational choices. These factors operate before entry into a specific organization.

One explanation for the under representation of women in powerful positions is the under-supply hypothesis that too few qualified women are available to fill positions. An under-supply of women could reflect a shortage of women who enter work force or deliberate choice made by women that lead them into less power positions.

However, it is observed that a large number of women enter the work force. It is plausible that the self-selection process operates. Women may be more likely than men to make choices that lead them to jobs or careers unsuited to advancement to powerful positions. Three types of self-selection may operate (a) the choice of job versus career (a job requires little training, with little chance of advancement, whereas a career requires training but has possibilities for advancement), (b) the choice of a gender-typed occupation (a career traditionally occupied by women and associated with little power, such as nurse or teacher, versus a career traditionally occupied by men and associated with greater power such as doctor or administrator), (c) the choice of a gender-type specialty associated with great power such as a production executive.

Job Verses Career

The choice made by a large number of women of jobs instead of career could help explain an under-supply of female applicants for powerful positions. Whereas credentials for a powerful position may require the development of a career, economic pressures may force some women to seek jobs that require less training. For a substantial number of women, the decision to enter the work force may be based to a large extent upon economic necessity.

The choice of a job over a career has implications for the type of power. A career provides more positional power and greater chances for advancement.

Gender-Typed Occupations

A gender-type occupation is defined as an occupation congruent with sex-role stereotypes and dominated by one gender. Example of female gender-typed occupation includes elementary school teachers, nurses and social workers. Male-typed occupations include administrators, doctors, lawyers, and business executives.

Despite the increase in the numbers of women in the work force, they still tend to occupy gender-typed occupations. Female-typed occupations generally have less pay, less power and less prestige than male-typed occupations.

Gender-Typed Specialties

Even with careers with good prospect for advancement, women may tend to occupy female-type specialty. In management, for example, women may gravitate to female-type sub-fields such as health administration, office management of food services, whereas man may specialize in engineering, production, or operation. Female-type specialties are associated with relatively little influence in organization. The concentration of women in such specialties may result in an under supply of acceptable female candidates for powerful positions in male-typed specialties.

Self-selection into gender-type specialties may reflect social forces that are beyond the individual's control. Early sex-role socialization may prepare women for such positions and may create external pressures to accept them. At the same time, socialization may lead women to prefer such positions because of familiarity or perceived competence.

Of course, increasingly positive attitude towards women in the work place are indicative of healthy social change. The continuation of this trend in future is likely to reduce job-segregation along sex lines. Yet, a considerable amount of time gap is needed to rectify the existing inadequacy. Another source of inadequacy stems from organization factors.

Organizational Parameters

The organizational parameters operate at two key transition points: entry level and promotion. Every organization has specific policies governing the selection and promotion of its employees. Specific features of these practices may not work to the advantage of women vis-à-vis men.

Entry Level Analysis

Differences between gender may occur because women enter organizations through positions with lower ranks on average than men. Rank is directly related to power.

One factor related to entry level under the control of organization is job publicity, or information about job openings. If publicity concerning high-ranking jobs is more accessible to men than to women, then relatively few women may apply. Because powerful positions already tend to be dominated by men, it is possible that access to notices about openings of powerful positions may be relatively more accessible to men. There are some evidences that men are more likely than women to obtain information about job openings and to receive assistance in obtaining them.

Organizations that recruit outside their boundaries may rely in informal networks to publicize job openings. Old boys associations may tend to be primarily made up of men. It may become more important as rank increases. The absence of women from informal networks and the limitation of publicity of job openings may lead to restriction primarily to men of information about high level openings in organizations.

Organizations may inadvertently or deliberately exclude women from powerful positions through recruitment. They may actively recruit male candidates in preference to females or recruit women for positions with relatively less influence. Even among those who ootain information about job openings, discrimination may occur in the selection process. Some researches indicate that in comparison with men, equally qualified women are extended fewer job offers, receive lower salaries, and are seen as less desirable for managerial positions. Interviewers tend to give lower evaluations to women who are considered for jobs. Furthermore, some research indicates that the gender of the interviewer does not make a difference, both male and female interviewers tend to give lower evaluations to women than to men.

The development of an individual power in an organization may depend in part upon the amount of power held by the department or sub-unit in which the individual's job exists. Power may flow to departments capable of making important contributions. Such contributions may involve control over resources critical for the organization's survival, control over information, or control over the decision making process.

By some accounts staff support departments have less power than production departments. There is evidence that women are disproportionately employed in staff departments, such as public relations and personnel, rather than in marketing and production departments.

It is possible for an individual to enter an organization in a high-ranking job in a powerful department and still have little position power. Position power involves at least three key factors: (a) discretion, the opportunity to plan, design and implement, (b) visibility, in tangible results of work and in physical location, and (c) relevance, activities that are central to resolving organizational problems.

Research concerning gender difference in positional power has generally shown that men have more positional power than women do. A study found that men were more likely than women to have authority at work, one quarter of the men had authority over others' pay and promotions, whereas only one-tenth of the female employees surveyed were in similar positions of authority. Another study defined authority as the perceived amount of control over other individuals in the work place. The researchers investigated whether gender differences in authority were best predicted by women's qualifications, attitudes, and behaviours or by the behaviours and politics of employers. They found that women had less authority than men in general and most of the differences in authority were best predicted by the behaviours and politics of the employers. Men were more likely than women to obtain authority associated with their positions. Traditionally male occupied positions were associated with greater authority than were female-typed positions.

Kanter (1977), in a case study of single organization, found three sources of power less available to women than to men: (a) supplies having access to materials, money and resources needed to meet the unit's goals and reward its members, (b) information having access to and can use information, and (c) support having the opportunity to make decisions with the assurance that important people within the organization will back them. An independent investigation replicating Kanter's observation found difference between men and women. With respect to supplies, male managers reported having greater control over assets than did their female counterparts. With respect to information, male managers attempted to get early information about decisions and changes in policy more often and were more successful than female managers. Men also had broader informal networks that included top executives and outside contacts. With regard to support, men were more likely than women to seek favours from top executives, previous supervisors, colleagues outside the area, and personnel. Women were more likely to approach their current and previous supervisors.

Difference in Promotion

The other major transition in an individual's career and the development of power involves promotion within the organization. Research evidence points to the major differences between men and women regarding promotion. First, several studies show that men are advanced at a faster rate than women do; women also report less satisfaction with opportunities for promotion. One explanation of difference in rates of promotion concerns the permanence of jobs. Because women tend to have less permanence on average than do men, they have less time to advance.

A second finding is that promotions have different implications for power among men and women. A study found that women needed a greater number of promotions than did men to reach the same rank. This may be interpreted as an organizational strategy to pacify women without giving them real power.

Several organizational factors might account for the difference between the genders in the rates of promotion and the power associated with promotion. These factors involve three systems within the organization that may influence an individual's progression to a powerful position: performance appraisal, selection, and training.

Performance appraisal system and administrative decisions regarding salary and promotions provide guidance for decisions about careers. Performance appraisal is clearly instrumental in promotion and career development in the organization. One hypothesis is that women tend to receive lower rating on pertormance than their male counterparts. However, some studies found that women received higher evaluations than men did. Still other studies found no difference between the gender. Difference between men and women in rated performance has been independent of the rater's gender.

The inconsistency of the finding on ratings of performance may reflect a variety of factors relevant to promotion. Some reviewers of literature opine that women receive lower evaluation when the rater has to rely upon inferences rather than from behavior. Women may receive negative evaluations when they violate sex-role expectations by performing male-type jobs.

Another explanation of the inconsistent finding on evaluation of performance concerns a tendency to reward women for mediocrity. Competent men receive better ratings than equally competent women; but incompetent men receive lower ratings than equally incompetent women. if so, women with the best record of performance are less likely to be promoted than those with mediocre records. In consequence, the pool of qualified women candidates for promotion would shrink at each step in the hierarchy, and eventually the qualified women would be eclipsed by better qualified men.

Female managers may not only receive unfavorables evaluations, but they may also receive less useful evaluations from their supervisors. In a study, it was found that in comparison with men, women were less likely to receive critical feedback regarding the real job objectives, and incentives to improve. Supervisors also expected less professional commitment from women than from men. The supervisors reported that they felt uncomfortable in giving negative feedback to the female managers for fear of an emotional response.

Many of the same factors that prevent women from entering powerful positions may also prevent them from being promoted to powerful positions, Women may have restricted access to information about job opening, because of exclusion from important informal networks. Personal contacts have been found to be particularly important for selection to managerial positions. Executives may rely on personal contacts in the belief that they provide reliable information about job candidates and reduce the uncertainty involved in filling powerful positions.

Women may be seen as unlikely candidate for powerful positions because of their dissimilarity to those responsible for making decisions regarding selection. Job performance may not be sufficient or even necessary for career advancement. Moreover, selection and evaluation may be based more on similarity of social background than actual job performance or competence.

Training and development programmes offered by the organization are often directed at preparing employees for promotion. However, training may also represent a source of power and a consequence of having power. The connection of training with difference between genders in promotion may be complicated by differential access to training or access to different training among men and women. Because of difference in background, women and men may be seen as requiring different kinds of training to reach the same level of skill. They may also be offered different kinds of training because of difference in the type of jobs they occupy.

A second issue concerns the utility of training for promotion. Training can provide formal skills and knowledge and can give the trainee valuable credentials and credibility. These may be seen as a source of expertise and therefore, aid promotion, On the other hand, some kinds of training may be seen as signs of deficiency and therefore impede promotion.

When training is helpful for promotion, there may be built-in bias in the organization to restrict it to men only. In contrast, "specialized" training meant for women is viewed as signs of deficiency–filler and therefore impediments for promotion.

Thus, organizational promoters at the levels of entry into job and promotion bring possibilities of gender difference in power and position. In addition, non-organizational factors may also creep into the system. An important set of factors is embedded in the interpersonal matrix.

Interpersonal Matrix

The interpersonal matrix focuses on perception and social relationships that may influence career transitions. These factors operate at the levels of entry into the job as well as promotion. Critical factors of interpersonal nature include stereotypes, prototypes and attributions.

Perception of Power

Perception of an individual's power probably depends upon an individual's position in the organization. However, perceived power may exceed or fall short of positional power depending upon perception of others in the organization. Perception of others, in turn, may depend upon stereotypes, prototypes, and attributions.

Stereotypes are characteristics imputed to the members of identifiable groups. Female stereotypes tend to include such traits as gentleness, submission, dependency, and nurturance. In contrast, male stereotypes usually include such traits as forcefulness, dominance, independence, ambition, and competitiveness. Stereotypically masculine traits have been found more socially desirable than the stereotypically feminine traits (Broverman et al., 1972). An early study of men's attitude towards female executives found that male executives perceived female managers as temperamentally unfit for management and as having a negative effect on employee morale. Similarly, a survey found that virtually every perceived difference between male and female employees was viewed as unfavorable to women aspiring for high-level occupations. Some studies indicated that managers believed women had inadequate experience, drive, and motivation. Women were seen as working only to supplement the family income, not because they were committed to a career.

Stereotypes related to sex role might adversely affect an individual's relationship with supervisors, peers and subordinates. In an early study, male executives reported that they would feel uncomfortable with a female boss. Men who had female coworkers had more strongly negative reactions towards women than those who lacked female coworkers.

Relevant research suggests that gender-based stereotypes associate power with men but not with women. If this is so, women seeking powerful positions face the possibility that stereotypes might diminish perception of their potential power. In this way, perceived power of women may be distorted through gender-based stereotypes.

Sex-role stereotypes imply that the power is stereotypically male. To be a man is to be powerful. Thus, a powerful woman is a contradiction in terms. Incompatibility between the female stereotype and power in an organization may result in role conflict in women.

Stereotypes and associated sex-role expectations held by subordinates may be problematic for female managers. It is shown that female leaders who display behaviours incongruent with sex-role expectations receive lower evaluations from their subordinates, than do women who display traditional sex-role behaviours. Thus, stereotypes may foster negative attitudes towards women and create gender difference. Women in powerful positions face two types of role conflicts. The first form of role conflict is related to the incompatibility between work expectations and gender-role expectations.

Prototype is another factor in interpersonal situation. It is defined as idealized mental image or cognitive category that specify the behaviours expected of someone in a particular role. Actual behaviour is compared to the prototype to evaluate the individual's performance. In work setting, prototypes involve idealized expectations of the incumbents of jobs.

Leadership prototypes and implicit theories of leadership may influence expectations and evaluation of leadership. Some researchers suggest that prototypes of leadership include stereotypically male traits and characteristics. If so, prototypes concerning powerful positions may also be male-typed.

In addition to prototypes, attributions may play an important role in the gender difference. Attributions refer to perception of causes of behaviours. Attributions may be important for expectation about performance. If successful performance is attributed to an internal and stable cause such as ability, similar performance is expected in future. If the successful performance is attributed to an external and unstable cause, such as luck, similar performance is not expected in the future.

Difference in attributions associated with gender is fairly well documented. In comparison with men, women make more external attributions concerning their own success and more internal attributions for their own failures. Differences in attribution may reflect difference in expectations for performances. Women with low expectation may tend to attribute success to temporary or unstable causes, such as luck.

Research on attributions made about women's and men's performances indicates similar results. Women's successful performance tends to be attributed to effort and luck, whereas men's successful performance tends to be attributed to skill and ability. One potential moderator in the relationship is the gender typing of the task. In comparison with male-typed tasks, female-typed tasks are perceived as requiring less skill and ability and are more prone to external attribution of success. To the extent that the development of power depends upon perceived skill and ability, power may depend upon attributions. For example, Kanter (1977) suggests that power depends upon "recognized competence". Consistent with this view, it is found that causal attributions associated with perceived power, attributions of promotion to the individual's ability are correlated with evaluation of power and responsibility.

The factors such as stereotypes, prototypes and attributions do not operate in a simple and straightforward manner. There are a few other factors that complicate the picture. The minority status of women is one such condition.

Minority Status

Women constitute a minority status in the organization. The visible minority becomes salient in view of the relative scarcity of women in the upper rank of management. This may lead to exaggerated publicity of individual activity. When a member of minority experiences a success or a failure, more people within the organization may learn of it than if the same success or failure involves a member of the majority. The publicity attending on individual may increase with the rarity of others in the same activity. If so, salience may be a handicap.

One well-documented effect of minority status is an exaggerated perception of difference. This applies to differences between the genders, and it may affect expectations. For example, male managers exaggerate the difference between themselves and women. Men believe that women cannot be depended upon to act in accordance with the organizational norms. If this is so, men may close ranks to exclude women. Because of the importance of peer groups as sources of information, isolation from peer networks could be a serious handicap in developing power.

A major construct that seems to have relevance for development of career is the "Power-begets-power" concept. Its working is manifest in different forms of relationship as individual develops in the organization.

Relationship Types

Relationship with supervisors, peers, and subordinates may affect the development of an individual's power in the organization. Each of these relationship types presents opportunity to gain a specific resource for power and to capitalize on existing resources. Individual can use relationships with peers to gain access to coalitions and networks. Relationship with supervisors can allow autonomy or a mentoring relationship. Relationships with subordinates can be used to gain a loyal base of power and support.

These types of relationships relevant to power may be independent and mutually reinforcing. A general hypothesis in this context is that power begets power. Power may be seen as synergistic in that gaining power in one relationship may increase the possibility of gaining it in others and that losing power in one relationship may lead to its loss in others. For example, an individual who gains power from a supervisor could use it to increase influence with peers or subordinates. Similarly an increase in power gained through efficient subordinates could increase an individuals value in the coalition of peers. Building power in lateral and vertical relation may enhance a person's credibility in the organization.

Relationship with supervisor is a primary source of power enhancement. The supervisor's possible role as a mentor is a primary consideration. Mentors have been defined as higher ranking, influential, senior organization members with advanced experience and knowledge who are committed to providing upward mobility and support to a protege's professional career. Mentoring relationships are generally long-term, and are characterized by substantial emotional commitment by both parties.

Mentoring relationships may serve a number of functions. First, mentors may provide training and inside information on the organization and its political functions. Second, they may provide psychosocial support and increase the protégé's self-confidence by serving as a counsellor, friend, role-model, and coach. Third, they may serve as a buffer between the organization and the individual by running interferences for the protege and providing special access to information, contacts and resources. In short, mentors may serve to provide for the protégé's upward mobility in the organization by providing support, visibility, resources and direction.

Some researchers suggest that women are less likely than men to obtain mentors. However, a mentor may actually be more important for a female manager than for a male manager. Research indicates that women who have mentors fare better in organizations than those who do not. A study found that women who had mentors advanced more rapidly in the organization then those who lacked mentors. Women who were evaluated in an assessment center as lacking middle-management potential advanced as far with a mentor as those who had potential but lacked mentors. Female managers reported that their mentors assisted with promotions, information, and support.

Several studies indicate that successful female managers recognize the importance of mentors for their careers, but several barriers prevent women from finding mentors. Female managers may have fewer formal and informal opportunities to meet potential mentors than their male counterparts. They may be also less likely to initiate relationship with potential mentors. The rarity of female mentors may restrict their availability to female managers. The few female executives available may be unwilling to be mentors for female managers. Moreover, because female executives are less powerful than their male counterparts, they may not be in positions to provide necessary support for their female protege.

Sex-role socialization may discourage men from acting as mentors for female managers. Men may be more comfortable as mentors to other men, perhaps in part to avoid rumours or potential sexual involvement. Both mentors and proteges have reported sexual tension as an issue. Cross-gender mentor relationships have been found associated with problems related to jealous spouses and resentful coworkers. Although mentors contribute to the development of the individual's power and have been found to be associated with advancement in women, women may be less likely than men to have such relationships.

Relationship with Peers

Relationship with peers may provide horizontal power through access to information or through alliance. Relationship with peers can involve coworkers within organization or outside of it. Two types of relationships are important: coalition or alliances between coworkers, formed for purpose of influence, and networks, or relationship based on mutual exchange of information.

Coalition in organization may be either ongoing or short-term. Ongoing coalitions are stable, institutionalized elements of the informal structure of the organization. They consist of a set of people who bargain among themselves to distribute organizational power. Short-term coalitions form around current issues and problems for limited period of time and dissolve when the goal is achieved.

Ongoing and short-term coalitions have different advantages and disadvantages for the development of power. Ongoing coalitions provide stable, consistent bases of power. Long-term alliances may increase the accessibility of some high-ranking positions while limiting the accessibility of others. Short-term coalitions may provide more immediate gains or losses of influence but may be less likely to support an individual's development of power over time.

Early laboratory research found that women adopted anti-competitive and accommodative strategies in coalitions, whereas men adopted exploitative and success-oriented strategies. However, later research found that women adopted the same competitive strategies as men.

Low-power group members have been found to strive towards equality. They tend to develop relationships in cooperative rather than competitive manner. Because women tend to have less power than men in organization, research on behaviour in coalitions by people with little power may apply to women. These predictions are confirmed by research finding that in comparison with men, women form stronger commitments to their partners in the equal power situations.

The comparison of behaviour of men and women in group situations provides useful information. It is observed that men tend to be more verbally active and influential than women and are more likely to be seen as group leaders. Men also initiate more task-oriented behaviours; women initiate socio-emotional behaviour. The researchers argue that gender is associated with status in-groups; so men initially gain status because of gender. Once in position of power, men may adopt behaviour consistent with their position. Difference between the gender on behaviour in-groups may reflect status-role expectation as much as gender-role expectation.

The gender-composition of the group has been related to power-related behaviours. The exercise of power, as defined in terms of the amount of verbal interaction, is greater in all-male groups than in all-female groups. Men in mixed-groups tend to dominate and women verbalize less than they do in all-female groups. Men in mixed-groups are more personal in their expositions, address others more often and are less concerned with expression of commitment.

The network is another level of analysis. A network is a collection of people who regularly exchange information, support, and favours within and across the organization's boundaries. Networks may be more stable than coalition and may have less potential for conflict.

Network can be a source of power by disseminating information. Two general types of information may be exchanged in networks. First, information about job openings may be acquired through networks. Information may increase access to powerful positions in organizations. Second, information needed to perform job functions may be obtained. One way that this may occur is through informal training for individuals entering a position. Gaining access to networks may be particularly crucial for high-technology field in which the rapid change of information requires informal means of transmission.

There is not much empirical research on the relationship among gender, network and power. In general, networks are segregated by gender. Women usually have their own networks and so do men. Men and women are equally adept in building organizational network, but men are apparently more adept in developing outside contacts and interacting with organization's dominant coalition. If women are under-represented in male networks, their exclusion could reflect both intentional and unintentional influences. For example, women may be seen as disruptive intruders in all-male groups and excluded for that reason. Women may also be excluded because men feel uncomfortable in dealing with them in informal setting. Women may also be underrepresented in informal networks by choice. A study found that women were less willing than their male counterparts to share relevant data with colleagues. Another study found that 67% of the female managers reported that their primary source of information was superiors or subordinates. Similarly, women reported less use of informal mechanisms to advance their careers. These findings suggest that women may be less likely than men to use informal peer networks as sources of information.

Apart from relationship with peers, relationship with subordinates is another potential source of power. Theories concerning influence in organizations suggest that relationship with subordinates represent an important source of power.

Relationship with Subordinates

Acceptance by subordinates is an important condition for securing power. A manager's ability to influence his or her own superiors may depend upon acceptance by subordinates. Conversely, upward influence may be important to a manager's ability to exert leadership with subordinates.

There is research evidence to suggest that subordinates can influence the power of their supervisors by providing or failing to provide a dependable base of support. Although perceived leader power has been found to be related to subordinates' reaction, few empirical studies have been carried out to examine the relationship between gender and subordinates' acceptance-rejection behaviour.

In a field study, the findings indicated that male supervisors gave more promotions to their subordinates than did female supervisors. Women's apparent lack of ability to meet their subordinates' needs reduce their ability to gain power through subordinates.

The literature concurring the relationship between gender and power highlights another set of factors. These are individual difference factors. A detailed analysis of these factors provides several clues.

Individual Difference Factors

A common explanation for differences between the genders in power concerns individual characteristics. These characteristics influence individuals' interaction in organizational setting. These factors include background factors, stylistic dimensions, personality features, and career aspirations.

Background Factors

In the context of exercising power, a number of factors seem relevant. Factors such as education, family structure, birth order and other demographic features play their roles. Kelly (1983) used archival biographical data to compare 236 eminent men and 81 eminent women who were political or organizational leaders. The men and women did not differ on factors related to home background; relationship with parents or siblings, or birth order. However, the public roles of their parents did differ. In comparison with powerful men, powerful women were more likely to come from families in which the mother was professionally successful and the father attained little success either in career or income. This finding implies that the powerful women may have had mothers who served as competent role model. Moreover, the apparent role reversal at home suggests that the mother served as a role model in the family as well as in work. The study also found that the eminent women had better relationships with peers at school, disliked their teachers less frequently, and finished college more frequently than did the comparison group of eminent men.

One interpretation of Kelly's (1983) finding is that successful women are socialized in ways that make them psychologically more similar to the average man than to the average woman. Consistent with this interpretation, a study found that a group of women in male-typed business roles saw themselves as having more male-typed characteristics. They saw domestic roles as less important, they were more achieving. In effect, women in male-typed occupations seem to have accepted male gender roles for themselves. Another study found that women had fewer years in a career and had less education than men.

Research concerning education shows that it is associated with power but the association is much stronger for men than for women. A comparative study found that education was correlated with the likelihood of attaining position of authority, but the relationship was three times as great for men as for women.

Stylistic Dimensions

It is possible that men and women have different patterns of management style and this variation may be a source of power. Other researchers view that men and women use similar pattern of management, but women use it with less skill than do men. McClelland (1975) suggested that men use directive behaviours such as manipulating and restructuring the environment, whereas women use interpersonally-oriented behaviours concerned with process and contextual issues.

Few studies have directly investigated gender-difference in power-related behaviours. A study found that women were more likely than men to report role models, contact with other women, and attempts to appear feminine. In another study, it was indicated that men tended to use threatening and coercive tactics, whereas women tended to use rational discussions and verbal confrontation. However, there is no difference between male and female manager in methods of rewarding and punishing subordinates.

There is some evidence to suggest that female managers may make greater use of participative methods, show more empathy, and feel less comfortable exerting power than do their male counterparts. A study found that subordinates perceived female managers as more receptive to subordinates' ideas and more encouraging of their efforts than were male managers. Female managers' style of communication was perceived as more "concerned and attentive" than that of male managers. Men were seen as more "dominant and directive" and quicker to challenge others. Thus, there is not much difference in management styles though gender differences are noted in the areas of using participation and styles of communication, However, no definitive conclusions with respect to power differentials have been derived from these studies.

Personality Features

A hypothesis sometimes used to explain differences between men and women concerns personality that women have more or less of certain traits believed to be related to power. These traits include need for power, motivation to manage, aggression, self-confidence, and need for achievement.

Need for power, as is defined by McClelland (1975), has been found to be closely associated with managerial success. It has also been found to differentiate executives from non-executives. Research from field and laboratory setting suggests that men and women do not differ on need to power. However, one study found that male teachers reported a higher need for power than did female teachers. Another study found that female managers expressed greater need for power than did their male counterparts.

Difference between men and women in types of need for power is observed. It is found that female managers express a higher need for "socialized power" than do their male counterparts, but there is no difference for "personalized power". Socialized power is beneficial for the organization, whereas personalized power is beneficial to the individual. It is likely that women suppress their needs for certain types of power or express them in ways consistent with sex-role stereotypes. Overall, research suggests that men and women may not differ in need for power and the behavioural differences in the expression of power may be due to sex-role socialization and situational constraints.

Some research suggests that male and female managers differ in their motivation to manage. Donnell and Hall (1980) studied 136 matched pairs of managers and found that women exhibited a motivational profile indicating lower basic needs and higher needs for self-actualization than those for men. Women were concerned with opportunities for growth, autonomy, and challenge and less concerned with pay, work environment, and strain avoidance. However, it has not been demonstrated whether motivation to manage is significantly related to advancement.

Meccoby and Jacklin (1974) concluded from review of relevant literature that aggression is the only trait relevant to management on which men and women differ. Men are more aggressive than women in a variety of situations. However, the relationship between aggressiveness' and power has not yet been thoroughly investigated.

Reviews on difference between genders in self-confidence generally suggest that women have lower self-confidence than do men. Self-confidence may be one of the few characteristics that differentiates male from female managers.

Low self-confidence among women may reflect attributions regarding success and failure. Women may be less likely than men to expect successful outcomes, even when their performance is superior. When they are successful, they may attribute their success to temporary or external causes, such as luck, rather than to lasting, internal causes such as ability. One result may be that women's external attributions and low expectations for success may not only lead to low self-confidence, but also to a lower probability of successful performance. Unsuccessful performance may, in turn, reinforce external attributions, low self-confidence, and low expectation for future success. The result may be a cycle of powerlessness, in which failure to reach powerful positions and a habit of internal attribution for failure leads to low self-confidence and low aspiration.

Differences between men and women on self-confidence may vary with the situation. Self-confidence among women has been found to be partly based upon comparison of their own ability with that of others. Female-typed jobs have been found to be correlated with self-confidence and positive self-evaluations among women.

Self-confidence may be associated with seeking or using power in organizations. People who lack self-confidence may hesitate to seek or use power. On the other hand, those who lack power may eventually develop low self-confidence. This cycle may be more of a problem for women than for men in organizations. Because women have relatively less power in organizations, their positions are less likely to provide a basis for self-confidence.

There is another explanation to account for gender difference. According to some researchers, "fear of success" is a major construct in this context. Women associate success with loss of femininity and with social rejection (Horner, 1973). In otherworlds, women are seen as reluctant to behave inconsistently with sex-role expectation for fear of criticism. So fear of success, if it occurs, may represent an attempt to satisfy gender-role expectation. The original research that formed the basis of the fear-of-success hypothesis has been criticized on methodological ground. Fear of success has been found among male and female managers and among young employees of both genders.

Another domain in which much research has been undertaken involves career aspiration. Although career aspiration is conceptually related to achievement motivation, its specific analyses provide much insight.

Career Aspiration

The under-representation of women in top-ranking jobs has been explained by some researchers in terms of gender difference in career aspiration among women but not necessarily other types of aspiration, such as those related to family and home. One study found that, in comparison with men, women placed less importance on success in a career. Another study found women were less likely than men to express a desire for further promotion.

Women also appear to have lower expectation then men with regard to salaries and career. In a study of male and female management students, women had significantly lower expectation regarding career entry, pay and peak-pay than did men.

It may be misleading to take the evidence of low aspiration levels among women at face value. Women may have lower career aspirations than men, but women aspire to succeed in both family roles and job roles. In this sense, women's aspiration is a part of their total aspiration. Moreover, women may express lower aspiration because of social barriers to their advancement. They may make their aspirations consistent with realistic expectations. Finally, an area that deserves analysis concerns non-work roles.

Nonwork Roles

Individuals have roles other than work roles. Gender difference in nonwork roles may bring some possibilities of power differentials.

One explanation for diminished development of power among women with families is overload. Research on dual career couples indicate that women tend to take responsibility for a majority of dc ...tic chores and child-rearing activities. A study found that 33% of the female managers reported being primarily responsible of child-care duties and 33% of male managers reported that their wives took primary responsibilities of child-care activities. Such a disproportionate division of household labour may help men by allowing them to concentrate on their careers, but hurt women by creating extra demands on their capacity. In short, an inequitable division of household labour may hurt a female manager.

Second, employers may have lower expectation from a married woman. It is assumed that a married women would place her family before her job. It is also apprehended that a woman would give-up her career after marriage. Accordingly, employers have hesitation to recruit and promote women.

Third, women may lose potential for advancement through career interruptions. A study found that 31% of women, but only 5% of the men had non-continuous work experiences, It was also found that women who had interrupted their careers in comparison with those who had not had significantly fewer promotions and reached lower ranks. The relationship between interruptions and advancement was more pronounced at higher levels in the organization.

One line of research deals with a wide range of individual characteristics in an attempt to characterize successful female executives. The executive group tends to be first-born, with close and supportive relationships with their fathers. They tend to use their fathers as role models as teenagers, report disliking "traditional" women and prefer coeducational activities. They develop skills and expertise through training and rely on mentors early in their career. With advancement, they typically become independent of mentors and refine interpersonal skills.

A second study found that female executives described themselves as highly intelligent, confident, assertive and competent. A third study used interview method and successful female executives expressed that they recognized the importance of interpersonal skills for success in the corporate world.

In conclusion, it can be said that factors in four levels of analysis do not operate in isolation. There are many interactions amongst them. Gender differences in power seem to reflect divergent paths to power traversed by men and women during the development of their career. For women, the paths of power contain many barriers and can be described as an obstacle course. In contrast, the path to power for men contains few obstacles that derive from their gender. Although wind of change has started to blow and many forms of social changes are giving a new shape to the evolving pattern of egalitarian management style, a time gap is needed to make correct evaluation of the current status of female managers.

Box 6

Recapitulation at a Glance

Analysis of gender difference in power calls for four levels of analysis:

Social System Level

1. The larger social system incorporates several potential sources of influence on the development of power and gender differences in power in organizations.
2. Underrepresentation of women in powerful positions reflect women's choice of jobs over careers.
3. Gender-role socialization also forces women to get into female-typed occupations only.

Organizational Parameters

4. Organizational practices involving publicity and recruiting explain, atleast in part, the low-level entry position of women into positions.
5. Factors involving performance appraisal, selection, and training system prevent women from being promoted to higher positions.

Interpersonal Motives

6. Distorted perception of power decreases women's access to mentors, coalitions, and networks. This may, in turn, lessen their ability to gain power in organizations.
7. The lack of power may impair women's ability to meet their subordinate's needs and reduce their ability to gain power through subordinates.

Individual Difference Factors

8. Women seem to have lower self-confidence than men.
9. Women appear to explain success in terms of external factor (luck) and failure in terms of internal (ability) factor. In contrast, males tend to explain success in terms of internal (ability) and failure in terms of external (luck) factor.

10. Although men and women do not differ with regard to overall aspiration, men have greater work-role aspiration whereas women have greater family (social) role aspirations.

Stress, Depression, and Emotional Intensity

The successful management of personal life depends upon the efficacious handling of stress and depression. Stress is experienced when demands exceed the resources. Every individual has a number of physical resources such as bodily health, assets or money; the individual has personal resources such as skills and confidence, and the person has social resources such as support of the family, relatives, friends and colleagues. On the other side of the scale, the individual encounters demands. The physical demands may be in the form of excessive heat or extremely low temperature. The personal demands may take the form of completing an important assignment or facing a job interview. Similarly, social demand may spring in the form of meeting a social obligation. When demands are encountered, the individual evaluates his or her resources. If resources exceed, the stress is averted. If demands exceed, the stress is experienced. Thus, what seems to be important in the experience of stress is the subjective evaluation of threatening conditions.

Researchers have typically operationalized environmental stressors as the incidence of negative life events, such as loss of job or death of a friend. However, it is important to recognize that stressors may spring from various domains of an individual's personal life such as the conflict between his or her belief system and the job held. Stress may originate in family life in the form of the incompatibility with the spouse. The individual may also experience occupational stress in the work place. In a broader environment, it may be encountered in the form of cataclysmic stress (floods, famine or cyclone).

Irrespective of the domain of the origin of stress, individuals are mobilized to handle it. The manner of appraising stressors and the particular coping mechanisms used to handle stressors play a pivotal role in life. There is a wide variety of coping mechanisms that individuals use. Efforts to classify coping responses into clusters or categories have not yielded uniform patterns. In general terms, coping responses can be classified into three domains: (a) appraisal-focussed coping-efforts to define and redefine the personal meaning of a situation, (b) problem- focussed coping-responses that seek to modify or eliminate the source of stress by dealing with the realty of the situation, and (c) emotion-focussed coping-responses that control stressor-related emotion and attempt to maintain affective equilibrium.

In the context of gender difference, a fundamental question concerns whether men and women differ with regard to the magnitude of stress encountered. The question also involves the types of stressors encountered and styles of coping used. Similar questions are also pertinent in the domain of depression–a common syndrome of contemporary life. Many of the insights derived from our discussion on stress and coping can as well be applied to the analysis of sex difference in depression.

Stress and Coping

As outlined earlier, life stressors are associated with a wide range of disorders, whereas coping resources are compensatory factors that help to maintain health. However, life events may encompass only a small portion of the ongoing stressful aspects of an individual's environment. Higher rate of ongoing life difficulties constitutes an important aspect. The long-term strains associated with social roles and daily-living also constitute important component of the stress domain. Strains in nursing, child rearing and household economics are associated with stress experience. Beyond psychological domain, physical illness among individuals and their family member is a significant stressor. Characteristics of the physical environment such as noise, crowding, inadequate lighting, heightened temperatures, and dirt can also create discomfort and stress.

The stress and coping paradigm points to social support factors (e.g., informal social networks and relationships with intimate partners and family members) as responses for managing stress. It has been observed that sociodemographic factors may be related to coping responses. For example, personas of low socioeconomic status (SES) may use fewer active and preparatory coping responses and more fatalistic or avoidance-responses than persons of high SES do. In comparison with persons with low education, persons with more education may develop higher levels of cognitive complexity that shape more realistic appraisal processes and active problem-solving. Although some investigators have suggested that the coping responses among older persons become more restricted and are characterized by passive and less flexible responses, the empirical results have been mixed. The other aspect involves examining the empirical characteristics of coping indices used by men and women.

Sex Difference

Sex differences found in the incidence of depression suggest potential sex difference in the rate of stress and resource factors. Because fewer men than women receive treatment for depression, men and women are believed to differ in mean levels of stressors, coping and social resources. In this regard, there is some evidence that in comparison with men, women are more exposed to environmental stressors, have lower supportive social resources and use less efficacious coping patterns (Billings & Moos, 1984). It is found that both stressful life events and social resources have impact on the functioning of women. However, Pradhan and Misra (1996) found no sex difference amongst medical professionals, with respect to born-out (stress) phenomenon.

Billings and Moos (1984) examined the relationship between sex and stress in an empirical investigation. The investigators used an expanded concept of multiple domains of life stress to develop several indices of ongoing life stresses. The measurement of stress included negative life events, physical illness, children's illness, negative home environment, family strains, and work stressors. Similarly, the measurement of coping strategy contained measures of appraisal-focussed coping, problem-focussed coping, and emotion-focussed coping. Social resources measure included number of friends frequency of network contact, strength of close relationship, and the quality of personal relationship. Men and women were compared on each of these indices.

Although generally small, some consistent pattern of sex differences emerged. Although men and women were exposed to comparable levels of stressors, such stressors affected them differently. Functioning among men was more strongly related to negative life events, children's illness and spouses' stress symptoms and work stressors. Functioning among women was more strongly affected by family strains and a negative home environment. The coping responses of men and women were generally similar although women made more frequent use of emotional-discharge coping. A similar pattern of women's use of less efficacious forms of coping has been observed in community setting.

There was no sex difference in mean levels of social resources. However, social support was more strongly related to the functioning of women. Thus, previous reports about the importance of supportive personal relationship based on samples of women may not apply to men. However, different sources of social support may be salient to men's adjustment. For instance, the quality of support obtained from relationships with coworkers and supervisors has been related to adjustment among men. In a study carried out in the Indian context, Pattnayak, Panda and Mohanty (1997) found that males manifested better coping behaviour than females in stressful situations.

While the examination of sex difference in the context of stress and coping has been rather limited, a great deal of research interest has been generated in the domain of occupational stress. This is a natural outcome of the impact of the influx of women into work place during the past decades.

Occupational Stress

In line with the current changing scenarios in the work place, research on the effect of work stress on men and women has generated many research topics. The effects of stress have been shown to have a negative impact not only on the individual worker's life, but also on the employing organization's economic costs.

Recently some qualitative literature review has examined the relationship between sex and stress. Conflicting conclusions have been obtained. Some studies indicate that unemployed women experience greater stress than do employed ones. The authors opine that the homemaker's role presents greater psychological demands and lesser level of control than do positions held by employed women. These greater demands combined with lesser control are postulated to lead to greater stress in unemployed women. Another review concludes that employed women experience greater stress than both unemployed women and men because of several unique stressors faced by employed women. These factors include the interface of marriage and work, social isolation, and stereotyping.

A second conflict in the sex-stress literature centres around whether stress is manifested in the same way by men and women. Some authors suggest that women experience psychological stress (e.g. depression, emotional discomfort) more frequently than men, whereas men experience physiological stress (e.g. coronary heart diseases, cirrhosis of the liver) more frequently than women. Other investigators maintain that employed women experience both psychological and physiological stress owing to unique stressors both at home and work places.

In view of these conflicting results, Martocchio and O'Leary (1989) undertook a meta-analytic review of sex difference in occupational stress. The literature search identified all published articles. The search yielded 65 studies. Each study was classified by the type of stress measure used. Eighteen measures were found among the studies, These measures were categorized into two distinct groups: (a) physiological measure of stress manifestation and (b) psychological measure of stress manifestation.

The first step in the meta-analytic method was the calculation of the weighted average observed correlation and its variance. The weighted average serves as an estimate of the population parameter corrected for the sampling error artifact. The next step was to determine whether the magnitude of the relationship between sex and stress varies as a function of a moderator variable.

The widely held belief that there are sex differences in occupational stress was not supported. In addition, the type of stress measures used (i.e., psychological vs. physiological) was not found to moderate the sex-stress relationship. In other words, there was no support for the belief that women experience greater psychological stress than men, and men experience greater physiological stress than women. In a recent study (Nagartnamma, 1999) comparison of mental heath status in three different Indian organizations revealed the absence of sex difference in occupational stress. Ushashree, Shasu Reddy and Vinolya (1995) also did not find sex difference in job stress and job satisfaction.

While evaluating the findings of this meta-analytic review it is important to recognize some of the problems and limitations of existing measures of stress. Apart from the classic problems of reliability and validity, there are other issues too. An important issue is the fact that social desirability affects the individual's report of his or her experienced stress. A future research question involves the examination of expression versus repression of the reporting along female-male line. Similarly, it could be argued that when stress is assessed through psychological measures, researchers are measuring perceived stress. On the other hand, when stress is assessed by using physiological measures, researchers are measuring manifested stress. The important question is whether there are sex differences within perceived stress and within manifested stress, not whether type of stress acts as a moderator variable in the sex-stress relationship.

Closely related to stress is the domain of depression. A large body of evidence indicates that women are more likely than men to show unipolar depression. The examination of sex-depression relationship and analysis of possible explanations are important for providing clues to its etiology.

Unipolar Depression

According to the third edition of the Diagnostic and Statistical Manual of Mental Disorder (OSM-III: American Psychiatric Association, 1980), the common symptoms of depression include loss of motivation, sadness, anhedolnia, low self-esteem, somatic complaints, and difficulty in concentrating. The opposite of depression is mania. Mania symptoms include greatly increased energy, racing thoughts, pressured speech, wild and extravagant behaviour. Persons who suffer manic episodes also suffer episodes of depression, whereas the majority of persons who suffer depressive episodes never experience mania. Thus, in DSM-III, the affective disorders are broken down into bipolar affective disorder, which is characterized by alternating episodes of mania and depression, and unipolar depression.

To date, almost all of the discussion on sex differences in depression has been concerned with sex differences in unipolor depression. It has been generally assumed that there are no sex differences in bipolar disorder. The DSM-III divides unipolar depression into major depressive disorder (MDD) and dysthymic disorder (DD). The diagnosis of MDD is given to patients who have the acute experiences of severe depressive symptoms for a period of 2 weeks or more. There are two subtypes in DD. Major depressive disorder with melancholia is characterized by marked anhedonia, the somatic symptom of depression (e.g. early morning waking, psychomotor retardation) and extreme guilt. The subclass "MDD with psychotic features" is used when the patient shows gross impairment in reality testing. The diagnosis of DD is given to a person who chronically experiences moderate-to-severe depressive symptoms for at least a 2-year period.

There are two sources of data on rates of depression in men and women: records of persons treated for diagnosed affective disorders and surveys of general population in which respondents are asked about symptoms of depression they are experiencing. Many clinicians and researchers argue that clinically severe level of depression and sub-clinical levels of depression are two distinct types of depression, with different characteristics, causes and courses. From this standpoint, studies in which self-report questionnaires are used to detect depression in a community sample tell us nothing about the etiology of true depressive disorder. Others argue that clinical depression and subclinical depression are simply two points along a continuum of severity in depressive symptoms.

Despite such difference in opinions, a comprehensive examination of relevant studies provides mean female-to-male ratio across studies. In most of the studies, women significantly preponderate among depressives. Walloons and Spitzer (1983) report a large study. Which indicates the female-to-male ratio of 2.1 and 1.9 for MDD and DD respectively. In the United States, the overall picture indicates a clear and significant preponderance of women among depressives.

However, a number of studies conducted in developing countries do not show a large magnitude of sex difference. In India, Mohan (1972) reports female-to-male ratio 1.6. Yet, Rao (1970) points out that access to psychiatric treatment is more restricted for women than for men in many developing countries. Although the ratio of females to male depressives varies greatly from county to country, there is a consistent tendency for women to preponderate among depressives across a wide variety of nations. Upamanyu and Upamanyu (1994) examined depression among male and female Indian adolescents. They found results similar to western findings. In a recent survey based on the report from the World Health Organization, Gater et al. (1998) examined sex differences in the prevalence and detection of depression and anxiety disorders in general health care centres. A two-step design in a sample of 25,916 patients attending primary care centres in 15 countries from 4 continents (Europe, Asia, South America, and North America), revealed similar odds-ratio for women. The findings did not support local psychosocial effects; the role of biological or psychosocial factors having similar effects across cultures was stressed. The populations in which sex differences in depression have not been commonly found include university students, the bereaved, the elderly, and residents of some rural, nonmodern cultures.

Several explanations have been offered to account for sex differences in depression. However, despite impressive evidence regarding sex differences, a number of critics view that sex differences found in studies are simply the artifacts. These are artifacts of differences in the socioeconomic status of men and women, or differences in the willingness of men and women to show the common symptoms of depression.

Some researchers believe that it is an income effect, not a gender effect. By most indicators, women's economic status is lower than men's. Women do not attain same level of education as men. It could be that the difference observed in rates of depression in men and women is the result of socioeconomic status instead of gender differences.

Some investigators have been concerned that the sex differences in depression result from men's unwillingness to admit to and seek help for depressive symptoms. The hypothesis holds that men and women experience depressive symptoms equally, frequently, and to the same degree, but because depressive symptoms are perceived feminine, men are less likely to admit to them.

There is also a third artifact explanation. According to this hypothesis, men and women are equally susceptible to depression, but depression in men, often takes the form of acting out behaviour instead of sadness, passivity and crying, which are symptoms commonly included in self-report inventories. In particular, it has been suggested that male equivalent of depression is alcoholism. Proponents of this argument point to studies showing that twice as many men as women are diagnosed as alcoholics. It suggests that the rates of alcoholism in men make up for the absence of depression in men.

Biological Explanation

It has been posited that women's greater vulnerability to depression may be the result of biological characteristics unique to women. Two general types of biological explanations for the sex difference in depression have been proposed. The first group of explanation arises from evidence that women are particularly prone to depression during periods in which they experience significant changes in hormonal levels. Several investigators have suggested that depression in women is brought about by changes in the levels of estrogen, progesterone, or other hormones.

The second group of biological explanations of the sex differences in depression attributes the difference to a greater genetic predisposition to depression in women. According to these explanations, women are more likely to inherit the disorder, because the genetic abnormality that leads to depression is somehow linked to the chromosomes that determine gender.

Hormones and Moods. It is widely believed that hormonal fluctuations strongly affect moods in women. Women are believed to be more prone to depression during the premenstrual period, the postpartum period, and menopause, each of which is characterized by changes in the levels of a number of hormones. Specifically, after the onset of puberty, levels of estrogen and progesterone rise and fall sharply during the menstrual cycle. During the first 2 weeks of the cycle, arbitrarily defined as the first 2 weeks after the onset of blood flow, levels of progesterone and estrogen remain quite low. Around the end of the first 2 weeks, the level of estrogen rises and peaks, then declines again. Near the 21st day of the cycle, the level of estrogen peaks again and the level of progesterone peaks for the first time. Then, during the last few days before the onset of the next menstrual flow the levels of both estrogen and progesterone drop and remain low until after the menstrual flow. Mathur (1997) has observed and documented various forms of disorders before and after menstruation of women in India. Levels of estrogen and progesterone also change dramatically during pregnancy, the postpartum period, and menopause. During pregnancy, both estrogen and progesterone are produced in large amounts. Then, shortly after a woman gives birth (the postpartum period), her estrogen and progesterone levels drop sharply. Similarly during menopause, estrogen and progesterone productions decline to a very low level and remain there for rest of a woman's life.

If women commonly experience depression during these periods of hormonal changes, this suggests that their greater vulnerability to depression in general may be the result of the negative effects of changes or imbalances in female hormones on moods. The notion that depression during periods of hormonal fluctuations is common is not well supported. Menopausal depression was once thought to be common; some contemporary studies show that levels of self-reported depressive symptoms seem to drop in women as they pass through menopause.

Estimates of the incidence of postpartum symptoms are high ranging from 30% to 60%. Yet the great majority of women experiencing postpartum depression symptoms recover fully from them within a few days. The rate of premenstrual depression is estimated by some studies to be very high. Yet, there is a methodological flaw somewhere. Although women reporting on retrospective questionnaires indicate that they feel more depressed during their premenstrual period than during other times, daily diaries show that most women do not experience significant premenstrual mood changes.

It is still possible that abnormalities in hormonal fluctuations in women account for their higher rates of clinically severe depression. Many hypotheses have been proposed for exactly how hormonal abnormalities would affect mood in women. Most of these hypotheses have focussed on the two ovarian hormones estrogen and progesterone. Because those periods during which women have been thought to be more vulnerable to depression (e.g., menopause, the premenstrual period, and the postpartum) are characterized by decreased estrogen levels; it has been proposed that estrogen withdrawal triggers depression and other premenstrual syndromes (PMS). The evidence for this hypothesis is indirect, some studies report reduction of depressive symptoms in depressed women given estrogen therapy. In addition, some women ingesting estrogen in oral contraceptives also show decreases in depression.

Another estrogen-related hypothesis holds that high levels of estrogen in combination with low levels of progesterone are what lead to tension and dysphasia. One study found that women suffering from PMS had higher estrogen/progesterone ratios then women not suffering from PMS. Others have argued that declines in levels of progesterone, not estrogen, trigger depressive symptoms. Increases and decreases in levels of progesterone are correlated with increases and decreases in depression. Some studies have found correlation between the degree of depression in some women and the amount of progestin in the oral contraceptives they are using.

Thus, there are multiple interpretations. Yet, it is premature to conclude that hormonal fluctuations have no effects on moods in women. In addition, it must be explained why sex differences in depression do not emerge until after puberty, why cyclic changes in hormones and other biochemicals begin in women.

One other biological explanation of sex difference in depression has been proposed. According to this explanation, women's greater vulnerability to depression can be attributed to a genetic predisposition towards depression.

Genetic Factors. Affective disorders run in families. This aggregation of affective disorders within families could be due to either genetic or environmental factors shared by family members. Yet, in a review of twin studies of affective illness, Allen (1976) found that in dizygotic twins, the average concordance rate for unipolar depression was 11%, but in monozygotic twins the concordance rate for unipolar depression was 40%. The substantially higher concordance rate for monozygotic twins indicates some sort of genetic transmission of the disorder. Could it be that the sex differences in depression are due to a greater gender predisposition to depression in women? A number of investigators have argued that serious affective illness is the result of a mutant gene on the X chromosome. Because females have 2 X-chromosomes, they should be more at risk for depression than men.

One way investigators have tested the X-linkage hypothesis of affective disorder is to examine the correlations between affective disorders and two abnormalities known to result from mutations on the X chromosome, red-green colour blindness and the Xg blood group. If affective disorder is caused by mutations on the X chromosome, then we should see significant high correlations between the presence of affective disorder and the presence of either colour blindness or the Xg blood group. A number of studies have examined the family pedigrees of persons suffering from affective disorder and have found that the relatives who show affective disorder also tend to have the Xg blood group or colour blindness. However, some investigation note that the family pedigrees used in studies have been incomplete and the statistical significance of the relations observed are often marginal.

Another way to test the X-linkage hypothesis is to examine the transmission of affective disorder from parents to children. Specifically, if a father carries the mutant gene on his X-chromosome (and therefore manifests affective disorder), all of his daughters will carry the mutant gene, because the father always gives his daughters an X chromosome. Yet none of affected father's sons will carry the mutation, because carry father always gives his sons an Y chromosome. If a mother carries the mutant gene on one of her two chromosomes, then her daughters and sons have equal chances of carrying the mutant gene. In short, if affective disorder is linked to X chromosome, we should see father-daughter pairs of affected individuals, but no father-son pairs. We should observe equal numbers of mother-daughter and mother-son pair.

However, most family history studies of the X-linkage hypothesis have discovered more father-son pairs of affective disorder individuals than is comparable with transmission via the X chromosome. There is no consistent evidence that the observed sex difference in depression is due to a genetic predisposition to the disorder in women. Furthermore, the biological explanations do not explain the absence of sex difference in certain subgroups such as college students, the elderly persons and the bereaved individuals. Theorists have been prompted to count on psychosocial factors.

Psychoanalytic Explanation

According to classic psychoanalytic theory, women are more vulnerable to the depressive process than men because of the personality structure that results from women's psychosexual development. During the oedipal stage, while castration anxiety is motivating a boy to develop a superego, a girl realizes she and all other females have been deprived of a penis and all the power and status that accompany being male. The girl's realization leads to hostility towards her mother for own self-worth, and the growth of envy of her father and all males.

A girl's fixation on her father, which is the model for later love relationship with men, is a weak one based on narcissistic love, rather than an object attachment, because it is motivated by a desire to get back a part of herself she feels she has lost. It is this tendency towards narcissistic love relationships, driven by penis envy that puts women in greater risk for depression. The woman looks to men to make up for her losses, but she is inevitably and frequently disappointed. After such disappointments, she is prone to turning her energy back to herself rather than reattaching it to new objects. Her already injured ego is confronted by the hostility she feels against the object just lost and depression is likely to result.

The psychoanalytic description of the development of female personality has received almost no solid experimental support. For example, there is no support for the oedipal shift in girls from attachment to the mother to the father. Similarly, there is little evidence of either castration anxiety in boys or a penis envy in girls, although many women acknowledge an envy of men's social power.

Late psychodynamic theorists down-played notions of biological determinism in personality development, emphasizing instead the interaction between biological roles and cultural restrictions on women's behaviours. These and many more contemporary psychoanalytic writers point to the restrictions placed on female sexual expression, power and personal freedom by patriarchal cultures as sources of frustration for woman. Further women's roles as child-bearers and child-rearers conflict with their needs for self-development and independence. To the extent women renounces her role as mother, she suffers the disapproval of others. According to most of the neo-Freudians she denies the primary component of female self-definition. These restrictions on female expression, the inferior status of the female role, and the conflicts between the innate desire to bear children and needs for independence all contribute to a greater tendency towards self-injury in women.

However, a number of the suggestions offered by the Neo-Freudians on how women's roles as passive wives and mothers affect mental health have been incorporated in contemporary sex-role explanation of female psychopathology.

Sex-Role Explanation

It has been argued that a central element of women's roles in society is the nurturing of relationship. Women's greater concern with relationship has been viewed by traditional psychology theory and moral development theory as an indication that women do not advance to as high a stage of moral development as do men who are more concerned with issues of justice and rationality.

Yet, these theories suggest women's concern with relationship make them vulnerable to despair and depression. It has been suggested that the desire for relationship is an inherent aspect of female personality. Women who attempt to succeed in jobs will be continually faced with disturbing conflicts between their natural propensity towards relationship and demands to be independent and competitive in the job.

A number of other sex-role theorists have been concerned with the incompatible expectation put on women when she enters the workplace. Women may be expected to be both passive, unselfish and supportive in line with her feminine role and assertive, self-sufficient, and demanding if she is to achieve in her work. These dual sets of expectations are difficult because the women may feel forced to violate one set, ignore one set, or perhaps live up to both sets of expectations in the same time. Deviance from sex-role expectations may result in social rejection.

Some support for the role conflict hypothesis comes from epidemiological studies of depressive symptoms in the general populations. It is found that among persons, who are married and employed, women report significantly more depressive symptoms than men; this is not true among unmarried employed persons. This pattern is in line with the assertion that having dual roles can be a risk factor for depression in women.

However, some investigators find that both working wives and nonworking wives report more depression than working men. In addition, other studies show that nonworking wives are more depressed than working wives. These data do not support role conflict hypothesis. Even it is suggested that having two sets of role in one's life actually protects one against depression. One may be protected against depression because when one source of gratification is taken away, either the family or work, one has second source to fall back on. Data in which women who have both a family and a job are less depressed than nonworking wives lend partial support to this hypothesis.

Other sex role explanation stresses the subjective value of a women's role in society compared to the value of a man's role. At a very young age, girls are more likely to say they wish they were boys than boys are to say they wish they were girls. This understanding of the female sex role relative to the male sex role has been attributed to the greater prestige, power, competence, size and strength associated with men. It is argued that the traditional female role as homemaker is becoming increasingly boring and undervalued as more modern conveniences are introduced. It is suggested that the sex difference in depression can be attributed to the lesser value put on the female role and the resulting lesser gratification women receive from fulfilling that role.

The biggest problem with sex role account of sex differences in mental health is the frequent absence in these accounts of well-described processes by which role conflicts might lead to depression or other disorders. It is particularly difficult to explain why sex role pressures would put some women and not others into depression. Other psychologists and sociologists suggest that the female role contributes to greater feeling of lack of control and helplessness.

Learned Helplessness Explanation

Learned helplessness has been defined as a set of motivational, cognitive and affective deficits that occur when uncontrollable negative events are experienced. In humans, these deficits include lower response initiation, an inability to learn new response-outcome contingencies, sadness, and low self-esteem. According to the original learned helplessness theory (Seligman, 1975), these deficits are the result of the expectation that outcomes will be uncontrollable, because no response can be found to control them. Seligman (1975) documented the similarities between depressive symptoms and helplessness deficits.

A reformulation of the original model (Abramson, Seligman & Teasdale, 1978) employed attribution dimensions to account for inadequacies in the original model. The thrust of the reformulated model was on the explanatory styles. People who blame themselves instead of others for bad events will experience a low self-esteem. People who explain bad event by causes that are stable rather than unstable in time will expect to be helpless in future. People who tend to explain bad events by causes that influence many areas of their lives (global causes), instead of causes that influence only one area (specific causes), will expect to be helpless in many areas of their lives. Thus, according to Abramson et al., people who habitually tend to explain bed events by internal, stable and global causes (and explain good events by external, unstable and specific causes) will be more vulnerable to depression than people with the opposite explanatory (attributional) styles.

The epidemiological trends in the incidence of depression in different groups may be explained by the learned helplessness theory. High rates of depression are found among the poor, the undereducated, the unemployed, the ill, and women. How does learned helplessness explain the preponderance of women among depressives?

Women may receive more uncontrollable (bad) events during their lifetime than men. Maccoby and Jacklin's (1974) review suggests that boys are trained to be more self-reliant and active, whereas girls are trained to be dependent. As adults, women also expect that their action will be less successful at generating desired outcomes than man's. In several experimental studies, men's performance at laboratory tasks were rated higher than equally good female Performances, Successful women are often rated as less acceptable and likable than unsuccessful women or successful men. Achievements of women are rated as less valuable than the achievement of men. On another level, women have more difficulty having their ideas taken seriously by groups than do men.

Besides experiencing more events that could give them a sense of helplessness, women may also be more prone to the maladaptive explanatory styles. A number of studies on children have found that girls are more likely to attribute success on academic tasks and other positive events to luck or the favours of others, and to attribute failures to a lack of ability and other stable global factors (Dweck & Reppucci, 1973). Such attribution patterns are associated with a greater tendency to become helpless after failing at tasks.

Although a wide range of studies have supported the hypothesis that a maladaptive explanatory style is a risk factor for the depression (Peterson & Seligman, 1984), most of the studies have used populations in which sex differences in levels of depression are usually not found (e.g., university students, children, and hospitalized depressives).

Of course, it is neither necessary nor sufficient under the helplessness theory to have a maladaptive explanatory style in order to become depressed. It is sufficient that one expects to be helpless in controlling the environment. There is considerable evidence that women in many areas of the world are trained to have this expectation. Learned helplessness model could explain the preponderance of women in depressives across cultures. Direct tests of this explanation have not been undertaken, however.

Since the evidence currently available for each of the explanations considered above in not strongly supported, one other view is presented. Nolen-Hoeksema (1987) explains the sex difference in terms of contrasting response sets in depressive episodes.

Ruminative Response Set Explanation

Nolen-Hoeksema (1987) puts forward a new explanation for the sex difference in Depression. It is argued that, regardless of the source of a depressive episode, how an individual responds to his or her own depressed state may contribute to the severity, chronicity, and recurrence of the episode. Specifically it is posited that the men's responses to their depression are more behavioural and dampen their depressive episodes, whereas women's responses to their depressive episodes are more ruminative and amplify them.

Most people occasionally experience mild-to-moderate episodes of depressive symptoms. For some of us, these episodes last only a few hours or days. Yet we somehow bring ourselves out of such episodes before we reach the point where we would seek professional help. For others, however, initially mild depressive symptoms often become more severe until they are moved to seek professional help.

There is reason to believe that the ways we respond to cope with our moods affect the severity and chronicity of our moods. In particular, persons who tend to respond to their own episodes of depression by engaging in activities designed to distract them from their moods appear to recover faster from depressive episodes than those who tend to be inactive and to ruminate about the causes and implications of their depressed mood. Evidence is emerging from a number of studies that men and women show different pattern of responding to their own feelings of depression. It is indicated that men, when depressed, tend to engage in activities designed to distract themselves from their moods. Women, when depressed, tend to be less active and to ruminate more about the possible causes of their mood and the implications of their depressive episodes.

Researchers draw inferences regarding the sex differences in responses to depressive symptoms on the basis of several evidences.

Nolen-Hoeksema (1986) presented college students with a "list of things people do when depressed" and asked them to rate how likely they would be to engage in the behaviours or thoughts described when depressed. The subjects were instructed to be sure to "rate these items according to which you think you would do, not what you should do". The men in the sample had significantly higher scores than women on 4 of 37 items. "I play a sport," and "I take drug" each of these responses would tend to distract the individual from this depressed mood. The women in the sample scored significantly higher than men on "I try to determine why I am depressed". "I talk to other people about my feelings"; and "I cry to relieve the, tension." These responses tend to focus and maintain the individual's attention on her mood.

There is also evidence that there is sex difference in activity level during childhood depression. Observational evidence indicates that girls appear to engage in self-evaluation and rumination about the failure, regardless of whether or not they were asked to, whereas boys do not.

There are atleast three mechanisms by which a ruminative inactive response set for depression should amplify and prolong an episode, whereas an active response set for depression should dampen and shorten an episode. First, rumination interferes with attention, concentration, and initiation of instrumental activity. These difficulties lead to increased failures and a greater sense of helplessness in controlling one's environment. On the other hand, engaging in active behaviour increases the individual's chances for controlling the environment.

A second mechanism by which a tendency to become ruminative when depressed would amplify depression involves the accumulation of negative memory. Mood state has a powerful effect on individual's recall of past events. Persons who are depressed show greater access to negative memories and easier learning of negatively toned new material.

Finally, ruminative response sets during depressive episodes may increase the likelihood that an individual will consider depressogenic explanations for future negative events, thereby increasing expectations of helplessness and hopelessness. Although both the ruminating and nonruminating individuals express same depressive explanations for their failures, the ruminating persons invoke these depressive explanations more frequently than the nonruminators.

With respect to the origin of the response style, it may be postulated that socialization practices in line within sex-role stereotypes reinforce these differences. Rumination in women may not be encouraged directly by parents and teachers, but these socialization agents do not reward them for activity as they do it for boys.

If a ruminative response style amplifies women's vulnerabilities to depression, then the recommended interventions for depressed women should be ones that help to distract them form their mood and intensify activity. It is useful to educate the depressed women about the distorting effects of mood on thinking and memory. She should be encouraged not to make a decision or try to solve a problem when she is depressed, because she has particular access to negative memories. Others have recommended setting aside a half-hour at the end of the day to do one's worrying. The ruminator often feels that her worries diminished in size and number by the time "worry-hour arrives".

The preponderance of women among depressives raises another question regarding negative affect such as anxiety. Although some studies indicate such sex difference, there is also a paradox. Not only women are more vulnerable to depression, women also report greater capacity in experiencing joy. Most surveys indicate that women report as much overall happiness as do men (Myers, 2000). The resolution of this paradox requires specific analysis of sex differences in emotional intensity.

Emotional Intensity

Women frequently report being just as happy as men. In 1960, American national sample in which women expressed having more emotional difficulties, they reported nearly the same overall level of happiness as did men. To the item " taking all things together, how would you say things are these days-would you say that you are very happy, pretty happy, or not too happy?", women responses were similar to men's. In a European sample, women reported being more satisfied with their overall life than did men (Haavio –Mannila, 1971). In a cross-cultural study, Michalos (1987) surveyed 6000 college students in 23 countries and his data revealed that women reported being as happy as or happier than men. Larson (1978) reviewed the well-being literature and found "No consistent sex differences in well-being for older persons on any type of measure".

Thus, the findings that women report being as happy as men and women report being depressed at twice the rate that men do seem contradictory, Some researchers argue that women are actually unhappy, but they report in surveys that they are happy because of a need to conform to social norms–one of which is being happy. This explanation, however, makes it difficult to account for women's self-reported higher negative affect. If women falsely report being happy only to appear being happy they would not accurately report experiencing high levels of negative affect.

In view of this complexity, Fugita, Diener and Sandvik (1991) proposed that gender differences in affect intensity can explain the paradoxical presence of both the greater prevalence of negative affect and the equal (or greater) overall happiness reported by women.

According to Fujita et al. (1991), affect intensity is the individual difference variable that refers to one's response intensity to a given level of emotion-provoking situation. People who experience high levels of negative emotion intensity also tend to have very intense positive emotions. One of the costs is the experiencing of more intense negative emotions.

If people who experience high levels of positive affect also experience high levels of negative affect, it is possible that these people would report much more distress while also reporting equal levels of overall well being. Fujita et. al. (1991) posit that women are more affectivity intense than men. This allows them to experience both more joy and more sorrow. These gender differences in affective experience can be used as a basis for explaining the gender differences in depression. Moreover, the concept of affect intensity is equally proficient in explaining women's equal overall well-being.

In order to provide empirical support for the construct of affect intensity, Fujita et al. (1991) carried out a study. They measured positive intensity, negative intensity, and global happiness in different ways. Three affect intensity measures and three hedonic level measures were used. Affect intensity was measured with the self-report Affect Intensity Measure (AIM). The AIM is a 40-item instrument that measures how intensely participants feel emotions. The AIM asks participants to answer questions like "When I feel happy it is a strong type of exuberance" and "When I am nervous I get shaky all over". It is important to note that these items do not assess how frequently the participant experiences an emotion, but rather the intensity of the emotion experienced. The AIM yields both a positive and negative affect intensity score.

In addition to the self-report AIM, the AIM was also modified for the Fujita et al. study for observer use by changing the instructions so that the observer answered the questions as he or she imagined the participant would answer them. Furthermore, participants were asked to recall positive and negative emotional experiences in a timed period. In each memory category, participants were given 2 to 3 minutes to write down as many memories of events as they could. The four memory category tests were lifetime happy events, lifetime unhappy events, last year happy event, and last year unhappy event. A simple count of the number of positive memories recalled in the fixed time period was used for the positive affect intensity measure. The negative affect intensity measure was found using a simple count of negative memories recalled. Thus, affect intensity was measured in three different ways. AIM, modified (observation) AIM and memory performance.

The hedonic level measures were obtained in three different ways. First daily mood reports were collected. For 42 consecutive days, participants returned a form that asked them to rate on a 0 to 6 scale (0=*not at all*, 6= *extremely much*) how much of several positive and negative emotions they had experienced that day. Each participant completed the entire form for both positive and negative emotions each day. Scores for each emotion taken were averaged across the 42 days for each participant. The positive affect measure was constructed by averaging four positive affect adjectives (happy, pleased, enjoyment/ fun and joyful), and the negative affect measure was constructed by averaging four negative adjectives (depressed, worried, unhappy and hostile). Like the AIM, this measure was also modified so that observers answered as if they were the participants. Thus, hedonic level measures were obtained in three different ways: daily adjectives, summary adjectives and observation summary adjectives.

The findings of the study supported the basic propositions of Fujita et al. (1991). On five of the sex intensity measures (both positive and negative), the women's mean level was found to be more intense than the men's mean level. In contrast, on only one of the six hedonic level measures did women differ from men. This difference was on the self-report affect measure on which women reported more positive affect than men did.

The pattern of correlation also was in line with the prediction. In the complete sample matrix, a significant positive correlation was found between the positive intensity and negative intensity measures. This implies that persons experiencing high levels of positive emotion also experience high levels of negative emotion. Further, significant negative correlations were-found between the hedonic level measures within measurement method. This finding was expected because affect intensity has been found to be unitary across valence, whereas positive and negative hedonic level make up a bipolar affect balance dimension. All affect intensity measures correlated positively with each other across valence and methods. In addition, all of the hedonic level measures correlated in the hypothesized direction.

The result of the study offers support for the proposition that women experience emotion more strongly than do men. The statistical comparison of groups (men versus women) provided evidence that women differ form men in the intensity of their emotion. However, there is little evidence of affect balance difference between the genders. The principal component analysis used as a condensation of the complete sample correlation matrix, provided evidences that affect intensity is unitary across valence. This means that if a person experiences strong negative emotions, that person is more likely to experience strong positive emotions.

The result of these studies helps clarify past anomalies. Although women scored significantly higher on almost all of the intensity measures, they did not differ form men on most of the hedonic level measures, Based on these findings, one would predict that, if researchers only collect negative emotion data and the items tap both hedonic level and affect intensity, they would find women experiencing more negative affect (e.g., depression) than men. One would also predict that, if researchers collect data that balances the positive affect against the negative affect, then the gender differences would disappear. Thus, the paradox of past research is replicable; women score higher on negative affect even though they are not lower on global happiness. It appears that more intense positive emotions tend to counterbalance the more intense negative emotions when subjects report their global happiness.

With respect to the mechanism that allows high affectively intense people to experience more negative affect than low affectively intense people, researchers draw on Beck's idea of cognitive operations. Beck's (1976) operations are personalizing, over generalizing, and selective abstraction. Personalizing is a cognitive operation in which a person interprets events in a self-referential manner. Over generalizing is the cognitive operation in which a person takes a single event as being representative of the events in the world at large. Selective abstraction is the cognitive operation in which a person focuses his or her attention on the specific, emotion-provoking aspect of events. A person who interprets events in self-referential manner, takes single events as being representative of the world at large, and focuses attention on emotion-provoking aspects of events will probably experience more intense emotional outcomes than a person who does not.

Finally, there are two important observations in this context. In order to identify the link between maladaptive cognitive operations and gender, more studies are needed to draw definitive conclusion. There is some evidence that women use maladaptive cognitive operations, but more studies are needed in this area. Second, as indicated earlier, Nolen-Hoecksema (1987) has argued about the causal role of ruminative response style in depressive symptoms. It appears that her explanation is more applicable to community level depression, not to clinical depression, In contrast, the role of cognitive operation seems more plausible in the context of clinical depression.

Box 7

Recapitulation at a Glance

Stress and Coping

1. There are three broad classes of coping categories: (a) appraisal-focussed coping (b) problem-foccused coping, and (c) emotion-foccused coping.
2. There is some evidence that in comparison with men, women are more exposed to envioronmental stressors, have fewer supportive social resources, and use less efficacious coping patterns, such as emotion-focussed coping.

Occupational Stress

3. The meta-analytic review of the sex-stress literature reveals that there is no sex difference in occupational stress.

Depression

4. There is preponderance of women among depressives. Women report depression at a rate twice as much as men do.
5. It appears plaussible that women's ruminative response set amplifies and prolongs their depressive systems, whereas men's active response style dampens and shortens depressive symptoms.

Happiness and Well-being

6. Women report as much global happiness as do men.

Affective Intensity

7. Women indicate greater affect intensity than do men. That is, women experience high levels of positive affect as well as negative affect.

8

Cross-Cultural Evidence and Etiology of Sex Differences

The preceding chapters bring home a couple of major points. First, the magnitude of sex difference is not consistent across domains. While the magnitude of difference is substantial favouring males in the area of aggressiveness, the gap is very small with a female advantage in the domain of affiliation behaviour. There is almost no difference in the domain of happiness. Second, there is also variation of the magnitude of difference across subdomains. For example, there is female advantage in computational skills whereas there is male advantage in problem-solving in the context of mathematical performance. Third, a gradual narrowing of difference across time is clearly visible. While sex difference existed in some of the domains in the past, the difference is disappearing in recent years.

The decline of difference reflects the impact of social change. Although it is not difficult to implicate the role of social change in the narrowing of gaps between the genders, a more comprehensive understanding of the process requires the analysis of socio-cultural parameters.

Furthermore, it is important to recognize that an adequate analysis of the role of socio-cultural parameters is possible only through cross-cultural investigations. There are distinct advantages in adopting cross-cultural research in the context of sex difference. First, cross-cultural contexts provide quasi-experimental design. For a large number of pertinent variables such as social structure or individuals' mobility, it is not possible to manipulate them in laboratory to study cause-and-effect relationship. There are many ethical constraints to manipulate social and human variables. Yet, researchers can use various social and/or cultural groups that vary in these dimensions.

Second, cross-cultural evidence provides unique opportunity for theory testing. For example, Bushmen males have been shown to have fairly high levels of estrogen (Tobias, 1966). If they are closer to females in levels of estrogen than are males in some other societies, the variation among human population may help us to test some theories about the effects of hormones on observed sex differences.

While reviewing cross-cultural evidence on sex difference, we intend to delineate the etiology of sex difference.

One of the most difficult problems facing researchers is to untangle the possible influence of biology and social factors. Biology, sex and social behaviours are not confounded quite the same ways in different societies. Hence cross-cultural research has tremendous potential for helping us to test theories about etiology of sex difference. Prior to explicating cross-cultural studies of sex difference and their implication for etiologic inferences, it is useful to have familiarity with biogenic explanations.

Biology and Behaviour

A number of reasons are usually cited to make the case that a particular sex difference is probably biologically determined. It is posited that sex difference is consistent across culture. It is also claimed that a sex difference appears in non-human primates as well as humans. In addition, a sex difference appears early in life. These claims have their limitations. Yet, we can first discuss the specific ways in which biological influence operates.

Male Vulnerability

The important biological fact that distinguishes the sexes is that males are more physically vulnerable than females. This differential vulnerability is particularly pronounced at the beginning and end of the life span.

Many more males than females are conceived, but many more males than females die before birth. Many males than females experience difficulties during the birth process resulting in more males than females with birth defects. Even in unproblematic deliveries, the births of male offspring take an average of an hour longer than the births of females. The length of labour, in turn, has been shown to be more predictive of later problems in infants and young children's behaviour than the drug a mother receives during labour and delivery.

In a review article detailing greater male vulnerability across the life span, Gualtieri and Hicks (1985) hypothesized an immunoreactive theory of selective male afflictions. They suggested that there is "Something about the male fetus that evokes an inhospitable uterine environment" (p.427). Simply stated, they believed that the mother's body is stimulated to produce a kind of antibody against a male fetus, but not against a female fetus that is generally more similar to he and that these antibodies lead either directly or indirectly to fetal damage.

The fact of male vulnerability is well-studied. The possibility that male vulnerability may influence late behavioural predispositions has not been extensively explored in research.

The Role of Hormones

The results of early studies with animals have prompted many to propose that sex steroids are causing many of sex differences. Research with rats and primates has indeed linked levels of sex-steroid hormones and male and female differences in hormone concentrations to some sex-related behaviours such as aggression (Maccoby & Jacklin, 1974).

In the last decades, considerable advances have been made in studying hormone-behaviour linkage directly. Technological developments have made work with human populations much less difficult. It is now possible to obtain reliable measures of sex-steroids and other hormones from saliva. Many of the recent studies have been carried out on normal populations of children, particularly adolescents, measuring endogenous (i.e., normally circulating) hormone levels.

Exactly how hormones affect and are affected by human behaviour is still not well-understood. The working theory has been derived from animal research. The theory posits two types of effect, sensitization and activation. Sensitization is believed to occur during the prenatal period, when circulating hormones function to programme the fetal brain in a number of ways. The early sensitization may itself affect later behaviour. During the puberty, circulating hormones then activate or interact with the sensitized brain to produce behaviour affects.

It is still very difficult to obtain hormone measures in humans before birth. Thus, studies to test sensitization effects in normal humans have had to rely on hormone measures taken from the umbilical cord blood in birth. One recent study of intellectual abilities in young children provided support for the sensitization theory. In this study, the amount of androgen (testosterone and androsteindione from the umbilical cord blood) was found to be negatively related to girls spatial abilities at age six. That is, girls with high levels of androgen in their blood at birth had lower scores on tests of spatial ability when they entered school than did girls with low levels of androgens at birth. However, circulating hormone measures were not available when the children were tested at six years of age. Hence, it was not possible to determine whether prenatal hormones actually sensitized the brain, resulting in differential cognitive abilities. An alternative hypothesis is that hormone levels at birth are related to hormone levels throughout childhood, and the circulating hormones themselves influence cognitive development.

More data are available linking emotional behaviour and hormones. In research on adolescent emotional behaviour, relations have been found between high variability of circulating testosterone and anger in both boys and girls. That is, children whose circulating levels of testosterone vary widely from day-to-day are more likely to show anger. It is the changability or variability that produces anger, not the mean level of hormones.

Thus, it is important to note that (a) daily variation in hormone measure is substantial, (b) the variability itself is a stable indicator difference, and (c) the variability of an individual's hormone level may be more important to behavioural outcomes than the absolute magnitude of circulating hormones.

The evidence generated in the context of the biology-behaviour linkage does not lead to conclusive formulations. Many of the arguments advanced may not be strong enough to stand cross-cultural tests. For example, consistency of a sex difference across cultures may occur because most societies face similar life problems and socialize for similar behaviours. Similarly, it is entirely possible that some sex differences may be the result of differential socialization in non-human primates and humans. There is some evidence that rhesus monkeys treat their male and female infants differently.

Researchers advocating a biogenic approach often cite early onset of sex difference in favour of their claim. Yet, there are cross-cultural studies that suggest sex differences in socialization of the newborns.

On the other side of the phenomenon, there are also arguments to convince one of cross-cultural diversity. Just as human populations differ in culture, they may differ in the frequency of certain physical traits. If certain biologic differences between the sexes like hormone levels are implicated to produce sex differences in behaviour, then some populations might have more of a sex difference than others, because of greater or less differences between the sexes in genetic make-up or nutritional factors that may affect physiology. It is also possible that there is cross-cultural variability in sex differences because some societies seek to socialize against biologic predispositions. It is not correct to assume that socialization will work to create sex differences, it may also be used to obviate them.

Finally, it is observed that many of the sex differences appear only later in childhood period. The inference that appears to be made here is that the later a difference appears, the more it is likely to be directed to socialization pressure. The argument, of course, takes on more plausibility if it can be shown that the sex differences appear only after the onset of a particular socialization practice that varies by sex of target. However, late-appearing sex differences are not necessarily nonbiologic. If, for example, a particular trait is tied to hormonic control, then sex differences might not appear until boys and girls begin to differ in hormones.

In sum, an examination of distributional pattern of sex differences across cultures would be valuable in unpackaging the contributions of biologic and social factors. Cross-cultural examination of sex difference can be attempted in three broad areas: (a) physical and physiologic differences, (b) role-related differences, and (c) psychological differences.

Physical and Physiologic Differences

It is a common observation the all animals that reproduce sexually have sex differences at the level of anatomy. Although the sex difference in reproductive organs is easily understood, the difference at the level of secondary sex characteristics is not well-understood. However, it is conjectured that human sexual dimorphism has some implications. First, attention can be directed to the examination of differences in life span development.

Developmental Differences

Probably the most documented male-female difference is in height. For any given human population, adult males, on the average are taller than females. The gap for any given human population is important. Males in some populations are not necessarily taller. Body weight, bone weight, the proportion of face and muscle, and physical fitness has been less often studied. Nonetheless, the evidence from different cultures suggests that within a culture, males generally have heavier skeletons, greater bone densities, greater aerobic work capacity (greater maximum oxygen uptake during exertion), and a larger proportion of their total body weight. Females have a generally larger proportion of fat and a proportionately wider pelvis.

Research conducted in North America and North Western Europe has documented that men have greater grip strength, greater strength of arm pull, proportionately longer hearts and lungs, greater capacity for carrying oxygen in the blood, and a greater capacity for neutralizing the chemical products of exercise. Assuming that these differences are found in other populations, they indicate the relatively greater strength of males and their greater capacity for high-energy exertion.

Data from western countries suggest that certain aspects of adult sexual dimorphism are negligible until puberty. Although newborn boys are slightly taller than newborn girls are, there is generally no sex difference in height in childhood. Around ages 12 and 13, girls may temporarily be taller than boys, but the typical adult male pattern of greater height asserts itself later in adolescence.

Some aspect of development appears earlier than puberty. From infancy through adulthood boys have on the average, larger and stronger muscles (except when girls have their adolescent growth spurt), higher basal metabolism, and higher calorie intake. Girls have a larger proportion of fat.

The fact that some of the physical sex differences are not constant across all ages might be due in part to the different rates of physical maturation in boys and girls. Girls appear to mature earlier than boys. Girls reach puberty about 1 year earlier and reach the peak velocity of adolescent growth 2 years earlier. Studies of embryonic and infant development suggest that both in utero and among newborns, females surpass males in physical development. Thus, the precocity of girls may partly mask dimorphism in childhood. However, the earlier physical maturation of girls does not include earlier sitting, crawling and walking. It appears that ages of sitting, crawling and walking are a function of social factors. It has been observed that African children, as compared with Western children, may walk earlier because of greater encouragement by their mothers.

Explanation of Dimorphism

As indicated earlier, adult males in any given population tends to be taller, heavier and have proportionately more muscle. It is conjectured that the differential growth is due to the different effects of androgen and estrogen on the formation of bones and muscles. Until they are about 8 years of age, boys and girls do not differ in their hormone levels. As androgen production increases in males around puberty, there are not only changes in sex organ but also there are increment of muscle-formation and bone protein. Perhaps androgen facilitates the synthesis of protein necessary for bone growth and muscular development. Androgen is also implicated in the increased production of red blood cells a factor, which may enhance aerobic work capacity. On the other hand, estrogen production which increases in girls around puberty and appears responsible for many of the sexual changes in girls, seem to have a different effect on growth. The increased estrogen production appears to inhibit growth, except the growth of pelvis. It is around the time of puberty that linear growth stops in girls and the deposition of fat increases. If the sex hormones are largely responsible for sexual dimorphism, then such dimorphism is probably under genetic control.

Some degree of sexual dimorphism may also be influenced by social learning. Work and physical activity could certainly influence degree of muscle strength. If males in a society typically engage in more physical activity, then their muscular strength may be enhanced. Aerobic work capacity may also be influenced by training. It has been shown that both male and female athletes show higher maximal oxygen uptake than non-athletes of comparable ages. Hunter-gatherers are shown to have higher aerobic capacity than people of sedentary population. However, these conclusions are not definitive in the sense that genetic factors remain uncontrolled.

In the context of genetic control, the why of natural selection may be looked at. It may be postulated that it would be adaptive for females to be fully developed skeletally in the birth canal by the time they could reproduce. If they were not, then chances of surviving childbirth would be greatly reduced. It is also possible that were the female to continue growing substantially after she began to reproduce, her fetus might have reduced chance of surviving because of increased internal competition for nutrients. Natural selection then may have favoured a growth time for females, which ends shortly after puberty.

The male advantage in post-puberty growth may have a reason. It has been suggested that the greater size and strength of males in many animal species relate to their aggressive behavour on the one hand and their low investment in the care of young on the other hand. The argument is that where males' parental investment is high, males compete with each other for females. As a result, males that are bigger, stronger, and more aggressive have greater reproductive success. Where male investment in parenting is less, dimorphism is expected to be less.

It is interesting to recognize that several cross-cultural studies can be undertaken to evaluate these possible explanations of dimorphism. For example, if human populations vary in the degree to which males and females differ in hormone levels, we can ask if that variation corresponds to the degree of height, weight, muscular strength or work capacity. In other words, are populations with higher levels of estrogen in males less dimorphic? Intra-cultural comparisons in other cultural settings may also be useful. Similarly, the "exercise" hypothesis can also be examined. We can ask whether or not those societies with equal work for boys and girls have the least sex difference in aerobic work capacity. We can investigate if sexual dimorphism is pronounced in societies where male invests little in parental care.

Parallel to the possibility of relevant cross-cultural studies to examine sexual dimorphism the analysis of role-related differences offers possible hypothesis.

Role–Related Differences

The ethnography is a rich source of data on sex difference. The relationship among sex, social roles and social institutions provides some clues for an understanding of sex differences. The examination of roles in the context of subsistence activities and studies in the context of social organizations provide key elements.

Subsistence Activities

All human societies have the distinctive features of sexual division of labour in obtaining and processing food and other resources. Child care is predominantly a female activity. Offence and defense are primarily male activities.

An extensive cross-cultural survey (Murdock & Provost, 1973) has documented the subsistence activities that are characteristically performed by males and females across a world wide sample of societies. Hunting, trapping, and catching large aquatic animals are almost exclusively men's activities. Men usually predominate in herding large animals, fishing, collecting honey, clearing land and preparing the soil. Apparently there are no exclusively "feminine" subsistence activities although women generally predominate in gathering wild plant foods. No sex consistently predominates in agricultural activities, milking and gathering small land or aquatic fauna.

A consistent sexual division of labour is also apparent in crafts. Men almost exclusively work with metal (mining, smelting), wood, stone, bone, horn, and shell. Murdock and Provost, (1973), observed that men predominate in house building, net making, rope making although these are not always exclusively their domains. As with subsistence, there appear to be no craft and manufacturing activities which are exclusively "feminine" cross- culturally. One activity spinning is predominantly feminine, although men do more of it in some societies. Some activities such as weaving and making baskets, mats, clothing, pottery are useful feminine activities. Murdock and Provost (1973) hypothesized that men predominate when crafts become specialized. There is some statistical support for this hypothesis with respect to a few crafts.

However, the contribution of women in the area of "secondary" subsistence activities are prominent. With the exception of butchering which is predominantly a male activity, women consistently predominate in the preparation of food, dairy production and cooking. Women also preserve meat and fish. Thus, women contribute substantially in the area of secondary subsistence activities.

Furthermore, tasks necessary to the maintenance of the housework and its activities are women's work. With the exception of house building task women usually gather fuel, fetch water and do the laundry. The greater involvement of women in childcare is one of the most distinguishing characteristic sex difference in a variety of human cultures. In most societies, mothers are the principal caretakers of infants. The female role in care taking is even more pronounced if we consider societies where girls are the principal caretakers of infants.

While no systematic survey has been undertaken to document sex difference in fighting, there is probably no society where females regularly participate in armed combat, even in societies like Israel where women are rarely sent to the front line.

There are three possible explanations for the universal pattern of division of labour. Some activities (e.g Murdock & Provost, 1973) suggest that these patterns can be explained in part by the superior strength of males and probably their superior capacity to mobilize strength in quick bursts of energy. Others stress the incompatibility between certain subsistence activities and childcare. Recently it has been suggested that economies of effort may play some role in explaining the performance by one sex of activities that are adjacent in the production sequence or physical location.

To support the strength hypothesis, Murdock and Provost (1973) point to the nature of men's versus women's activities. Activities which require running (hunting, herding, warfare), the throwing of weapons (hunting, warfare), or lifting heavy object (catching large animals, clearing land) appear to be consistently performed by men. The work more characteristically assigned to women-gathering, most secondary subsistence activities, most household tasks, and childcare does not seem to involve the same degree of physical strength and quick bursts of energy. However, a number of authors are critical of "strength" hypothesis; they argue that women can and sometimes do heavy physical work such as agricultural activities.

Perhaps the "incompatibility" argument could better explain why men usually collect honey and fish (both of which are dangerous but generally do not require that much strength). The incompatibility hypothesis probably could also explain why men usually engage in full-time craft specialization – producing large quantities of items for sale or exchange, it precludes interruption.

There is no evidence to choose between the "strength" and the "incompatibility" hypotheses. Support for both of these interpretations are based on same data. What is needed is the independence of the supposed predictors.

Certain work patterns do not seem to be predicted by either the "strength" hypothesis or by "incompatibility" hypothesis. Recently it has been suggested that certain tasks may be performed because they are adjacent in the production sequence or because they are clustered in the same physical locations. The argument is that men may make nets and ropes because they are needed for fishing (which men principally do). The argument also suggests that musical instruments may be made by men because they lumber wood. Women primarily do secondary subsistence work and housework because men are often occupied in far-away contexts. The economies of effort require women to do the work closer to home. In addition, men probably could not gather as well as hunt if the collected flora and fauna are located in different places.

The ethnographically derived sex differences point to another aspect of sex differences. Apart from role-related differences, status-related variation across sex is also explicated.

Sex and Social Organization

Most societies favour one sex over the other in structuring social groups and access to resources. The Ethnographic Atlas shows that 89 percent of the societies in which married couples live with or near kin have a unilocal rule of residence (a rule stipulating that the couple lives with or near the kin of one sex). It is also shown that 85 percent of societies with inheritance of real property have unilineal inheritance rules (only one sex inherits), 82 percent of societies with movable property have only one sex inheriting such property, and 89 percent of societies with lineal descent groups have unlineal groups (inheritance in such groups is passed through only one sex) Moreover, these social rules tend to be consistent (structured around the same sex).

Where one sex is chosen as the core of the residential group, as the core of the unilineal descent group, or as the inheritor of property, it could be either male or female, but by far most societies favour males of the societies with unilocal residence; 81 percent have married couples living with their husbands' kin. Of the societies with unilineal descent, 75 percent have membership assigned through fathers. Of the societies with unilineal inheritance of real property, 87 percent assign it to male heirs. Of the societies with unilineal inheritance of movable property, 85 percent assign it to male heirs.

It is observed that most societies structure social groups and access to resources around male sex. The why of this preponderance of male sex is an important question. After all, some societies do have bilocal residence (where married couples live with either husband's or wife's kin). Some researchers view this post-marital residence changes are key to understanding other changes in social organizations. To explain why institutions are structured around males it would be helpful to ask why most unilocal societies have patrilocal residences.

The cross-cultural evidence suggests that nonunilocal residence appear only in special circumstances. Neolocal residence seems to be associated with the development of money or commercial economy. It is observed that pattern of residence (patrilocal, matrilocal or bilocal) is a function of which sex (males, females or neither respectively) contributes the most to subsistence. However, there is another hypothesis as to why the most societies structure their social organizations around males. The role of men in warfare is cited as one explanation of patrilocal residence. It posits that internal fighting among language groups or other social groups within the community induces expectations that sons live near by for the propose of security; this reason overrides which sex is contributing most to subsistence. In other words, internal warfare (which is very common in most communities) determines patrilocal residence; in the absence of warfare, the pattern of residence is determined by the sex contributing most to subsistence.

In the context of organization, status is another key element. Traditionally anthropologists define status as individual characteristics valued in a society. Others emphasize the aspect of control while some others stress power and authority. The sex difference across these dimensions needs to be examined.

It does not need documentation to note that women have rarely occupied superordinate positions in decision-making domain. Even in matrilineal societies where women may have relatively more authority and influence, men usually occupy the political offices. For example, among the Iroquois, woman seem to have relatively high status (woman could influence the selection and deposing of ruling elders and influence the discussion of the political council and have occasional power over the conduct of man). But women could not serve in political council and speak only through male speakers.

There are two hypotheses to explain male dominance. The first hypothesis is based on the concept of warfare. It posits that role of men in warfare brings males control over resources. Consequently men enjoy greater status owing to the enhanced control over resources. The second hypothesis implicates mobility of men and explains males' superiority in the absence of warfare. It is suggested that mobility expand experiences with outside world. Male's greater mobility and contact with outside world bring knowledge and status-enhancement. This hypothesis predicts that women in sedentary societies have lower status in comparison with women in migratory societies. However, none of these hypotheses has yet been systematically tested against data from the cross- cultural record.

While some of the explanatory concerns have surfaced because of the cross-cultural explanation of sex differences in physical and physiologic domains as well as social organization domains, the analysis of sex differences in psychological and behavioural areas is likely to offer valuable insights.

Psychological Differences

The possibility of concepts explaining sex difference could be enhanced by surveying pertinent cross-cultural evidence. Although the domains include a wide variety of concerns such as infancy, childhood, adulthood, perception learning, thinking, and many other psychological functioning, only some of the representative areas would be discussed, These include life span considerations and stylistic dimensions.

Life Span Consideration

The life span considerations encompass infancy, childhood, adolescence, adulthood, and old age. Only a few researchers have observed infants in non-Western societies. Yet, findings obtained from studies carried out in North America and other Western societies suggest some interesting features in sex difference.

There is some evidence that newborn females discharge their energy more in smiling and other facial movements, whereas male newborns discharge it more in total body activation. Male infants (few weeks to few months old) are more fretful than female infants. Some studies indicate that female newborns indicate greater tactile sensitivity than male newborns. At about 1 year of age, girls look and vocalize more towards their mothers than their fathers; boys look and vocalize more towards their fathers than mothers.

Although not many sex differences have been indicated for infants, it is important to know which of them would hold across cultures. The universal differences appearing at newborns may very well represent biologic differences. Such differences could potentially condition parents to respond to boys and girls in different ways that may produce personality differences between the sexes. For example, if it turns out to be true that female infants smile more, parents might be apt to look at them more directly. As a matter of fact, research on parent-infant interaction in the Untied States suggests that mothers may hold female infants more face-to-face (Maccoby & Jacklin, 1974). Parents might also feel that female infants are more content and therefore spend less time attending to them. Research suggests that parents spend more time handling, attending and stimulating male infants.

The study of sex difference in infancy and differential parental behaviours may affect sex differences later. For example, greater parental attention to male infants might reinforce egoistic behaviour which is generally more characteristic of boys. It would be interesting to investigate whether or not differential attending produces cross-cultural variation in the degree of egoism boys and girls exhibit. Similarly, the inference that infants look and vocalize more to same-sex individuals carry important implications. It suggests cognitive gender identification at a very early age.

The period of childhood is also an area of research concern. Most of the observational data come from six-culture project in which children were observed in Kenya, Mexico, Philippines, India, Okinawa and the United States. The sex differences observed were summarized by Whiting and Edwards (1973) and by B. Whiting and Whiting (1975).

A sex difference in aggression is perhaps the best-documented difference that emerges from cross-cultural research. Boys usually display more aggression than girls and this difference seems to appear by 8 years of age. Whether males continue to be aggressive in adulthood is not clear. Experimental and projective research in the United States suggest that the childhood sex difference continues into adulthood (Maccoby & Jackin, 1974). Rohner's (1976) ethnographic survey does not show consistent sex difference in adulthood aggression in nonwestern societies.

In addition to aggression, there are other sex differences in childhood behaviour. The evidence suggests that girls are more apt to conform to others, particularly to adults. In an analysis of the six cultures data, it was found that girls were consistently more likely to conform to mothers than boys. Research conducted in Israel and Russia is also suggestive of girls' somewhat greater conformity.

In play, boys seem to show a preference for boys and girls show a preference for girls. Some studies do indicate that boys and girls tend to play in different size groups. Boys are more likely to play in large groups; girls prefer small groups of two or three.

Personal space (the space between individuals) also seems to differ by sex. Boys maintain greater distance between themselves and other children. There are often sex differences in social behaviour. Girls exhibit more nurturant behaviour than boys. Data from the six cultures study show that 7-11-year -old girls are consistently more apt to offer help and support. The kibbutz girls of 1-4 years of age are more likely to aid, assist, share and cooperate. However, the age of onset of nurturant behaviour in girls is not clear.

Research shows that boys and girls may exhibit different styles of dominance and dependence behaviour. Boys seem to exhibit more egoistic dominance, girls more prosocial dominance (responsible behaviour). As for dependency behaviour, boys may seek attention and material goods more; girls may seek help and physical contact more. Girls are more oriented towards adults and believe in ways that are socially adaptable. Boys are more oriented towards peers and behave more selfishly. Although there is no evidence that girls are more sociable, girls may engage in or seek closer, more intimate social contacts, whereas boys may be more expressively sociable, yet more distancing.

There seems to be somewhat more cross-cultural variability in nurturance and proximity to parents. Data from the United States suggest little sex difference in nurturance or depending behaviour. However, data from other cultural systems suggest that girls usually are more nurturant or more likely to stay closer to home and adults.

As indicted earlier, biological explanations in general and hormonal levels in particular have been suggested as explanations of sex differences in human life span development. However, anthropologists and cross-cultural psychologists point at the direction of social factors. We would examine the role of possible social factors after we review some cross-cultural studies of sex difference in other areas.

Perception and Cognition

Cross-cultural psychologists have looked for differences. Agrawal and Agrawal (1999) explored sex difference in creativity and intelligence among Indian children. Boys were significantly more creative and intelligent than girls. Khanama and Sen (1996) also found similar male advantage with respect to creativity. With respect to a different domain such as haptic perception, Gupta and Gupta (1997) found that females made significantly more haptic perceptual judgement in comparison with males.

Ember (1977) suggests this cognitive development (in terms of Piagetian tasks) generally shows no sex differences, but sex differences do appear both intra-culturally and cross-culturally in measures of field independence—dependence and other spatial-visual abilities

The terms "field independence" and "field dependence" refer to different perceptual styles and more broadly to different cognitive styles. Field independence refers to the tendency for parts of the field to be experienced as discrete from the field as a whole; field dependence refers to the parts being fused with field, or experience as "global" (Witkin and Berry, 1975). Cross-culturally perceptual style has been measured by the embedded figures test, rod and frame test, and the Koh's block design test. The summary of data from the cross-cultural project of Witkin and Berry (1975) provides a consistent picture. Males are more likely to be field-independent while females are more likely to be field dependent. Witkin and Berry (1975) also suggest that sex differences appear greatest in sedentary, agricultural societies and least in migratory, hunting societies. No or few sex differences have been found among Eskimos.

Many researchers think of field independence/dependence as indicative of analytical/global ability. However, whether or not field independence/dependence measures are merely measures of spatial-visual abilities has not yet been determined. But other measures of spatial-visual ability show superiority of males.

Dawson (1972) has presented a theory that normal male cognitive style (higher spatial numerical and field independence scores) is in part influenced by neonatal androgen programming of the brain and in part by the appropriate male socialization process (p. 22). Androgen then, is presumed to account partly for greater visual spatial abilities. In support of the hormonal part of his theory, Dawson cites evidence that West

African males feminized by a Kwashiorkor-induced endocrine dysfunction (which increases estrogen) are significantly lower on spatial-visual abilities and significantly more field - dependent than normal males.

There is another physiological explanation in terms of lateralization of the brain. There is evidence that the left cerebral hemisphere dominates verbal functions and the right cerebral hemisphere mostly but not as strongly dominates nonverbal functions (Buffery & Gray, 1972). It is proposed that this supposedly innate "lateralization" develops earlier in girls than in boys and the earlier lateralization in girls could account for the known cognitive style differences between the sexes. There is some evidence supporting some part of the theory. However, the evidence is not complete enough to support the notion entirely.

Berry (1971) advances an eco-cultural model to account for the data. On the basis of his data obtained from a wide variety of cultural groups, Berry shows that a particular cluster of eco-cultural dimensions is associated with field independence, whereas a different cluster is associated with field dependence. The low accumulation of food, hunting-gathering exploitative economic mode, nomadic settlement pattern, low population density, low social stratification, and assertion-oriented socialization emphasis are related to field independence. In contrast, high accumulation of food, agricultural exploitative economic mode, sedentary settlement pattern, high population density, high social stratification and compliance-oriented socialization emphasis are related to field dependence. As predicted by this eco-cultural model, Eskimos were found to have field independent cognitive style and Temmes of African were found to have field-dependent cognitive style. It is also important to note that eco-cultural explanation represents a functionalistic approach. The people in hunting gathering societies (e.g, Eskimos) are expected to be field-independent (with greater perceptual discrimination), so that they can fish and hunt effectively. However, all of the variables in a cluster are packaged; hence it is difficult to ascertain the specific contribution of a particular dimension (such as settlement pattern) on cognitive style.

The application of Berry's (1971) eco-cultural framework generates some of the predictions and these predictions have been tested in intra-cultural and cross-cultural setting. For example, Berland (1977) investigated the cognitive styles of Khanbadosh, a subsistence society in Pakistan. This subsistence society of street musical entertainers is partly sedentary. As predicted, it was shown that there was less sex role segregation in this society as compared to mainstream population. Similarly, the people had intermediate positions on field independence-dependence dimension.

Recently Mishra, Sinha and Berry (1996) have examined a similar group in India. Data obtained from the study on Birhors, a semi-nomadic tribe in the state of Bihar, (India) also demonstrated intermediate position on the dimension of field independence—dependence as predicted by Berry's eco-cultural model.

Consistent with the interpretation that migration is associated with field independence, boys are expected to be better at spatial visual skills because of their greater experience with movement through physical environment. Apart from mobility factor, there is another important consideration. It is generally observed that education, especially contemporary education, aims at fostering field independence (making individuals autonomous of external referents). In many parts of the world, boys and girls are not given the same amount or the same kinds of education. It is likely that sedentary, agricultural societies may show more of a sex difference in field independence/ dependence than hunter-gatherers because the former has more special education by sex. Where education is voluntary, girls might be more often kept out of school when there is a great deal of work to be done around the house. Whether this is true or not, the factor of education certainty has to be statistically controlled for in future cross-cultural research on sex differences in perception and cognition.

The analysis of behavioural differences has been mostly approached through observation and administration of standardized tests. However, there are certain areas of differences where direct observation and/or measurements are relatively difficult. In these cases, we have to count on indirect ways of knowing how people feel and experience. The use of indirect methods has provided some clues on difference in expressive behaviour.

Expressive Behaviour

Males and females have characteristic personality differences that are reflected in a number of expressive moods in art, in music, game preference and in dreams.

Asthana and Mandal (1998) examined posed social expressions of emotion. The significant sex x emotion interaction revealed that female expressions were more expressive than male expressions in expressing sad emotion. Sex difference in the expression of happy emotion was not significant in another study; Tauvab (1999) found that women show greater perceptual defense than men. Women had higher recognition threshold for taboo words than men.

The bulk of the dream research has focussed on the sex of the character in males' and females' dreams. It has been suggested that there is a tendency for males to dream more about males than females, whereas females tend to dream about the sexes equally.

The same tendency is found by Grey and Kalsched (1971) in India. The sex difference in dreams reflects male's greater unresolved problems with men. As a partial support for this hypothesis, it is observed that in men's dreams males have a higher proportion of aggressive interaction with males, whereas in women's dreams females divide aggression equally between both sexes.

An alternative hypothesis is that dreams reflect real-life difference in interaction rather then an unconscious conflict. Grey and Kalsched (1971) cite some supportive evidence for these hypotheses from India. Pointing out that traditional Indian society is quite segregated by sex, they find that more traditional individuals (both males and females) have significantly lower number of opposite-sex characters in their dreams and males who have more opposite-sex friends have a higher proportion of opposite-sex dream characters.

The "reality" hypothesis seems to explain the apparent cross-cultural tendency of males to dream more about male characters. As reviewed earlier, there is tendency for boys and girls to choose same-sex peers for play. Nonetheless, it may be generally true that girls who are more often at home see males and females in more equal proportion than boys do. Boys who may be more often free to play might spend more of their time in all-male groups. The greater tendency of males to have aggressive encounters with males in dreams may thus reflect a greater frequency of aggressive behaviour in males. Additional support has been Provided by another study that examined words in dream. A study involving 75 tribes indicated that men were significantly more apt than women to mention weapons, death and animals in their dreams. This tendency may reflect men's greater involvement in the occupations of hunting, herding and war. Men are more apt to mention large aspects of their dream setting (e.g., landscape), while women are more apt to describe interior setting and small spaces. Men also are more apt to mention non-relatives and aggressive encounters. It is expected that the sex difference in dreams would be proportional to their role segregation.

Some researchers have examined sex differences in drawings. One study examined sample designs prepared by college students. It was found that men were significantly more likely than women to close designs, enlarge or expand designs upward, emphasized sharp or angular lines.

Women, on the other hand, were significantly more likely to leave designs open, elaborate designs internally, blunt or enclose sharp lines or angles. Although this sex difference in drawing was obtained from a study in the United States, future cross-cultural investigations are likely to offer much insight. For instance, Mathur (1994) has documented significant sex difference in spontaneous art of high school boys and girls in India, although specific dimensions of differences have not been identified.

There is also reason to believe that cross-cultural sex difference will appear in game preference. It is expected that in societies with strong pressure for obedience, games of strategy is preferred. In contrast, games of physical skill is preferred in societies with strong pressure on achievement. Generally girls are socialized in the direction of obedience and responsibility; boys are in the direction of achievement and physical development. In conformity with these expectations, boys are found to prefer games of physical skills, whereas girls are found to prefer games of strategy.

Another area that deserves cross-cultural examination is the two sex differences in the domains of adjustment and maladjustment.

Adjustment and Maladjustment

There is not much cross-cultural research on how males and females feel about themselves. One particular aspect of self-concept provides some clues using Rotter's external-internal "locus of control" Scale. Sinha (1972) found that male college students in India had higher internal locus of control scores than female college student. Similar findings were also obtained in Japan. Males appear to feel that they have more personal control over their lives than females. Although this finding has not been replicated across a large number of cultural systems, trend is visible. The societies that are most strongly male-dominated have the greatest discrepancy in male-female concept of personal control.

The cross-cultural examination of sex difference on anxiety does not offer uniform picture. In some societies males indicate greater anxiety than females in other societies. It is likely that women in Western societies may have more anxiety because traditional women's roles (i.e. housewife and mother) are no longer valued. Hence they may suffer from anxiety because of role conflict. Men may have anxiety in other society because they may be subjects of another kind of role conflict induced by acculturation pressures.

Role conflict and acculturation may affect roles of mental illness. When the sexes are affected differently by these stresses, different patterns of sex differences in mental illness may result.

Changing values may be one source of role conflict. In a comparative study, it is reported that women have lower rates of mental illness in the community where women are isolated from the sentiments of the larger society about changing women roles, whereas women have higher rates of mental illness in the community where they are beset by conflicts about their roles. In the United States, it is only among married persons that women are significantly more likely to be mentally ill. They suggest that they may be so because the "housewife" role no longer has much prestige and married women who work have the burdens of two roles.

But changing values themselves may not be sufficient to produce role conflict. Perhaps it is really the result of a discrepancy between what one values and what one can achieve. For example, a study found that in Eskimo community, women (who had higher rates of mental illness than men) had identified highly with Western culture but unlike men had no real contact with that culture. This conflict springs from the inability to achieve what people want.

The bulk of evidence generated by cross-cultural research underlines the significance of social factors in sex difference. While the possible role of biology is not ruled out, the manifestation of sex difference is explicated through sociocultural factors.

Socio-Cultural Explanations

Probably most cultural and social anthropologists believe that sex differences are socially or culturally induced products of differential socialization. The evaluation of this proposition is possible when we examine the evidence of mediating mechanisms such as sex-linked emphasis and task assignments.

Reward and Punishment

Most people probably think of socialization in its most direct-sense the encouragement and discouragement of particular behaviour through rewards and punishment by socializing agents. For many behaviours, it is observed that if societies exert differential pressures on boys and girls to believe differently, then socialization may account at least partly for sex difference in behaviour.

Although the cross-cultural evidence is largely indirect, there is suggestion that differential socialization pressures on the sexes could account for some of the sex differences in behaviour. There are three areas in which both sex differences in socialization and actual sex differences have been observed. These areas include aggression, nurturance and responsibility. The main sources of cross-cultural data are provided by Barry, Bacon, and Child (1957).

Box 8.1

Sex Differences in Socialization Pressure

Area of Socialization	*Stage*	*Percentage of Societies with Evidence of Sex Difference in Socialization in the Direction of:*			
		Boys	*Girls*	*Neither*	*No. of Societies*
Fortitude	Early childhood	18%	1%	81%	130
	Late childhood	28%	1%	71%	143
Aggressiveness	Early childhood	18%	2%	80%	116
	Late childhood	24%	3%	73%	125
Self-reliance	Early childhood	24%	3%	74%	151
	Late childhood	44%	2%	54%	151
(in 1957 study)	Combined	85%	0%	15%	82
Achievement	Early childhood	Negligible difference			
	Late childhood	Negligible difference			
(in 1957 study)	Combined	87%	3%	10%	31
Industriousness	Early childhood	2%	32%	65%	
	Late childhood	4%	48%	47%	173
Responsibility	Early childhood	3%	24%	73%	147
	Late childhood	6%	38%	55%	154
(in 1957 study)	Combined	11%	61%	28%	84
Obedience	Early childhood	1%	14%	84%	159
	Late childhood	3%	13%	84%	158
(in 1957 study)	Combined	3%	35%	62%	69
Sexual Restraint	Early childhood	1%	23%	76%	152
	Late childhood	2%	45%	52%	160
Nurturance	Combined	0%	82%	18%	33
(in 1957 study)					

Barry Josephson, Lauer and Marshall's 1976 data suggest that, where there are sex differences in socialization, boys rather than girls are pressured to be aggressive, whereas girls rather than boys are pressured to be nurturant and responsible.

There are also two areas in which socialization pressures may correspond to behaviour differences. Boys are generally farther from home and girls come to comply more with adult's wishes. These two sex differences in behaviour seem to correspond to two sex differences in socialization–that boys are pressured to be self-reliant and girls are pressured to be more obedient.

An important gap exists with respect to the magnitude of differential socialization as reflected in Barry et al.'s (1957) study vis-à-vis Barry et al.'s (1976) study. For example, earlier study suggested that most societies (85 per cent) pressured boys to be self-reliant but the later study indicates that most societies (74 percent in early childhood and 54 percent in late childhood) do not differentially pressure boys and girls on self-reliance. Barry et al. (1976) report that the later sample includes modern technologically advanced societies. If such societies have less differential socialization by sex, then the later sample might be expected to show fewer sex differences in socialization pressures. More studies are needed to draw definitive conclusions.

The socialization process assumes a conscious effort on part of parents and other caretakers to shape specific behaviour. But there are other ways in which caretaker behaviour can shape child and adult social behaviour. The task assignment is one such mechanism.

Task Assignment

In many societies, parents assign a great deal of work to their children. Such assignment probably parallels the adult division of labor by sex as much as possible. Boys and girls are assigned different work; girls far more work than boys.

A number of different theoretical orientations would lead us to expect that sex difference in task assignment might produce sex difference in social behaviour. First, learning theory would predict that behaviour learned in the course of task assignment would tend to generalize either because of parental reward and punishment for appropriate task-related behaviour or because of the intrinsic rewards of performing a task well. Behaviour may also be learned during the course of task assignment.

Second, identification and imitation theory would provide that a child might be likely to identify with and imitate the behaviour of the task model. Third, a cognitive theoretical orientation would suggest that children assigned sex-typed chores may behave in ways consistent with how they think others expect them to believe.

A number of analyses from the six-culture-study suggest linkages between task alignment and social behaviours. B. Whiting and Whiting (1975) have shown that, in those societies in which herding is important, boys score high on responsible social behaviour as compared with societies in which herding is unimportant. B. Whiting and Whiting (1975) have also shown that in those societies in which children are assigned more work (probably because of their mother's greater workload) children exhibit behaviour profiles with more nurturant and responsible behaviour. The six culture data indicate unequal assignment of chores to boys and girls. Girls are significantly more often assigned responsibility of all works and girls show significantly more responsible social behaviour (B. Whiting & Whiting, 1975).

There are few studies that have examined direct linkage between specific aspects of socialization and particular sex difference in behaviour. Most of the evidence in the areas of studies of socialization are indirect. There is another area of research in which some subtle aspects of sex difference in socialization have been investigated.

Subtle Aspects of Socialization

There are some subtle aspects in sex difference in socialization. Data from the United States suggest a few early and subtle differences in socialization by sex. This difference seems to have a role in inculcating egoistic behaviour. For example, U.S parents spend more time attending to male infants in physical ways–holding them, touching them, and stimulating them. In particular, parents are apt to elicit gross motor behaviour (Maccoby and Jacklin, 1974). Boy infants seem to be handled more roughly, girl infants seem to be treated as more fragile.

These socialization differences in handling and attention could subtly reinforce the habit potential in boys of egoistic behaviour. If parents attend more to boys when they fuss, boys might learn more than girls to seek attention and other satisfaction of their own needs. If parents are usually rougher with male infants, this might lead boys to be more prone to rough-and-tumble play, both to engage in it and to expect rough handling from others. If fathers in particular handle their male infants more roughly, such infants might be led to expect greater roughness from males in general.

Of course, it is possible that potential reaction to infants may themselves be a response to biologic difference in male and female infants. Perhaps male infants are more fretful generally, causing parents to attend to them more or perhaps male infants are "rougher" so those parents are rougher with them. Future research will have to try to control variables to generate definitive conclusions.

The other subtle sex difference in socialization refers to greater parental tolerance of aggression in boys. There is some evidence of an interaction between the sex of the parent and the sex of the child with regard to the display of aggression towards parents. A few studies suggest that fathers may be more permissive of aggression from girls and mothers may be more permissive of such behaviour from boys. Of the 13 companions of tolerance of cross-sex aggression cited by Maccoby and Jacklin (1974), ten significantly indicate cross-sex permissiveness. Greater punishment of boys and cross-sex permissiveness could conceivably increase the aggressiveness of boys. The more severe physical punishment could generate increased anger, which may be displaced in the form of increased aggressive behaviour to peers. The greater cross-sex permissiveness may further increase habit potential of boy's aggressiveness if mothers are the primary socializers.

An important factor, which might influence differential socialization, is the extent to which boys and girls may be around adults. Parents may have similar ideas about how both boys and girls should behave, but if boys are not as often around, parents may have less of a chance to influence boy's behaviour. It is possible then that boys are less apt to inhibit egoistic behaviour including aggression and dominance behaviour; they are less apt to learn responsible and nurturant behaviour. If reward and punishment are successful in shaping social behaviour, then differential exposure of boys and girls to parental influence might function as a mediating factor.

More generally, it may be that the social context of learning contributes to the extent to which certain behaviours are learned. Girls, if they are more often around the home, will not only have adults around as overseers, they will also have a larger number of younger children around. Boys, if they are more often away from home, are probably more likely to have peers around. These different targets of interaction are likely to induce different forms of social behaviour in boys and girls. Because of greater contact with adults and young children, girls learn to be obedient, responsible and nurturant. Boys, on the other hand, learn to be aggressive and dominant because of their frequent encounter with peers.

These cross-cultural empirical findings may be conceptualized within specific theoretical frameworks.

Current Theoretical Positions

Although several theories have been advanced to explain the development of sex role behaviour, the four most important theories have come from biogenic, psychoanalytic social learning, and cognitive developmental approaches.

As already discussed, the relationship between biology and behaviour implicates the role of genetic factors in general and hormone levels in particular. In general, higher androgen levels in males are presumed to stimulate higher aggression, dominance and other traits associated with men. In contrast, greater levels of estrogen in females are presumed to inhibit aggression and dominance in women. Although researchers adopting this approach cite consistency of sex difference across cultures and species, as supporting evidence, the interaction of biogenic factors with socio-cultural conditions can not be ruled out.

There is not much empirical work to support psychoanalytic theory. Kakar (1981) has analyzed aspects of Indian society such as myths, rituals, fables and arts to explicate childhood in Indian socio-cultural system. While his study generated a number of predictions, especially in terms of Erikson's psychosocial development, empirical testing and assessment have not been adequately undertaken. In recent years, Chodorow (1978) has been responsible for the revival of psychoanalytic orientation. Using psychoanalytic orientation, she points out the basic difference between the core structure of self–concept of girls and that of boys. Basing on these differential therapeutic programmes for men and women, Davar (1999) adopts a similar position (feminine agenda) in the context of mental health of Indian women. However, psychoanalytic views including those of Chodorow (1978) need further empirical support for the viability.

Social learning theory, as it describes the learning of gender-related behaviour, is articulated by Mischel (1966). Briefly, from the very beginning of life, parents and other care-takers treat boys and girls differently. Children are believed to choose to imitate models of some sex (often their parents, but also other children, other adults, and even characters from print or visual media). By and large, social learning depicts that identification with and imitation of same-sex parent and other adults play a large role in the acquisition of sex-typed behaviour.

However, the extensive review of Maccoby and Jacklin (1974) does not provide conclusive evidence in this context. Identification with the same-sex parent and imitation of other same sex adults seem to be much more likely in traditional societies. But research in developed countries such as the United States shows little correlation between same sex parent and the child. Perhaps children in contemporary modern societies do not consider the work of the same-sex parent as relevant for them and for their future. Hence, they are less likely to imitate. In contrast, children still consider the work of the same-sex parent as relevant in traditional societies; hence there is tendency for imitation. Thus, social learning theory posits different predictions for modern and traditional societies under present circumstances.

Cognitive development theory as it describes the learning of gender-related behaviour is articulated by Kohlberg (1966). According to this theory children cannot understand generalized concepts such as their own sex and its accompanying gender-role expectations until their cognitive abilities are sufficiently developed to a stage or level at which they can understand the concept of gender. Kohlberg believes that gender development is analogous to the Piagetian theory of physical constancy. One of the hallmarks of cognitive development theory is the role of the child as an active processor of culturally transmitted information.

There is some disagreement about the age at which children are supposed to develop their gender identities. Kohlberg (1966) opines that it is absent in the first 2 years of life and becomes stable only by age 6 to 7 years. Critics believe that gender identity appears earlier in infancy. As supporting evidence, they cite infants' preferred looking behaviour at same-sex parents. They also cite the work of others on hermaphrodites who, when their genitals are altered to conform to their genetic sex, are reluctant (even at the age of 2 years) to change their sexual identity accordingly.

Some current work blurs the line between the two theories (social learning and cognitive developmental view). Fagot (1985) has shown that children currently do respond to reinforcement patterns, but they respond selectively. Reinforcement is not effective when given by some groups, but it is very effective when given by others. For example girls respond to the reinforcement given by female and male teachers and by other girls but not to the reinforcement given by the boys. Boys respond to the reinforcement given by other boys, but they do not respond to this given by teachers or by girls.

Similarly, research into the effects of models shows that children do model the behaviour of same-sex adults, but not when the adult is doing something different from other adults. Imitation may be "alive and well", but it is selective cognition.

A sophisticated version of cognitive development and social learning theories is Ben's gender schemas theory. It would be fully discussed in the context of androgyny. Briefly it regards the child as an active processor and organizer of gender-related cognitions. There is a considerable body of research findings documenting the existence of gender schemas, even though it is a new area of research. (Bem, 1985).

One additional field of research on the socialization of gender involved area outside of developmental psychology. It is psychological anthropology. In a landmark study, Whiting and Edwards (1988) have reanalyzed historic six culture sample by gender and have added five new cultures. These eleven cultures have been analyzed for differences by sex in dyadic interaction of adults with children and children with children of different ages. The authors concluded that we are the company we keep. If an individual spends his or her time with an infant, this infant itself seems to bring forth nurturing responses. If the individual spends enough time with infants, he or she will become a nurturer. In many cultures, but not all, young girls are given child-care responsibility, whereas young boys are not. As a function of these responsibilities, girls are more likely to become nurturant.

However, it does not explain why girls are given one kind of responsibility than another but it does explain other notions. For example, it has been claimed that people change over their life span. One of the determinants of such change may be through the company they keep. The notion that we are the company we keep is also congruent with the term self-socialization (Maccoby & Jacklin, 1974).

Thus, currently held theories point to several critical dimensions of socialization process. What is needed for the future is an integrative approach to the salient features of workable theories. For such an objective, further cross-cultural work would identify culturally-sensitive dimensions. Furthermore, analytic reviews of studies across dimensions (especially different segments of the past century) will delineate the changing pattern of workable theories in the context of changes in world societies. This is a challenging task that lies ahead.

Box – 8.2
Recapitualation at a Glance
Why Sex Difference?

Biologic Perspective

1. Biologic views claim the importance of sex hormones in sex difference. It posits that higher androgen level in males stimulate aggres-

sion, dominance and other masculine behaviour in men. In contrast, higher levels of estrogen in females inhibit such behaviour in women.

Physical and Physiologic Difference

2. Although there is no adequate explanation for the why of sexual dimorphism (difference between sexes with respect to anatomy), there are cross-cultural evidence of differences resulting from dimorphism.

Role-Related Differences

3. Cross-cultural evidence shows differential contributions of males and females towards subsistence activities.
4. Females seem to have less power and status in social institutions and organizations.

Psychological Difference

5. Females show greater nurturant and responsible behaviour than males. Males indicate greater aggressiveness and dominance than females.
6. Males are more field-independent than females.
7. There is sex difference in expressive behaviour. One indicator of this difference is the difference in dream content. Males' dream content reveals more encounter with males. Females's dream shows equal encounter with males and females in their dreams.
8. Cross-cultural research indicates sex-linked social factor (emphasis on responsibility and nurturance for girls and self-reliance for boys).

Socialization

9. Differential reward and punishment and task-assignment seem to work as mediators of socialization.
10. Social learning in form of identification with and imitation of model seems to produce sex difference in behaviour though there are moderator variables.
11. There is also evidence for developmental cognitive theory. It posits that the child actually processes and organizes gender-related information that is culturally transmitted.

Part II

Trend of Convergence

9

The Emerging Concept of Androgyny

The quality of life is fundamental concern of every society. All societies strive for their citizens's enrichment of activities and experiences. However, this objective presents a formidable challenge. Because of complexity of societal structure and global events, many factors complicate the process of social planning. Every society is like an organism. Its origin, growth, and enrichment are influenced by elements that constitute it. Men and women are elementary units of a society. The characteristics of men and women greatly influence the nature and quality of society.

Both men and women, in turn, are products of ongoing changes of external reality. The various roles they perform, the activities they endorse, and the ideals they emulate shape their behavioural patterns. In recent years, there are many events that have transformed the conventional standards regarding men and women. More specifically, women liberation movement and greater participation of women in workforce have brought about some tangible changes in developed societies. Similarly, a transition from rural and agricultural life style to urban industrialized pattern has modified standards regarding sex-appropriate roles in developing countries.

During the last few decades, the traditional society of India has been undergoing a series of changes. Multi-directional forces of urbanization, industrialization and socio-educational advancement are affecting various aspects of traditional Indian society. More recently, changes have become more pronounced as a result of political independence, constitutional measures, planned economic development, programmes of industrialization and social development, emergence of urban culture, western science and technology, secularization and rational outlook. The changes in socio-economic and political conditions have brought out changes in beliefs, attitudes, and value system.

In this transitional state of changing environment, both men and women are experiencing a psychological change in themselves. It is our fundamental concern to examine the pattern of these changing values, attitudes and roles, particularly in the context of present situation.

When we consider the psychological make-up of men and women, the term sex-trait-stereotype (the constellation of psychological traits) emerges as a focal theme.

The term sex-stereotype, according to Ashmore and Del Boca (1979), is usually considered to be cognitive. It is a set of beliefs; it deals with what men and women are like and it is shared by the members of a particular group. According to Williams and Best (1982), stereotype is the belief system containing generalization about the characteristics of the groups of persons. Sex-stereotype area has been confused by inadequate distinctions among different, but closely related constructs. Sex-trait stereotypes consist of those psychological characteristics of behavioural traits that are believed to characterize men with greater frequency or lesser frequency than they characterize women.

According to William and Best (1982), sex-roles (e.g., that there are more men than women engineers) are often explained by reference to sex-role stereotypes (there should be more women engineers) and often explained by reference to sex-trait stereotypes (e.g., men are strong).

Traditional View of Sex-Role

Linton (1936) used the term status in the sense in which we are using position. Role refers to the sum total of the culture patterns associated with a particular status. Thus, it includes the attitudes, values and behaviour ascribed by the society to any and all persons occupying this status. Among the various roles which human beings play, those that have received maximum attention of social psychologists are sex roles. There is no firm evidence that males and females are destined by nature for the arbitrary roles and characteristics frequently assigned to the two sexes in any culture. As Angarist (1978) and others (Spence, 1979; Spence & Helmreich, 1978) have noted, term sex-role has several meanings. Anthropologically, sex-role refers to how one's position in the societal structure is determined by sex. Sociologically, it refers to how one's relationships to other people are determined by sex; psychologically it refers to how one's personality and behaviour are determined by sex.

According to more traditional trait conception of sex-roles, sex-typed individuals are highly masculine males and feminine females, whereas non-sex typed individuals would be referred to as undifferentiated. Gender Scheme Theory (Bem, 1981a, 1981b, 1985), a contemporary conceptualization of gender as a personal construct, classifies people into four categories: (a) sex-typed (masculine men and feminine women), (b) androgynous (those who are both masculine and feminine), (c) undifferentiated (those neither masculine nor feminine), and (d) cross sex-typed (feminine men and masculine women).

The behaviours which are labeled as masculine and feminine are not inevitable consequences of biological differences between males and females. Masculine and feminine behaviours are culturally prescribed. Youngsters are socialized in the work activities and personality characteristics defined as differentially appropriate for males and females in their own culture. Everyone of us is so familiar with the social roles that there is no need to point specifically that the behaviour patterns expected of males are considerably same in almost all the cultures in the world. Similarly, behaviour patterns expected of females are also considerably same across many cultures.

One of the reasons often given for the difference in manifest as well as expected behaviour in males and females is based on the biological difference between sexes including their body builds, hormonal differences, reproductive functions, and chromosomal differences. However, many psychologists feel that part played by these biological difference in the behaviour of the sexes is minimal, and they can be better accounted in terms of social learning.

Historically, adult women and men have fulfilled somewhat different roles in all societies (Munroe & Munroe, 1975). In occupation outside the home, certain jobs, traditionally, are considered more appropriate for men and others for women. In the area of home making, women have automatically assumed the principal responsibility, while certain specific duties have been considered appropriate for men.

The sex-trait stereotypes not only affect the occupational opportunities of adult men and women, but at a much earlier age, may also determine the manner in which adults respond to children. These adult sex-trait stereotypes influence the children's perceptions of adult behaviour, talents and traits and their expectations for their future adult views. Both in psychology and society at large, masculinity and femininity have long been conceptualized as bipolar ends of a single continuum. Accordingly a person is either masculine or feminine, but not both.

Traditional sex role stereotypes assume that men and women differ in many respect: behaviour, ability, and temperament. Traditional male stereotypes include such traits as autonomous activities, discipline, logic, courage etc. According to Parson and Bales (1955), masculinity has been associated with an instrumental orientation, a cognitive focus on getting the job done, or the problem solved, whereas femininity has been associated with an expressive orientation, an affective concern for the welfare of others and harmony of the group. Bakan (1966) has pointed out that masculinity is associated with agentic orientation, a concern for oneself as an individual, whereas femininity is associated with a communal orientation, a concern for the relationship between oneself and others. Finally, Erikson (1964) distinguished between inner (female) and outer (male) space; this represents an analogue to a quite similar psychological distinction between masculine fondness for what works can what men and make and feminine commitment to resourcefulness in peace keeping and consoling.

Sex-role theorists and researchers have recently begun to focus upon cognitive processes that contribute to sex-typing (Bem, 1981a, 1982b, 1982; Crane and Markus, 1982). This emphasis on cognitive processes suggests that individuals develop a network of associations that surround their conceptions of maleness and femaleness. Individual differences are presumed to exist in the strength, saliency and availability of this sex-linked cognitive structure. Certain individuals may link a rich and varied network of culturally stereotyped associations to their construal of what being male and female should be like. As this cognitive structure develops, it may be invoked in order to process diverse kinds of information in a biased manner. Information processing task that is guided and organized by a pre-existing cognitive set or structure is termed schematic processing and the cognitive structure itself is called a scheme (Neisser, 1976). In terms of sex-roles, the cognitive structure consisting of sex-linked associations has been termed gender scheme and individuals whose gender scheme is richly developed and highly available have been described as sex-typed (Bem, 1981a).

According to the more traditional trait conception of sex-roles (Bem, 1974, 1977; Heilburn, 1976; Spence & Helmreich, 1978), sex-typed individuals would be different from androgynous and undifferentiated persons. Bem (1981a) found sex-typed individuals are more likely than non-sex-typed individuals to respond rapidly, recall more and make more highly differentiated judgements, when the stimulus information was sex-typed. Despite cross-cultural variation, there is impressive agreement within

American society concerning what constitutes masculine and feminine behaviour (Broverman, Vogel, Broverman, Clarkson & Rosenkrantz, 1972).

We expect men to adopt instrumental role that is to get things done and to take tasks that are physically strenuous or dangerous. Men are taught to be autonomous and independent, as well as dominating, aggressive and emotionally inhibited. We expect women to adopt expressive and passive dependent roles. They are taught to be warm and nurturant and to display their emotions. Despite the women's liberation movement, the Broverman et al's (1972) study found the traditional views of men as instrumental and women as expressive to be persistent and pervasive. An individual's sex is obviously both a biological and a social fact and a number of physical differences between the sexes are obvious and universal.

The term sex-typing sometimes refers to the process whereby social pressures are brought to bear upon the individual to make him or her conform to the social defined appropriate behaviour for his or her sex.

Frabel (1986) stated in his study that sex-typed individuals have a greater readiness than non-sex-typed individuals to engage in gender schematic processing. Further, the sex-typed individuals reject sex-inappropriate activities because of this gender-based processing. They readily categorize behaviours as male or female and then avoid the inappropriate category.

However, these differences may not be indicative of differences in abilities; it may be a product of perceived differences in abilities. Gender scheme theory of Bem predicts and the results of this study confirm that sex-typed subjects are significantly faster than non-sex-typed subjects when endorsing sex-appropriate attributes. These results suggest that when deciding whether a particular attribute is or is not self-descriptive, sex-typed individuals do not bother to go through a time consuming process of retrieving behavioural evidence from memory and judging whether the evidence warrants an affirmative answer which is what non-sex-typed individuals do. Rather sex-typed individuals "look up" the attribute in the gender scheme. If the attribute is sex-appropriate, they quickly say yes; if the attribute is sex-inappropriate, they quickly say no (Bem, 1981a, 1985).

There are some differences between boys and girls with respect to the extent to which they accept their sex-roles. Many theorists have indicated socialization as an antecedent variable to such differences. They view that sex-difference occurs through imitation where children choose same models (particularly same sex parents) and use the models more than opposite sex models for their behavioural modalities through praise or discouragement and through self-socialization.

The society has always considered masculinity to be a mark of psychologically healthy male and femininity to be the mark of healthy female. But recently, traditional view has been changed. According to modern view, sex typing prevents both men and women from developing as full and complete human beings. Supporters of this movement argue that people should no longer be socialized to conform to outdated standards of masculinity and femininity, but they should be encouraged to be androgynous. That is, they should be encouraged to be both instrumental and expressive, both assertive and yielding, both masculine and feminine depending upon situational appropriateness of these behaviours. On the other hand, the strongest sex-typed individuals might be seriously limited in the range of behaviours available to them as they move from situation to situation. According to both Kagan (1964) and Kohlberg (1966), the highly sex-typed individuals are motivated to keep their behaviour consistent with an internalized sex-role standard a global construct that is presumably accomplished by suppressing any behaviour that might be considered undesirable or inappropriate for their sex.

Thus, whereas narrowly masculine self-concept might inhibit behaviours that are stereotyped as feminine and narrowly feminine self-concept might inhibit behaviours that are stereotyped as masculine, a mixed or androgynous self-concept might allow an individual to freely engage in both masculine and feminine behaviours. In other words, a person's biological make-up does not demand that he or she be more or less disciplined, courageous, expressive or nurturant. Rather, they believe that these styles reflect a process of social influence. People adopt the styles in order to fit properly in the culture. Traditional styles are highly restrictive demanding certain kinds of behaviour. To demonstrate the strength of these arguments, investigators have developed measures that enable them to single out persons who are committed to traditional sex-roles and persons who are androgynous.

Research using this measure indicates that sex-typed people behave quite differently from androgynous people. The above view has been confirmed from an experimental investigation in which the participants were asked to prepare the first list that contains traits found in men and desirable for men. Secondly, they were asked to prepare the second list that contained the traits found in women and desirable for women. The participants were required to prepare the third list containing the items found in men, but desirable for both men and women. A similar fourth list was to be prepared containing items found in women, but desirable for both. As expected, the first two lists contained items that were considered masculine and feminine in stereotypic ways. However, the investigators were surprised to find a group of items included in the third and fourth list. Items such as independence, determination, and hard-working, though found in men, were considered desirable for all individuals. Similarly, traits such as conscientious, sympathetic, and helpful, though found in women, were regarded desirable for all individuals. Thus, the study indicated the possibility that an ideal individual is different from traditional men and traditional women.

Studies of Sex-Stereotypes

Mckee and Sherieff (1959) in California made a study employing a list of 200 adjectives in the assessment of sex-stereotypes and other related concepts. Their results indicated that there were a large number of traits that are differentially ascribed to men in general and women in general. Men were considered frank and straight-forward in social relations, intellectually rational, competent, bold, and effective in dealing with environment.

A study of sex-stereotypes was conducted in the late 1960 and in early 1970 by Broverman and his associates. These investigators developed a questionnaire called sex-role stereotype questionnaire (SRSQ) for use in their studies. The items of the questionnaire were obtained by asking college students to list behaviours, attitude and personality characteristics they considered to differentiate men and women. All items listed by more than one student were included in the questionnaire. The items were arranged into 122 bipolar attributes with each set up along a 6-point scale. In a typical use of this item pool, the subjects rate how characteristic each item is, first of the typical adult male, than of the typical adult female and finally of themselves.

The research of Broverman group served as a foundation for Spence, Helmreich and Stapp (1974, 1975) who developed personality attributes questionnaire (PAQ) as a measure of sex-role stereotypes and masculinity – femininity. These researchers were concerned with oppositeness of masculinity and femininity and they advised a procedure using whatever combination of male and female traits seemed appropriate.

Williams and Best (1982) studied sex-stereotypes with the help of adjectives checklist in which there were adjectives for men and for women.

The subjects were asked to indicate those traits that were characteristic of one sex than the other.

They began their second study to see if they would obtain generally similar findings concerning the male and female stereotypes, when an absolute judgement method was used. Two groups of Euro-American college students were employed. The first group of subjects was asked to consider the 300 ACL items and to indicate those that were descriptive of men in general. The second group of subjects was asked to consider the same list and to indicate those that were descriptive of women in general. After determining that male and female subjects in each group were responding in a similar manner, these data were analysed by obtaining a difference score between the frequency of endorsement of each adjective as a male or a female characteristic.

The relative magnitude of these difference scores was taken as an index of the degree to which the particular item carried a male or a female stereotype loading. For comparative purposes, difference scores were computed for the data obtained from the above relative judgement study. The difference calculated was between the number of subjects endorsing an item as more descriptive of men than women, and the number of subjects endorsing an item as more descriptive of women than men. The result indicated a high degree of correspondence between these two methods of stereotype measurement. The data from the two studies were then merged via standard scores to create a sex stereotype index (SSI) score for each of the 300 ACL items. In this system, scores above 500 indicate female stereotype loading. The greater the deviation from 500 the greater the loading. The SSI scores can be used to determine the degree to which any description employing ACL items is characterized by male and female stereotype traits.

Williams and Best (1982) also studied the development of sex-stereotype in children. They wanted to know at what age do children begin to ascribe different characteristics of women and men, and how does this learning develop across the childhood years. Children become aware of sex difference at a very early age and generally develop considerable knowledge of differential sex-roles before entering school (Edelbrock & Sugawara, 1978; Hartley, 1960; Hartley & Hardesty, 1964; Kagan & Lemkin, 1960; Kohlberg, 1966; William & Roberson, 1967). Most young children have strong preference for conventional sex-appropriate behaviours and seem to find the portrayal of sex-inappropriate behaviours puzzling and even upsetting. In order to assess knowledge of sex trait stereotypes in young children, they constructed a picture story known as sex-stereotype measure (SSM) (Williams, Bennett, and Best, 1975).

From the above discussion, it is clear that stereotyped ideas may influence the adult's perception of the child's behaviour in social interaction with the children. Moreover, stereotypic beliefs may have important consequences in areas related to the child's intellectual talents.

Lastly, sex-trait stereotype not only affects the occupational opportunities of adult men and women, but at a much earlier age, may also determine the manner in which adults respond to children, thus influencing the children's perception of their behaviour, talents and traits and their expectations for their future adult lives.

The different studies in sex-stereotypes stimulated the curiosity to study many interesting facts concerning the nature of trait of male and female. Soon after the early studies of sex-trait stereotypes, people became interested to know the definition of an adequate person. Many studies are conducted on this and many journals are published. Accordingly an adequate person or an 'androgynous' is one who is both masculine and feminine, both assertive and yielding, and both instrumental and expressive, depending upon the situational appropriateness of these various behaviours.

The Construct of Androgyny

The concept of androgynous individual (from andro-male, gyne-female) as a person who does not rely on gender as cognitive organizing principle and whose personality, therefore, combines both masculine and feminine elements was undefined and unarticulated (Bem, 1974).

Androgyny allows the individual to be both independent and tender, assertive and yielding, masculine and feminine. It greatly expands the range of behaviour open to everyone, permitting people to cope more effectively with diverse situations. The concept of androgyny proposes that instead of conceiving of masculinity and femininity as a duality, one should consider that any individual may have both masculine and feminine personality components regardless of gender. The possibility that masculinity and femininity can be integrated within a single individual has been documented (Bakan, 1966; Bem, 1974; Bem & Lenney, 1976; Spence, Helmreich & Stapp, 1975). Bem from her research finding has found out that androgynous individuals demonstrate greater maturity in their moral judgement, a high level of self-esteem, and a wider range of cross-sex behaviour and a variety of strategies for dealing with adverse situations, and they change their cognitions at a rate appropriate for the situation. Sex-stereotyped persons, on the other hand, are likely to demonstrate a greater degree of rigidity and they encounter difficulty in changing their existing cognitions.

Bem (1974, 1975) devised a new sex-role inventory (BSRI), in an effort to treat masculinity and femininity as two independent dimensions and thereby make it possible to characterise a person as masculine, feminine, androgynous or undifferentiated as a function of the difference between his or her endorsement of masculine and feminine personality characteristics. Items were selected by student judges and were assigned to the masculinity and femininity scales if they were judged to be more desirable in American society for one sex or the other. The male and female stereotypes defined in Bem's method are generally similar to those found in the other societies reflecting the usual male instrumentality and female expressiveness. The BSRI is a paper-pencil instrument. It includes both a masculinity scale and a femininity scale, each of which contains 20 personality characteristic selected on the basis of sex-typed social desirability. A characterstic was qualified as feminine if it was judged by two independent samples of undergraduates to be more desirable in American society for a woman than for a man (e.g., affectionate, gentle, understanding). Similarly, masculine characteristics were identified and included in BSRI.

When taking BSRI, a person is asked to indicate on a 7-point scale how well each of these masculine and feminine personality characteristics describes himself/herself. The scale ranges from 1 (never or almost never true) to 7(always or almost always true) and is labeled at each point. On the basis of his/her responses, each person receives an 'androgyny score' defined as student's "t" ratio for the difference between his or her endorsement of masculine and feminine personality characteristics. That is, the androgyny score is the difference between a person's endorsement of masculinity and femininity standardized with respect to the standard deviations of his or her masculinity and femininity score. The use of "t" ratio as the index of androgyny rather than a simple difference score has one advantage that it allows us to ask whether a person's endorsement of masculine attributes differ significantly from his or her endorsement of feminine attributes.

The personal Attributes Questionnaire (PAQ) is a self-report instrument consisting of 24 trait descriptions, each arranged on a bipolar scale. It is devised by Spence, Helmreich and Stapp (1974). The masculinity (M) scale contains eight items that are socially desirable characteristics (S) for both sexes, but that females are believed to possess a greater abundance than males (e.g., gentleness). The "M" scale and the "F" scale are largely independent of one another and permit a four fold classification of persons; high in both (androgynous), high in one or others (masculine, feminine), or low in both (undifferentiated).

Although different scales or different types of sex-stereotype inventory have been used to find out the nature and trait of masculinity and femininity, the BSRI has unique advantage. However, Spence and Helmreich (1978) suggested that PAQ has less of a social desirability bias than does BSRI.

It is pointed out from different studies (Bem, 1981a, 1981b) that androgynous individual is psychologically and socially adaptive. Bem's gender scheme theory predicts that sex-typed individuals are more likely to choose behaviours that are consistent with their own gender than are androgynous or cross sex-typed individuals who do not differ from one another in this regard. More specifically, sex-typed individuals are significantly more likely to select gender-appropriate activities even in a situation where many of the external barriers to gender-inappropriate activities have been removed. Furthermore, sex-typed individuals feel significantly worse after performing gender-inappropriate activity than androgynous or cross sex-typed individuals. Sex-typed subjects also report more nervousness following gender-inappropriate activities than androgynous and cross sex-typed persons who do not differ from one another in this regard.

The gender scheme theory demonstrates that gender-inappropriate behaviour is motivationally problematic for sex-typed individuals and so they actively avoid it. Sex-typed individuals are motivated to restrict their behaviour in accordance with cultural definitions of gender appropriateness as gender scheme theory implies. Boys and girls who are less sex-typed have been found to have higher overall intelligence, higher spatial ability, and higher creativity (Bem, 1981a, 1981b).

The androgynous self-concept may enable a person to freely engage in both masculine and feminine behaviours where as narrowly masculine self-concept may exhibit so called masculine behaviours. Bem (1974) stated that perhaps the androgynous person will come to define a more human standard of psychological health.

Studies of androgyny offer implications with respect to the relationship between sex-role orientation and psychological well-being. A number of empirical investigations also bring out the possible linkage between these two major constructs.

Androgyny and Psychological Well-Being

According to the traditional view, the psychological well-being is fostered only when one's sex-roles orientation is congruent with one's gender. However, the androgyny model proposes that well-being is maximised when one's sex-role orientation incorporates a high degree of masculinity and femininity regardless of one's gender (Bem & Lenney, 1976). Persons can incorporate a high degree of both masculinity and femininity in their sex-role orientation (androgynous orientation), or incorporate a high degree of one sex-role orientation and a low degree of the other (a masculine and feminine orientation).

The androgyny model proposes that one's psychological well-being will be maximised when one has androgynous sex-role orientation and it suggests that such an orientation would define a more human standard of mental health (Bem, 1974; Gilbert, 1981; Kaplan, 1976; Nickerson, 1977).

Self-esteem is chosen as the indicator of psychological well-being. It is related both theoretically and empirically to psychological well-being. Self-esteem refers to the positive or negative orientation towards the self. The individuals constantly evaluate themselves in different changing circumstances. High self-esteem expressed as a positive self-evaluation is considered by clinicians and researchers of differing theoretical orientations to be a healthy and desirable characteristic (Bradburn, 1969; Diggory, 1966; Mischel, 1970). In contrast, low self-esteem has been linked to such indicators or psychological distress as depression (Beck, 1967), neuroticism (Bagley & Evan-Wang, 1975), anxiety (Percell, Berwick & Beigel, 1974), poor general adjustment (Ellis & Greiger, 1977) and self-referal to mental health facilities.

Global self-esteem comprises a person's self-evaluation across a number of areas, such as feelings of adequacy and worth, feelings of being a 'good' or 'bad' person, physical appearance, personal skills and sexuality. Examples of global self-esteem scales are those developed by Berger (1952), and Coopersmith (1967). The second category, social self-esteem, refers to a person's sense of adequacy or worth in social interaction with people in general.

The concept of psychological androgyny has indicated a positive relationship with mental health. Androgynous individuals demonstrate greater maturity in their morale judgement (Block, 1973), a higher level of self-esteem (Spence et al., 1975), a wider range of cross sex behaviour (Bem & Lenney, 1976), and a variety of strategies for dealing with adverse situations.

The better psychological adjustment of androgynous individuals has been explained in terms of psychological freedom to engage in whatever behaviour seemed most appropriate in the situation, irrespective of its stereotype as masculine and feminine. An ideal personality is viewed as one which frees itself from boundaries marked by cultural stereotypes.

From the discussion, it is posited that androgynous individuals may have greater flexibility, and they change their cognitions at the rate appropriate for the situation. The androgynous individuals are likely to be more flexible and they demonstrate higher self-esteem, a wider cross sex behaviour, (Bem & Lenney, 1976). In varied situations of encountering adverse anedrogyneous individuals show a lower degree of stress (Sahoo & Dash, 1984).

A close examination of mapping flexibility indicates several domains of flexible thinking on the part of the androgynous individuals. Flexibility aids the individuals to adjust effectively with the problem of complex life. Persons who are flexible by nature usually find adjustments to new situations and experiences a lot easier. They operate from a base of relatively stable cognitions which relate them to the surroundings. As they encounter needs and experiences, they make changes in their cognitions to achieve a better match between their behaviours and environmental demands (Sahoo, Rout & Rout, 1985).

According to Bem (1974, 1975), androgynous persons are conceptually interesting, because they are not constrained by sex-role stereotype about what kinds of behaviour are differently more appropriate for men and women. Consequently they have a broader behavioural repertoire and can act appropriately and effectively in a wider range of situations. They can, for instance, be assertive in some situations and nurturant in others, or simultaneously assertive and nurturant in the same situations, even though prevalent social stereotypes stamp assertive actions as more appropriate for men and nurturant actions as more appropriate for women.

It is evident from American studies that a positive association exists between androgyny and mental health. Men and women generally need to possess the positive characteristics associated with both sexes. From the study of A.B. Heilburn (1981), it is found that androgyny is advantageous for college females. Androgynous females in his study are found uniquely high in self-esteem.

Androgyny has been readily accepted as promoting positive mental health and personal competence by allowing the person to circumvent the limitations of conformity to stereotyped sex-role behaviour (Bem, 1974; Block, 1973; Heilburn, 1978; Spence et al., 1975).

Taken together, we can conclude that there exists a distinct class of people who can appropriately be termed as androgynous whose sex-role adaptability enables them to engage in situationally effective behaviour without regard for its stereotype as masculine and feminine.

The Fundamental Issue

As argued earlier, androgynous individuals are likely to evince a greater degree of behavioural flexibility than do sex-typed persons. Androgynous individuals also demonstrate greater adaptability and psychological well-being compared with sex-typed persons.

However, these generalizations need not be considered definitive. These observations are mostly based on empirical studies carried out in western settings where attitudes towards women's role have been liberalized in the past decades. Western societies have provided greater opportunities and material resources to bridge the gap between men and women. In such a context, it is not unlikely that a combination of masculine and feminine characteristics are likely to meet greater social approval. In other words, there is a better match between androgynous functions and societal expectations. Even in the context of western societies, a different line of argument offers explanatory ideas concerning the better performance of androgynous individuals.

It is sometimes argued that masculinity is a desirable trait; women move towards masculinity when they become more androgynous. This explanation as to why androgynous females are favourably evaluated compared with traditional females requires more empirical investigation and the role of masculine traits in androgynous individuals requires specific analysis.

In developing societies, on the contrary, the match between androgynous functions and societal expectations is not marked as in the west. In these societies, there are taboos for cross sex-behaviour; social approval often follows sex-typed behaviour. Despite social change, the impact of tradition is pronounced in many spheres. Consequently, a fundamental question concerns the relationship between androgyny and well-being in India. It would be of great significance to investigate whether androgynous individuals experience psychological well-being; at the same time, it would be also useful to identify criteria along which androgynous individuals register greater well-being compared with sex-typed persons.

The present investigation is geared to examine such criteria of well-being. The other objective is to cross-validate the relationship between androgyny and well-being in our contemporary Indian society.

10
Theoretical Perspectives

The fundamental issues raised in the introductory chapter appear very substantive when we trace the evolution of the recent conceptualization regarding sex-role. As usual in a programmatic research, a number of changes have taken place prior to the emergence of the notion of androgyny. There are some precursors to the contemporary notions.

Sex and gender constitute perhaps the single most important dimension for discrimination between the types of human individuals. There are physical structures determined by chromosomes, gonads and hormones; hence these are considered by some as innate. That means, labelling of male versus female occurs at birth. Gradually, the individual develops gender identity. The early labelling of physical sex has marked impact on the child's psychological development, because from this labelling sex-typing starts, whereby a person acquires and values the particular characteristics considered appropriate for his or her sex in that culture. Sex-role is a multi-dimensional concept. Sex-typing is the process through which the developing child comes to match the template of preferences, skills, personality attributes, behaviours and self-concepts prescribed by the culture as appropriate for his or her own sex. It is the process through which a culture transforms male and female children into masculine and feminine adults. The sex-linked constellations of personality-traits and behaviours that a person learns through sex-typing processes are sex-roles.

The Evolution of Sex-Role Concepts

Sex is innate but sex-role for a person is learned. The results of sex-typing process is an individual's sex-role identity. The pattern and level of masculine and feminine characteristics adopted and exhibited in some manner by a person is indicative of one's sex-role. Various combinations of feminine and masculine characteristics could presumably be learned by a person, but not all combinations have been traditionally considered to be equally acceptable for men and women. A high level of masculine characteristics for men and feminine characteristics for women with relative exclusion of the other dimension represents the traditional sex-role identities. Men and women who display these traditional sex-role identities are sometimes labelled as sex-typed. The individual is aware of the characteristics typically associated with each sex.

Sex-role stereotypes are widely-held conceptions about the sexes that attribute certain sets of characteristics uniquely to one sex. In general, though men tend to view the characteristics typically associated with men as more descriptive of themselves than do women, the same pattern is true for women and feminine characteristics (Bem, 1974). The nature and characteristics widely associated with each sex in American society has been well-documented. Classic research by Broverman and associates (Broverman, Broverman, Clerkson, Rosenkrantz & Vogel, 1970; Rosenkrantz, Vogel, Bee, Broverman & Broverman, 1968) on sex-role stereotypes pointed out the existence of these highly consensus norms and beliefs about the differing characteristics of men and women (Broverman et al., 1970).

Traditional conceptualizations of femininity and masculinity maintained an emphasis upon the distinction between the sexes. Most earlier researchers postulated that gender differences result from differential socialization of men and women. The greater instrumental and dominance orientation of men are acquired aspects of femininity and masculinity. The girl is socialized to place great importance on personal relations and to cultivate such traits as sensitivity, warmth, and empathy. The boy, to put matters over simply, is trained towards activity and achievements; he needs to cultivate assertiveness and independence. Male dominance is built into the familial, economic, political, religious, and legal structures of society. Women's language is the language of the powerless. The greater power of men is reflected in their tendency to take more turns of speaking, to interrupt others more, to use more directive responses, and control the topics of conversation. One of the important arguments is that these gender differences are derived from traditional division of labour by sex which still has a powerful influence on women's lives, despite considerable sex-role change. Certain work activities, privileges and responsibilities are still assigned to individuals on the basis of sex. Men's place in the public sphere is associated with and generates power and authority. Women are assigned to domestic sphere, to child care and home related activities. Women's task centers around relationships and the interpersonal sphere. Men's task centers around work and the public sphere.

From the above discussion, it is clear that certain traits label a person as man and certain traits label a person as woman.

Despite the apparent diversity of the characteristics, there are some common threads linking them to one another. One conceptualization of masculinity and femininity that originates in familiar role is the distinction of instrumentality versus expressiveness. Instrumentality is defined as co-ordination of adaptation of the family system's need with the outside world. Expressiveness involves maintenance and regulation of emotional needs of the family and interaction within itself. Instrumentality connotes a goal orientation and general sensitivity to the responses that others have for the personal behaviour. Expressiveness connotes a sensitivity to other's responses and concerns interpersonal relationship. Men are assumed to have predominantly instrumental orientation, whereas women are expressive.

Skills necessary for expressive functions are emotional, sensitive, aware of other's feelings, tactful, interdependent, tender etc., and for instrumental functions are aggressive, independent, unemotional, assertive, and strong etc. A second framework was there to view masculinity and femininity, which is framed by Bakan (1966). He proposed two modalities of all human beings: agency and communion. Agency is concerned with the maintenance of the organism as an individual. It involves assertive activity, differentiation, self-protection, self-expansion and urge towards mastery and forming separation from others. Communion is aimed towards integrated participation of the organism as a whole. It involves selflessness, relationships, contact, cooperation, union with others and openness. Bakan argued that communion is the characteristic of femininity and agency is masculinity. From the above analysis, it is seen masculinity involves goal-orientation, assertive activity, self-development (instrumental/agentic) and femininity involves sensitivity, emotionality, selflessness (expressive/communal).

A feminine sex-role identity for women and masculine identity for men was the traditional sex-role ideal, although other identity variations are possible. A clear differentiation between the sexes in a wide range of characteristics was viewed as typical and desirable. More recent properties on sex-roles grew from these traditional views. Kaplan and Bean (1976) have pointed out that genetic differences, physiological differences and ultimately psychological differences somehow form a logical progression. This is called "linear model of sex differentiation".

In this model, masculinity is not typical in men, but expected and healthy; variation from the norm is viewed as deviant. The same reasoning is applied to femininity and women.

The biological basis for sex-differences posited in the linear model of sex differentiation has not been supported in research over years. Social scientists have generally recognised that learning beginning after birth is primarily responsible for enduring psychological differences. Traditional theories in sex-role development have still emphasized, however, that the ideal sex-roles for men and women are quite different.

Major Approaches

The theoretical perspectives on sex-role have focussed upon how children acquire a sex-role identity during their early years of life. Although some theorists have conceded that some changes in sex-role identity are possible, it has been generally assumed that once formed, sex-role identity is stable and persists into adulthood. Thus, adult patterns and problems of sex-role can presumably be linked to what was developed in those early formative years from where male and female children become masculine and feminine.

The primary theories can be distinguished in terms of what types of variables and processes are considered most crucial in sex-typing. The most important theories are identification, social learning, and cognitive developmental theories.

The first psychologist to ask how male and female are transmuted into masculine and feminine was Freud. Psycho-analytic theory emphasizes the child's identification.

Identification Theory. This theory emphasizes the child's identification with the same sex parents as the primary mechanism whereby children become sex-typed.

Identification is a concept derived from psycho-analysis and introduced by Freud. It refers to the process that leads the child to think, feel and behave as though the characteristics of another person, usually a parent in case of a young child, belong to him/her. It is not ordinarily a consciously initiated process. Mussen (1969) has pointed out that "identification is a particular kind of imitation: the spontaneous duplication of a model's complex, integrated pattern of behaviour (rather than simple discrete responses), without specific training or direct reward, but based on an intimate relationship between the identifier and the model" (p. 718).

By means of identification, the children feel themselves to be adequate and self-controlled. Freud proposed two types of identification. Analytic identification with the mother occurs in early childhood and is found upon the intense dependency relationship children have with their mothers. As mothers withdraw some of the intense nurturance characteristic of early infancy, the young child identifies with the mother in response to this: the threatened loss. In case of girls, they maintain this identification with their mothers over time and thus, they acquire traditional feminine characteristics. So far as analytic identification of boys is concerned, it is replaced by identification with the aggressor or identification with the father. In fact, psycho-analytic theory emphasizes the child's identification with the same sex parents as the primary mechanism whereby children become sex-typed.

Maccoby and Jacklin (1974) have pointed out some common elements concerning identification and initiation in sex-typing found in the literature:

(a) The rate and extensiveness of the sex-role acquisition process suggests that more than simple reinforcement occurs and imitation must be involved.

(b) Parents are most likely models in sex-typing processes, because they are highly available, powerful, and nurturant.

(c) The children are more frequently exposed to same sex, rather than other sex models; consequently, they acquire more sex-appropriate characteristics.

(d) Lastly, children like to imitate the models whom they perceive to be similar to themselves. They prefer to imitate same sex models than other sex models.

There is a point of difference amongst theorists as to whether identification and imitation are the same thing. According to Maccoby and Jacklin, they are interchangeable, whereas Bandura (1969) used the term as synonymous to refer to learning that occurs from modelling. Mussen says that for identification, intimate relationship between parents and child is important.

Despite the difference of opinion, both identification and imitation indicate that the child can learn sex-appropriate behaviour through observation of others without specific training and children acquire an extensive range of characteristics through an intimate relationship with their same sex parents.

Social Learning Theory. Social learning theory emphasizes the rewards and punishments that children receive for sex-appropriate and sex-inappropriate behaviour (Bandura, 1969). Mischel (1970) defined sex-typing as a process by which individuals learn to acquire value and adopt for themselves behaviour patterns considered to be most appropriate when expressed by their sex. Sex-typing is the example of socialization. The most important variable of socialization is cognitive process.

Sex-role behaviour is learned through child's interaction with others in the environment. This theory states that gender does not demand special consideration. Children become sex-typed because sex happens to be the basis of differential socialization in their culture. Early in the life, children learn to recognize gender by observing others through their own cognitive processes. They form unique synthesis of what they have observed. Observational learning and reinforcement by others are essential in developing child's sex-typing.

Social learning theory treats the child more as a passive recipient of environmental forces than as an active agent striving to organize and thereby comprehend the social world. Mischel suggested that the child may be more likely to imitate same sex-models because: (a) they perceive these models as similar to themselves, (b) those models have attributes and resources desired by the child and, (c) the child is reinforced more for learning sex-typed behaviour. He also argued that although observational learning and cognitive processes are essentially important for acquisition of sex-typed behaviours, but actual performance of behaviour is affected by reinforcement. The sexes rapidly learn the sex-linked expectation for behaviour by perceiving their parents and other's attitudes and attributes.

Kagan's Theory. In Kagan's theory (1964), the role of identification and social learning processes are important in sex-role identity. In the early childhood, the child differentiates the world of male and female and learns also which attributes and behaviour are considered desirable for the sex to possess. This publicly-shared belief about sex-typed characteristics is the sex-role standard. Some sex identification forms the foundation of sex-role identity. Parents' and other's rewards and punishments can facilitate the adoption of sex-typed behaviour. The more the children perceive themselves to possess sex-typed characteristics and its recognition by others, the stronger is their sex-role identity.

However, he did recognize that certain aspects of the sex-role standard creates unnecessary anxiety and restrictions for the individual.

Unlike social learning theory, cognitive development theory focusses exclusively on the child as the primary agent of his or her own sex-role socialization. Sex-typing follows naturally and inevitably from universal principles of cognitive development. Cognitive developmental theory links the progressive acquisition of sex-typing to more general maturation of children's thinking process. That is, it is the child who realizes what gender he or she is and in what behaviours he or she should engage (Lewis & Brooks-Gunn, 1979). In cognitive developmental theory, the content the child learns about sex-roles is determined by the environment, but the child's cognitive maturation affects the structure of thought about sex-roles (Huston, 1983). Child's cognitive understanding is essential for sex-typing because of need of cognitive consistency. Self-categorization as female or male motivates him or her to value whatever is seen as similar to the self in gender.

Kohlberg and His View-Point. Kohlberg (1966) said that sex-typing represents a child's increasingly sophisticated cognitive organization of the world around him or her in sex-linked terms. At first, the gender identity is not stable. Children appear to be confused about the sex. After a certain level of conceptual growth, they understand certain characteristics of physical objects. The sex-stereotypes become rigid over time. Once basic sex-role concepts are formed, the children develop personal stereotype preferences and values. After the development of a basic gender identity, sex-stereotypes and sex-typed values, they tend to identify with same sex-models, often their parents. Parents' attitude may actually interfere with developing appropriate sex-typing. Lastly, we can say that qualitative changes in children's thinking process lead to change in children's perceptions of themselves and others. These changes are reflected in their sex-related classifications, stereotypes, and values.

Mussen's View. Mussen (1969) has pointed out that learning identification and cognitive processes are all involved in sex-typing. He emphasizes that early year is more crucial. According to him, parents play many important roles. After sex labelling, parents promote sex-typing by providing models and rewards/ punishments for a sex-typed behaviour.

Analysing all the above theories, Huston (1983) provides a good summary of social learning and cognitive developmental theories. Social learning theory defines sex-typing as sex differences in behaviour. A person's role in the sex-typing process is more passive in that the mechanisms for change largely originate in the environment. Changes in sex-typed behaviour can occur if observational learning or reinforcement pattern is altered. In recent years, a growing dissatisfaction with the traditional methods of conceptualizing sex-differences has been expressed. In the early 1970's, social scientists rediscovered androgyny and started work against unsatisfactory model of sex-roles.

Gradually, because of social change and feminist movement, the raditional views were not appreciated by the modern society. Society became more liberal and the traditional arguments for women's proper role became less convincing. Newly emerging occupations demanded less of men's superior physical capabilities and more of training and educational opportunity that both sexes were capable of mastering. Modern occupations require feminine traits such as an ability to cooperate with others as well as masculine characteristics such as dominance. Along with the changes in the nature of work, the traditional role distinctions were not accepted. Family size has decreased and there is more time before and after birth of the children (Hoffmann, 1977; Marecek, 1979). Consequently, many women have recognized that home and family are the important sources of satisfaction in life, but these are not the only sources of satisfaction they need. Thus, widespread concern about sex-roles is a response to a shifting social climate.

Social scientists became interested to divide the sexes into two non-overlapping groups as the focus of comparison. A focus on male versus female differences in sex-role research observed how women and men can be similar to one another, and how they differ from each other of their sex. Kaplan (1976) argued that as a result of linear model of sex differentiation similarities were overlooked or dismissed. He said that female-male dichotomy failed to represent the diversity of personal qualities and the complexity of the culture. Today, social scientists and mental health practitioners are re-examining past formulations about sex differences in a new critical eye. They have now adopted the new value about how the sexes could and ought to behave. As a result of this new body of literature on the sex behaviour, the social scientists now emphasize similarities rather than differences. The concept of individual rather than male/female differences has occupied a privileged position.

Androgyny and Gender Schema Theory

Awareness of a broader sex-role change in society highlighted the inadequacy of traditional sex-role standards. A sophisticated model was needed then. Such model was available through reconceptualizing the traditional sex-role theories. The concept underlying this new view is simple in essence, but revolutionary in its implications. The concept of psychological androgyny is the blending of positive feminine and masculine characteristics within a given person. This concept of androgyny and related assumptions challenged the traditional views as a result of which the conventional ideas regarding the sex-role were not workable and enforceable. As a result, androgyny as an alternative conceptualization in theory and research received wide spread attention. The idea of androgyny is an ancient one. Long-back Carl Jung spoke of masculinity and femininity as inherent in every one.

Jung emphasized the need for all individuals to recognize and integrate within themselves those cross-sex characteristics that are inconsistent with dominant sex-role traits. Olds (1981) have pointed out this integrity is essential to personal wholeness. Bakan (1966) associated personal maturity with the integration of agency (masculinity) and communion (femininity) in a person.

Androgyny as defined by Block (1973) represents a successful balancing of agency and communion, a process that involves coping with demands of each dimension. Thus the term androgyny is viewed as a goal of all individuals irrespective of their gender. Kaplan and Bean (1976) defined androgyny not as building towards certain specific roles or personalities, but helping each person to overcome personal sex-role related constraints imposed on his or her own temperament and potential.

Secondly, androgyny is sometimes equated as the absence of any sex-role differentiation. Wesley and Wesley (1977) pointed out that it implies a zero difference between sex-stereotypes. But such a view fails to measure role differences. A truly androgynous world may have fewer inconsequential differences between the sexes. But the definition of androgyny can not be restricted to such a lack of differences. What is androgyny then?

The term simply denotes the possession of masculine and feminine characteristics by a given person. An assumption that masculinity and femininity have discernible dimensions have important consequences for human behaviour. Androgynous persons are described as independent and affectionate, assertive and understanding. The combinations of both masculine and feminine characteristics have desirable implications for an individual's behaviour regardless of sex. The combination of masculine and feminine characteristics afforded by androgyny is responsible for healthy adjustments in a variety of settings. Spence and Helmreich (1978) pointed out that the basic proposition underlying androgyny theory is that perception of traditional sex-role distinction is dysfunctional; rather, the androgyny can be the sex-role model of well-being. Bem (1974) emphatically stated that perhaps the androgynous persons will come to define a more human standard of psychological health.

So far as the meaning of androgyny is concerned, a number of formulations are there. The most commonly recognized view of androgyny is that of modulation or balance. According to the balance view, masculinity and femininity are extreme tendencies, when appearing individually without the presence of the other. On the contrary, androgyny represents a blending of masculine and feminine traits in a balanced proportion. This balance notion was the basic of Bem's first conceptualization and scoring of androgyny.

There are two other conjoint models besides the balance model which has been accepted widely. In this model, androgyny represents a summation of the independent influences of masculinity and femininity. Spence, Helmreich, and Stapp (1975) have pointed out that a high level of both sets of characteristics are more advantageous than low level.

The third model is multiplicative or interactive model which focuses upon the unique combination of masculinity and femininity and androgyny indicates emergent properties (Spence, 1983) that could not be predicted from masculinity and femininity. That means, androgynous person display special characteristics. As cognitive schema theory views, androgyny represents a particular way of processing information. In contrast to sex-typed persons, androgynous persons do not use sex-related connotations as guides in their information processing. In Spence and Helmreich's (1979) personality trait view, androgyny denotes a certain naturally occurring high level of masculine and feminine traits in one person. Behavioural androgyny was described in Kelly and Worell's (1977) review as representing high social competencies in that an individual has a wide reportoire of socially approved behaviours to draw form a variety of situations. This theory implies that a person may simply be skilled in selecting and performing behaviours, that successfully solve problems or obtain positive social reinforcement. According to Yagar and Bakar (1979), androgyny as a flexible behaviour should produce healthier and more adaptable persons in this complex changeable society.

So from the above analysis, it is clear that androgyny is defined and understood in different ways. Some have defined androgynous as those who possess both masculinity and femininity traits (personality traits), where others have emphasized socially appropriate behaviours or a particular type of cognitive processing (cognitive schema).

Although a number of theories have been established about androgyny, the theoretical statements by Bem and by Spence and Helmreich are unique.

Bem's View. Bem (1974) was originally interested in exploring how possession of masculine and feminine characteristics may have an impact on a person's flexibility of behaviour across situations. Masculinity and femininity were viewed by Bem as complementary groups of positive traits and behaviours. For her, sex-typing is the process through which the developing children come to match the template of preferences, skills, personality attributes, behaviours and self-concepts prescribed by the culture as appropriate for their own sex. In other words, it is a process through which a culture transforms male and female children into masculine and feminine adults. Sex-typed persons are more motivated to correspond the Society's definitions of desirable male and female behaviours in their behavioural expectations, self-descriptions, and actual behaviours. For the limited range of behaviours, they have problems in adjustments. Kagan (1964) assumed that traditional sex-typing is healthy and desirable.

However, Bem views that sex-typing process has a negative result. The desire to conform to these standards can prevent individuals from engaging in adaptive behaviours that are less sex-typical. The deviants from this process are likely to be healthier and these deviants are focus of attention of her research. She designed Bem's Sex-Role Inventory (BSRI) to categorise the persons whose self-descriptions include both feminine and masculine characteristics from those whose self-descriptions are limited to one dimension.

Although different theories provide explanation about the sex-typing, Bem's famous gender schema theory occupies the special position because of its uniqueness.

Gender Schema Theory. The gender schema theory is more specific about how the differences between male and female occur and what their implications for the behaviour are. This theory (Bem, 1981b, 1985) asserts that children become sex-typed because they come to perceive, evaluate and regulate their own behaviour in terms of gender templates that they come to construe and organize the reality in terms of gender.

The gender schema theory proposes that sex-typing derives in large measure from gender schematic processing from a generalized readiness on the part of the child to encode and to organize information about the self, according to the culture's definition of maleness and femaleness. Bem opines that sex-typing is mediated by the child's own cognitive processing which is derived from the sex-differentiated practices of the social community.

Thus, like cognitive developmental theory, gender schematic theory emphasizes the role of cognition in sex-typing and like social learning theory, it also assumes that sex-typing is a learned phenomenon. Therefore, it is neither inevitable nor unmodifiable.

Bem in her gender schematic theory has pointed out that the developing child invariably learns his or her societies' cultural definitions of femaleness and maleness. Individuals' information processing is aided by internal cognitive structures that permit them to perceive, interpret and organize incoming information effectively. The cognitive structures that assist individuals in their information processing are schemas. In other words, a schema is a cognitive structure, a network of associations that organizes and guides an individual's perception. A schema, therefore, functions as an anticipatory structure, a readiness to search for an incoming information in schema relevant terms. Therefore, schematic information processing is highly selective and it enables the person to impose structure and meaning into a vast array of incoming stimuli.

As a result of gender schematic processing, the individual spontaneously places the gender-related items in masculine and feminine categories. For example, the individual places the items like beautiful and rose in feminine categories and assertive and dominant in masculine categories. Gender schema theory construes perception as a constructive process in which the interaction between incoming information and an individual's pre-existing schema determines what is perceived. The theory also proposes that the phenomenon of sex-typing drives in part from gender schematic processing from an individual's generalized readiness to process information on the basis of sex-linked associations that constitute the gender schema. More specifically, the theory proposes that sex-typing results in part from assimilation of the self-concept itself to the gender schema. As children learn the contents of their societies, they learn which attributes are to be linked with their own sex. Simultaneously, the child also learns to evaluate his or her adequacy as a person according to the gender schema to match his or her preferences, attitudes, behaviours and personal attributes against the prototypes stored within it. Thus, the gender schema becomes a prescriptive standard or guide and self-esteem becomes its hostage (Kagan, 1964). Here, there is an internalised motivational factor that prompts an individual to regulate his or her own behaviour and the behaviour of others according to his or her cultural definitions of gender appropriateness.

Analysing the above view points, we can understand that Bem proposes a process of sex-typing by which children become psychologically masculine or feminine. It occurs in several steps:

(i) First, the children learn the existence of sex-based distinctions throughout society and which attributes are most appropriate to their own sex. This learning process teaches the children the network of sex-linked association which is the content of the gender schema.

(ii) Secondly, the gender schema functions to shape individual's evaluations of themselves. Children gradually learn that certain aspects of personality are appropriate for their sex alone and thus for themselves. As a result, they begin to evaluate their own adequacy as individuals in terms of gender schema they have developed recently. The individual also develops a standard of evaluating the personal characteristics and behaviour according to his or her cultural definition. By this, the differentiation of the self-concept is strengthened in the individual as a result of traditional sex-role identity.

Lastly, we can say that the gender schematic theory is a theory of process, not the content, because sex-typed individuals regulate their behaviour according to whatever definitions of femininity and masculinity their culture happens to provide. The central point of this theory emphasizes the process of dividing the world into feminine and masculine categories but not the content of the categories. In the early 1970s, there was a feeling shared by the culture that being sex-typed was not only normal but also desirable outcome of human development. Bem says that the concept of androgynous individual is the individual who does not rely on the gender as a cognitive organizing principle and whose personality, therefore, combines both masculine and feminine elements. She started her research programme on androgyny with the development of Bem's sex-role inventory (BSRI). Two years later in 1973, Jeanne Block published an insightful article about androgyny in the American Psychologist based on her research, and Ann Constantinople published a review article in the Psychological Bulletin criticizing the bipolarity assumption of traditional masculinity-femininity scale. (Constantinople, 1973). In 1974, Spence, Helmreich and Stapp published their instrument for assessing androgyny, the Personal Attribute Questionnaire (PAQ).

The review of literature pertaining to androgyny deepens the impression that the androgynous individuals demonstrate greater degree of mental health and behavioural flexibility compared to sex-typed individuals. The androgynous individuals appear to indicate less depression and less anxiety than the sex-typed individuals. They also demonstrate better work orientation and more effective coping strategy than sex-typed individuals. These empirical findings suggest better psychological adaptation on the part of the androgynous individuals. However, the recent conceptualization of psychological adaptation (psychological well-being) focuses on multicriteria nature of well-being, although traditional approach treats mental health in terms of absence of negative states such as anxiety, depression and tension. The contemporary approach stresses the presence of certain positive dimensions such as job satisfaction, perception of control, happy family life, and other attributes. Thus, the relationship between androgyny and psychological well-being needs to be investigated in the context of the recent framework of mental health. Therefore, a brief review of the pertinent literature on psychological well-being would strengthen this assertion. Prior to such examination, various approaches to operationalization need to be described.

11
Measurement Techniques

The social scientists have devised their own methods to study the human behaviour on sex-roles. Early measures of masculinity-femininity (MF) incorporated certain specific notions about men's and women's behaviour. Recently developed measures of androgyny are founded on new and quite different assumptions about sex-roles.

The BSRI was published as a research instrument. It is perhaps the most popular androgyny measure. The purpose of this instrument, according to Bem (1979), is to assess the extent to which the culture's definitions of desirable female and male attributes are reflected in an individual's self-description. The BSRI contains a number of features that distinguish it from other. One of the commonly used masculinity femininity scales, for example, involves the masculinity-femininity scale of California Personality Inventory (CPI). It includes both masculinity and femininity items.

Assessment Tools

Psychologists have used a number of assessment tools. A brief description of these measures indicates the contexts of their use.

Personal Attribute Questionnaire (PAQ). In contrast to BSRI, the Personal Attribute Questionnaire (Spence, Helmreich, & Stapp, 1974, 1975) is composed of scales of characteristics considered socially desirable for both the sexes, but more typical of one sex than the other. The PAQ was first developed as a modification of a popular instrument to measure sex-role stereotypes. This measures an individual's beliefs of how men and women differ on a specified set of characteristics (Rosenkrantz, Vogel, Bee, Broverman & Broverman, 1968). The full length PAQ is composed of those items that describe characteristics that are not only commonly believed to differentiate the sexes, but on which men and women tend to report themselves as differing (Spence & Helmreich, 1978). Items chosen for the femininity and masculinity scales were rated by undergraduate men and women to be ideal for both the sexes, but significantly more typical for one sex than other. Thus, masculinity scale items were rated as socially desirable for both sexes, but more typical for men than for women; men were also more likely than women to rate these adjectives as self-descriptive. A third scale contains a set of unique items judged to be both typical and ideal for only one or the other sex.

Spence and Helmreich's research to-date has found three basic areas :

(a) The validation of PAQ including populations of varying ages and socio-economic backgrounds,

(b) The relation to the achievement motivation hypothesized in previous research as related to sex (gender), self-esteem, and sex-role attitudes, and

(c) Familiar antecedents of masculinity and femininity (Spence & Helmreich, 1978).

The Andro Scale. The Andro Scale (Berzins, Welling, & Wetter, 1978) is a second generation androgyny measure. The rationale was explicitly patterned after that of BSRI. The purpose was to develop a measure with separate femininity and masculinity scales, composed of items positive in tone, but selected for their sex-typed desirability. This is similar to Bem's rationale. The items were selected if they were judged to be consistent with rationally derived concepts (Berzins et al., 1978).

The Andro Scale was developed by keying items from personality research form (PRF; Jackson, 1967). The 56 items on the scales (29 masculinity and 27 femininity) were selected from PRF item pool.

However, there are some differences among Andro Scale BSRI and PAQ, because Andro Scale utilizes mainly adjectives, and the respondent will put true or false. Both true and false items were selected to help control for acquiescent responding.

The ACL Scales. The masculinity and femininity scales keyed from Adjective Check List (ACL; Gough & Heilburn, 1965) were formed by rescoring a previously developed bipolar masculinity-femininity (MF) scale (Heilburn, 1976). Here items were chosen to discriminate between men and women and also between college males identified with masculine fathers and college females identified with feminine mothers (Heilburn, 1976).

Respondents were asked to check adjectives they view as characteristics of their own behaviour. Masculinity and femininity items are scored separately by the scale to which they belong. Heilburn appears to regard the new scales as a simple modification of the parents MF scale, as he had quoted research utilising the single bipolar scale as evidence for the new scale's validity (cf. Heilburn, 1981; Heilburn & Pitman, 1979b).

The CPI Scales. The femininity and masculinity scales keyed from the California Personality Inventory (CPI; Gough, 1967) were intended to supplement rather than to replace the CPI femininity scale which was seen by Baucom (1976) as having different purposes. Baucom also considered labelling females as masculine or males as feminine to mean that the person is behaving more like the other sex than the typical. His emphasis upon sex-based distinctions is unusual in androgyny research with the exceptions of the ACL scales.

Sex-Role Behaviour Scale. Orlofsky, Ransedan & Cohen (1982) developed the Sex-Role Behaviour Scale (SRBS) to assess sex-role related interests and behaviours. Orlofsky (1981) recognized the presence of essential distinctions between sex-role traits, attitudes and social roles and behaviours. The SRBS was designed to assess masculine and feminine behaviours in a manner analogous to other androgyny measures. The scale was designed to assess individual's role behaviour. It also exhibits interests stereotypically masculine and feminine, yet judged to be appropriate for both sexes.

In summing up the above scales, we have been impressed upon the fact that androgyny measures are based on views about masculinity and femininity quite different from those of traditional measures. Masculinity and femininity are independent dimensions that are present in members of both sexes and that operate together to furnish pleasant advantages to individuals who possess high degrees of both dimensions.

Bem Sex Role Inventory (BSRI)

Bem (1974) developed and validated Bem Sex-Role Inventory (BSRI) to operationalize androgynous personality. During its developmental phase, Bem prepared a preliminary pool of a large number of descriptors. With a view to identifying "masculinity" and "femininity" items in American society, she sampled male and female college students to participate in the study of constructing the scale.

The male participants were each provided with the list of preliminary items. They were asked to consider each item separately and decide on a 7-point scale whether the trait was more desirable for an "American man" than for an "American woman". Similar groups of male participants were also given the same list and were asked to indicate desirability ratings to show whether the traits were more desirable for an "American woman" than for an "American man". The 7-point scale ranged from "not at all desirable" to "extremely desirable". The responses of male participants generated desirability ratings separately for American men and American women.

The repetition of similar procedure with female subjects also generated desirability ratings for American men and American women. Bem compared desirability ratings for men and women. Three separate comparisons were made. The first comparison involved the ratings given by male judges, whereas second comparison consisted of ratings given by female judges. Finally, Bem compared desirability ratings obtained from all judges.

The significant statistical difference in favour of "desirability for men" identified masculinity items, whereas such significant differences in the direction of desirability for women delineated femininity items. Bem (1981) selected 20 masculinity items and 20 femininity items. She also selected 20 filler items where no significant difference was shown. The scale was validated to meet psychometric criteria.

Table 11.1

Masculinity, Femininity and Filler Items in Bem Sex-Role Inventory

Masculinity Items	*Femininity Items*	*Filler Items*
Acts as a leader	Affectionate	Adaptable
Aggressive	Cheerful	Conscientious
Ambitious	Childlike	Friendly
Analytical	Compassionate	Happy
Assertive	Does not use harsh language	Helpful
Athletic	Eager to soothe hurt feelings	Likable
Competitive	Feminine	Reliable

(Contd...)

(Contd...)

Defends own beliefs	Flatterable	Sincere
Dominant	Gentle	Tactful
Forceful	Gullible	Truthful
Has leadership abilities	Loves children	Conceited
Independent	Loyal	Conventional
Individualistic	Sensitive to the needs of others	Inefficient
Makes decisions easily	Shy	Jealous
Masculine	Soft spoken	Moody
Self-reliant	Sympathetic	Secretive
Self-sufficient	Tender	Solemn
Strong personality	Understanding	Theoretical
Willing to take a stand	Warm	Unpredictable
Willing to take risks	Yielding	Unsystematic

However, these 60 items are presented in a random order while administering the scale. Individuals are asked to indicate on a 7-point scale their self- endorsement. They indicate the extent to which an item is characteristic of the person. The self-endorsement ratings generate *two* scores for an individual: a masculinity score and a femininity score. Masculinity scores is the sum of scores of an individual across all 20 masculinity items. Similarly femininity score is the sum of scores across 20 femininity items. The difference score (M score-F score) is indicative of androgyny. Lower the score greater is the androgyny.

Sahoo Sex Role Inventory (SSRI)

Although BSRI has been extensively used in research and application, recent concern with cultural parameters and relevance has prompted some considerations. While many items may have their stereotypic nature across cultures, it is possible that some items may be indigenously masculine (or alternatively feminine). This possibility raises requirement of developing and validating a sex-role inventory relevant in Indian socio-cultural context.

Sahoo (1990a) adopted procedures similar to Bem's. However, due care was given to include some items (in the preliminary pool) that appeared relevant in India. As shown in Table 11.2, there is some amount of similarity between BSRI items and SSRI items. Sahoo (1990 a) employed this scale to examine its reliability and validity. The test-retest reliability ranged from .74 to .89. The Cronbach's alpha ranged from .84 to .91. The

SSRI was

Table 11.2
Desirability Ratings "For a Man" and "For a Woman" of Twenty Individual Items on the SSRI Masculinity Scale

Items	*Desirable for a Man*		*Desirable for a Woman*		*'t' Value*
	M	*SD*	*M*	*SD*	
Masculine	5.7	2.1	1.88	1.63	14.69
Ambitious	5.16	2.36	4.78	1.86	12.60
Independent	5.89	0.98	3.74	2.29	8.95
Courageous	6.15	0.8	4.72	1.68	7.94
Daring	5.32	1.51	3.67	1.54	7.50
Methodical	5.00	1.06	3.16	2.60	6.61
Energetic	5.71	1.04	4.38	1.84	6.33
Industrious	5.22	0.24	4.29	1.73	5.47
Takes Initiative	5.56	1.35	4.40	1.77	5.27
Progressive	5.80	1.25	5.01	0.86	5.26
Intellectual	5.90	1.03	5.24	0.90	5.07
Aggressive	2.70	2.20	1.86	1.37	5.60
Active	6.42	0.70	5.63	1.46	4.93
Has Leadership ability	4.82	1.29	3.41	2.62	4.86
Productive	5.48	2.01	4.06	2.32	4.73
Inventive	5.25	1.18	4.22	1.89	4.68
Strong Personality	6.25	2.20	5.03	1.75	4.35
Realistic	5.87	1.38	5.05	1.31	4.31
Willing to take a stand	4.69	1.52	3.76	1.67	4.22
Competitive	5.57	0.96	5.11	0.63	4.18

Table 11.3

Desirability Ratings "For a Woman" and "For a Man" of Twenty Individual Items on the SSRI Femininity Scale

Items	Desirable for a Woman		Desirable for a Man		't' Value
	M	SD	M	SD	
Feminine	1.64	1.33	5.33	1.83	16.04
Loves Children	5.15	.21	6.07	1.32	7.07
Likes Security	3.76	1.76	5.10	1.48	6.09
Dependent	2.09	1.76	3.79	1.84	6.80
Charming	3.99	1.71	5.39	1.66	6.08
Mild	3.69	1.61	4.76	1.37	5.09
Eager to soothe hurt feelings	3.47	1.75	4.71	2.04	4.76
Flatterable	1.88	1.41	2.84	1.51	4.57
Kind	4.83	1.49	5.52	1.17	4.31
Loving	4.95	1.69	5.85	1.28	4.28
Clear thinking	5.22	2.68	4.79	2.70	4.12
Modest	4.26	1.58	4.91	.83	3.82
Fashionable	3.23	1.76	4.15	1.91	3.53
Soft-hearted	4.47	1.45	5.34	2.13	3.48
Tender	3.74	1.46	4.53	1.87	3.43
Innocent	2.98	1.76	3.86	2.10	3.25
Emotional	3.18	1.80	3.99	1.83	3.11
Affectionate	5.29	2.28	6.08	.66	2.82
Attractive	4.31	1.94	5.03	1.55	2.76
Concerned about group harmony	4.45	7.21	5.00	1.59	2.75

SSRI was validated twice. The predicted pattern of its correlation with BSRI yielded statistically significant coefficient ($r = 0.53$, $P < 0.01$). Its correlation with femininity score on California Personality Inventory also provided supportive evidence regarding its validity. Thus, the SSRI is judged to have considerable amount of reliability and validity.

12
Androgyny and Adaptability

The androgynous individuals can remain sensitive to the changing constraints of the situation and engage in whatever behaviour seems most effective at the moment, regardless of its stereotype as appropriate for one sex or the other. In other words, for the androgynous individual, the traits of masculinity and femininity simply do not exist. The androgynous is a socially adequate individual in the sense that this self-concept may enable a person to freely engage in both masculine and feminine behaviours. He is both instrumental and expressive, both assertive and yielding, both masculine and feminine, depending upon the situational appropriateness of these various behaviours.

Androgynous sex-role, thus, represents the equal endorsement of both masculine and feminine attributes. On the other hand, a high femininity in females has consistently been correlated with high anxiety, low self-esteem and low social acceptance (e.g., Cossentino, Heilburn, 1964; Gall, 1979; Grey, 1957; Sears, 1970; Webb, 1963); high masculinity in males has been correlated during adolescence with better psychological adjustment (Mussen, 1962); it has also been correlated during adulthood with high anxiety, high neuroticism and low self-acceptance (Harford, Willis & Deabler, 1967; Mussen, 1962). In addition, greater intellectual development has been correlated quite consistently with cross-sex typing (masculinity in girls, and femininity in boys). Boys and girls, who are more sex-typed, have been found to have lower overall intelligence, lower spatial ability, and lower creativity (Maccoby, 1966). In an androgynous person, there is behavioural adaptability, whereas in case of non-androgynous individual, there is behavioural restriction. A review of literature from Bem's finding reports that whatever psychological barriers may turn out to be responsible for the behavioural rigidities of the sex-typed and sex-reversed subjects, there exists a distinct class of people who can appropriately be termed as androgynous. Their sex-role adaptability enables them to engage in situationally effective behaviour without regard for its stereotype as masculine or feminine. Bem has pointed out that when the artificial constraints of gender are eliminated, the person becomes psychologically healthy. By psychologically healthy, we mean a state of complete physical, mental and social well-being and not merely the absence of disease or infirmity. This is related to the feelings of subjective well-being derived from values of spiritual quality such as "being part of mankind", belonging to a common force, having moments of intense happiness, and having deep religious fulfillment in life.

Numerous studies have investigated the implications of traditional and non-traditional sex-role orientations for personal adjustment and social effectiveness in the last 10 years since Bem (1974), Spence, Helmreich and Stapp (1975) and others introduced sex-role scales that assess masculine and feminine traits separately.

The conceptualization of masculinity and femininity as independent dimensions rather than as bipolar opposites (Constantinople, 1973) and the development of dualistic sex-role measures have permitted researchers to compare empirically traditional assumption that sex-typing is necessary for psychological adjustment. More recently, it has been hypothesized that going beyond the sex-typing results in enhanced psychological functioning. These competing hypotheses have been referred by Whitely (1983) as congruence model and androgyny model respectively.

The congruence model implies that masculinity and femininity are opposite poles of a single dimension and mutually exclusive. It asserts that psychological adjustment is a function of gender by sex-role interaction, with well-being resulting from high masculinity and low femininity in men and low masculinity and high femininity in women (Whitely, 1983).

The androgyny model posits that psychological adjustment is best in individuals exhibiting high levels of both masculine and feminine characteristics. The androgynous individuals possess a broader range of social skills and competencies (instrumental and expressive skills) than individuals who possess one set of characteristics (masculine or feminine typed) or neither (undifferentiated) (Kelly & Worell, 1977).

Studies of social interaction and conversational skills have indicated superior social effectiveness in androgynous persons relative to sex-type subjects (Ickes & Banes, 1978; Kelly, O'Brien, & Hosford, 1981). The finding that psychological androgyny is superior to sex-typing with respect to self-esteem and other self-report measures has not been so consistent.

Coping with Stressful Life Events

More recently, work has been done to see if certain personality characteristics function as mediating variables for the effects of stressful life events. The study of Shaw (1982) was designed to investigate the possible mediating effects of sex-role. The previous work in the area of androgyny has indicated that androgynous subjects are more adaptable than sex-typed persons (Bem, 1975; Bem & Lenney, 1976; Bem, Martyna & Watson, 1976). Reflecting on these results, Baucom and Danker-Brown (1979) concluded that androgynous persons are more flexible and have a wider range of strategies for dealing with diverse situations than do the masculine sex-typed and feminine sex-typed persons, who rely principally on the set of strategies for obtaining reinforcement. Baucom and Danker-Brown (1979) also found androgynous subjects exhibit only dysphoric mood changes, when faced with a situation of helplessness in the laboratory. Undifferentiated subjects were unaffected, perhaps, according to Shaw, because they were less involved in the tasks. It was hypothesized to investigate that androgynous subjects will rate their stressful life events as less undesirable than other subjects and androgynous subjects will judge that they control their stressful life events more than other subjects. Previous work suggests that androgynous persons may either experience more stressful life events, because they experience more of everything or fewer events, if they have better control of their lives and things run smoothly for them. Results of their investigation showed that only androgynous female subjects rated their stressful life events as less undesirable than other subjects and only female undifferentiated subjects reported a greater number of stressful life events than subjects of the other sex-types. The results for males differed in direction from those of females.

There is another implication of these studies. The original supposition was that androgynous subjects have an advantage compared to other subjects in dealing with stressful life events. It appears that undifferentiated subjects are more disadvantaged than androgynous subjects. In case of females, androgynous subjects consider themselves happier and rate their stressful life events as less desirable.

Behaviour Flexibility

An androgynous person is able to engage in masculine-feminine or a blend of these characteristics depending upon what is appropriate for the specific situation (Bem, 1975). This flexibility should lead to more adaptive behaviour (cf. Heilburn & Pitman, 1979). Bem assessed that only an androgynous person would be able to exhibit flexibility across situations. In other research strategy, Bem and Lenney (1976) hypothesized that androgynous persons' flexibility would help them to feel comfortable about performing either feminine or masculine activities. Traditional sex-typed persons tend to show more avoidance of either sex-typed tasks than do androgynous or cross sex-typed persons. Sex-typing is seen to be associated with less effectiveness in cross sex-tasks.

LaFrance and Carmen (1980) observed frequencies of sex typical non-verbal behaviours during discussions with an instrumental or expressive flavour. Detailed analysis by BSRI sex-role category suggested that responses of androgynous persons revealed cohesiveness of behaviours within type (masculine or feminine), less cross sex-avoidance, less difference between display of each type of behaviours across situations, and fewer extremes of behaviour, especially in a sex-constant situation (e.g., an instrumental situation, for men).

Androgyny represents an ideal of human functioning, blending the best of masculinity and femininity. Some research findings suggested that a combination of masculinity and femininity provide maximum benefits rather than simple adherence of sex-typical standards (cf. Block, Vonder Lippe & Block, 1973; Heilburn, 1968; Mussen, 1962). Hinrichsen, Follansbee and Ganellen (1981) reported that androgynous persons consistently rated themselves higher on psychological health and self-concept scales than did those in other sex-role categories.

Locus of control is a trait referring to the degree to which persons believe that they can control events by their own behaviour (internal locus of control) versus events that are out of their control which is external (cf. Rotter, 1966). Locus of control measures have not proven to be helpful in documenting androgyny's superiority. Borderline or non-significant associations between locus of control and androgyny measures appear to be the rule.

Mental Health

Taylor and Hall (1982) reported on the size of masculinity and femininity's main effects for a heterogenous grouping of studies pertinent to psychological health. Bassoff and Glass (1982) provided a more extensive analysis on mental health. They concluded that androgynous and masculine subjects scored higher on measures of mental health over a range of studies than did their feminine peers.

Depression has been extensively studied in this connection and it appears to have negative relationship to masculinity. Baucom (Baucom & Danker-Brown, 1979) and Baucom (1980) explored how levels of femininity and masculinity may affect individuals' coping with situations that induce feelings akin to depression. Baucom and Danker-Brown (1979) concluded that differential susceptibility to helplessness is a function of sex-roles rather than of sex. Sex-typed persons may share a lack of flexibility and resilience following a loss of control, but masculine persons may have a history of greater success in avoiding the uncontrollable situations that may produce depression. Golding and Singer (1983) have pointed out that androgyny was associated with positive day-dreaming, fewest self-reported feelings of inefficacy, mind wondering and dependency, all of which are often related to depression.

All the studies share a common hypothesis that androgyny represents a stage of psychological development superior to that of non-androgynous persons. An early series of studies by J.H. Block (1973) suggested that higher levels of psychological development of self-concepts reflect an interaction of the agentic concerns, self-enhancement and self-extension with the satisfaction deriving from communion and mutuality.

In reviewing the literature on life quality, Campbell (1980) concluded that there are different categories of well-being. A major category involves affects and strains which focus on feelings flowing spontaneously from everyday experiences. Another category includes satisfaction which focus on relativistic cognitive judgements about the quality of experience. In analysing, interrelationships among a variety of measure of life quality survey, Andrews, Frank and Whithley (1976) found two separate factors that reflected positive and negative affect respectively, as well as a third factor, overall life satisfactions. This separation between evaluation of positive experience and negative experience is consistent with Bradburn's (1969) work that distinguished positive-affective life from negative-affective life. Other well-being researchers also distinguished between positive and negative feelings. Cherlin and Reader (1975) and investigators of job satisfaction, Hertzberg (1966), supported this position. More recently, two authors (Andrews & Mckennell, 1980; Mckennell & Andrews, 1980) have systematically examined hypothetical models involving two basic types of influences:

affective and cognitive on evaluation of life quality. Other empirical evidence suggests that besides the dimension of positive evaluations, negative evaluations, and cognitive appraisals of life satisfaction, there is another distinctly separate dimension of subjective mental health. In other words, personal competence in handling one's life is an important factor. Charlin and Reader (1975) compared the structure of self-evaluations of well-being in national survey data from 1957 and 1976, and found multifactor of well-being. Bryant and Veroff (1982) substantiated many of these points. They found that the same basic dimensions underlie men's and women's evaluations in both years. These dimensions were: happiness (an evaluation of positive experience), strain (an evaluation of negative experience) and personal inadequacy (an evaluation of personal competence) in handling negative experience.

Fred Bryant and Joseph Veroff (1984) have pointed four dominant dimensions which underlie people's evaluations of their own subjective mental health.

1. An evaluation of positive affective experience
2. An evaluation of negative affective experience
3. Feelings of personal competence in handling negative experience and,
4. Feeling of personal competence in deriving positive experience.

Bryant and Veroff (1984) have explicated these dimensions into six factors on the basis of factor-analytic studies.

The first one is the dimension of unhappiness and comprises of general unhappiness, past happier than present, happiest time in the past, low future morale and general dissatisfaction with life.

The second factor, lack of gratification, reflects indices of value fulfillment and life satisfaction derived from relevant role relationship.

The third factor, strain, includes a cluster of psychophysical symptoms (physical ill health, immobilization and psychophysical anxiety, frequency of drug-taking, and alcohol abuse). A similar psychophysical dimension of subjective mental health has been highlighted by other investigations (Bryant & Veroff, 1982; Langer, 1962; Macmillan, 1957).

The fourth factor, called feelings of vulnerability, is characterized by frequent feelings of being overwhelmed, feeling of nervous breakdown, and the perception that bad things frequently occur. Feelings of vulnerability correlate strongly with the strain factor for both men and women.

A fifth factor, labelled lack of self-confidence, involves depression, low self-esteem, feelings of anomie, the perception of problems and outcomes being uncontrollable, and lack of self-acceptance.

All the above factors have emerged for both men and women, except the sixth one which is uncertainty to accept the worrying immobilization, anxiety and self-doubt. This study points out that there is relationship between age, education, and marital harmony with subjective mental health.

As age is concerned, older people are generally more unhappy and show more strain, but they are much less uncertain and suffer less from feelings of vulnerability. This pattern makes sense when one considers people's adaptive struggles, as they move through the life cycle. People may become more unhappy and may suffer more stress especially because of failing health, but in the process they may learn to cope and align their aspirations with the possible and become more certain about lives.

Education is also related with subjective mental health. Higher education is associated with stronger self-confidence, but it is also related to greater feelings of uncertainty about one's life.

Thus, education may strengthen one's belief in one's own abilities. At the same time, it may lead to more worrying, anxiety and dissatisfaction about life to the extent that the latter represents foresightful coping. Kessler (1979) has demonstrated that more educated groups seem to cope better with stress, a fact that can build greater self-confidence as well as greater sensitivity to potential stress.

Marital harmony is another factor which is related to positive mental health. It is negatively correlated with unhappiness, but positively correlated with feelings of vulnerability.

Unhappiness can lead people to withdraw from marital bonding; feeling vulnerable to stress can push people into seeking marital support. Bryant and Veroff (1984) have shown that expression of marital unhappiness is more closely related to married people's overall unhappiness than are other specific sources of discontent. By contrast, feeling vulnerable to stress can push people into seeking marital support. Leaderar, William and Jackson (1968) have suggested that marriages are based on a vulnerable dependency of husbands and wives with each other. Therefore, a spouse can be a major source of comfort and assistance when stress occurs and for many men a spouse is the only source of intimate support.

More recently, the concept of psychological well-being has received added significance because of changing societal complexity and global problems. A state of complete health comprising of physical, mental, social and spiritual well-being is indispensable for healthy life. People who are mentally healthy exhibit several forms of balance, harmony and interrelatedness. Herzberg (1966) argued that mental health required both an adjustment to the environment, so that negative states are minimized, and also the occurrence of and potential for "psychological growth". The latter can be compared with "self-actualization" or self - realisation" (Maslow, 1970) where personal efforts to seek and achieve one's full potential are treated as central to mental health.

With the emergence of health psychology and the year 1960 designated as Mental Health Year in International World Health Organization, a general awareness of the concept is well-marked. The World Health Organization defines health as state of complete physical, mental and social well-being and not merely the absence of disease or infirmity (Nagpal & Sell, 1985). In the past, mental health's unanswering emphasis has always been of psychological dysfunction. Recently, people are becoming conscious day- by- day not only towards the curative process of mental illness but also to promote mental heath. Earlier mental health slogan "fight sickness" is now popularly replaced by "build health".

A full consideration of the topic of "psychological well-being" requires attention be directed to key sources of influences that advance or restrict such an outcome. Recently, it has become a matter of priority of mental health organization to identify and monitor indicators of mental health in all its facets, including subjective well-being and quality of mental life.

Traditional Dimensions

Traditionally negative mental states such as depression, stress and anxiety are considered to be important parameters of mental health, absence of which indicated that the person was mentally healthy. This approach originated from clinical psychology.

Stress. The phenomenon of stress is formally defined as the response to events that threaten or challenge a person. Human research spear-headed by Lazarus and his associates (e.g. Lazarus, 1966; Lazarus & Folkman, 1984), however, identified psychological appraisal as a crucial mediating process in the experience of stress. Events appraised as negative like death of spouse, unemployment, illness, ageing etc. are typically experienced as more stressful and organisms experiencing the events showed physiological reactions indicative of anxiety and arousal. Stress as the term goes, does not always indicate a negative aspect, though negative events result in greater detrimental consequences than positive ones (Sarason, 1978).

Anxiety. Anxiety is defined as a chronic complex emotional state with apprehension or dread as its most prominent component. In other words, it is an emotional condition in which there is fear and uncertainty about the future to such an extent that sometimes it leads to various nervous and mental disorders.

According to Sarason (1978), analysis of anxiety begins with the objective properties of situations and individuals' interpretation of them. Anxiety to him is thus a type of cognitive response marked by self - doubt, feeling of inadequacy, and self-blame. Sarason gives several characteristics of anxiety responses: (a) The situation is seen as difficult, challenging and threatening; (b) The individual sees himself as ineffective and inadequate; (c) The individual focuses on undesirable consequences of personal inadequacy; (d) The individual expects and anticipates failure and loss of regard from others.

Depression. Depression has come to be regarded as the "common cold" of the psycho-social functioning. This is because everyday life presents its share of adversities that are not always easily controllable. Depressive reactions seriously impair functioning when they become severe and prolonged. Literally, the term implies an emotional attitude, sometimes definitely pathological, involving a feeling of inadequacy and hopelessness, sometimes overwhelmingly accompanied by a lowering psycho-physical activity. Current trends conceptualize depression as a cognitive phenomenon (Beck, 1967).

Some studies emphasize that depressive symptoms occur when an individual experiences a negative life event that specifically matches the individual's personal motivational vulnerability. Some people get themselves into despondent states by faulty habits of thinking. Lewinsohn and his colleagues have centred this theory on depression arising from inability to produce pleasurable experiences and forestall aversive ones (Lewinsohn, Hoberman, Ter & Hautzinger, 1985). Under these disheartening conditions people become dejected, lethargic and find little pleasure in what they do. It seems from the analysis of cognitive theory of depression that negative life events have been found to enhance depression somewhat. Barnett and Gotlib (1988) suggested psycho-social variables like marital distress, low social integration to be involved in the category of depression.

As proposed by Abramson, Seligman and Teasdale (1978), depression is potentiated when uncontrollable bad events are seen internally, stably and globally caused and if such attributions are habitual, an attributional "style" that predisposes one to depression can be spoken of.

Contemporary View of Well-Being

The absence of negative states presents a picture of psychological well-being. But with the emergence of health psychology, personologists have indicated presence of positive aspects as more efficacious criteria of mental health. Most contemporary health psychologists have advocated the role of specific dimension of self-concept such as competence, job involvement, control, autonomy, social and family support., in well-being.

Perceived Control. Researchers and theorists have adopted perceived control as one central criterion of psychological well-being. Langer (1983) on the concept of perceived control shows that the belief that one can affect outcomes relevant to one's own life is of paramount importance to psychological well-being and physical health. She has shown experimentally that patients with more perceived control tend to respond better to treatment and live longer. She also found with age, self-esteem decreases because of decline of control.

Recent research work on "perceived control" suggests that perception of personal control results in positive reactions whereas perception of loss of control results in negative effects. Maintaining a sense of control has been found to enhance the ability to cope with stressors (Glass & Singer, 1972).

Researchers have suggested that increasing one's perceived control can satisfy a need to feel competent and masterful. The more control a person has, the better off he or she is. Thus an increasing sense of control enhances an individual's sense of adequacy and thereby fosters mental health which has been evidenced in a number of studies.

Loss of perceived ability to control aversive events develops profound feelings of helplessness and depression (Seligman, 1975). Unfortunately, there is also evidence that the malignant sequence associated with loss of perceived control, which often occurs among people who are ill, not only increases subjective suffering but also impedes physical recovery and sometimes leads to death.

Glass and Singer (1972) investigated the effects of negative outcomes in producing these feelings and helplessness. A group of people were put in situations wl re they had no control over some aversive events and another group of people, though put in the same aversive situations, were led to believe that they are doing so by choice. The two groups differ in their belief of control over the outcome. One group believed they could control the outcome, the other believed they could not. Although neither group exercised control, the group that believed that control was possible experienced less strain. A sense of control over the event seems to promote a higher level of well-being.

A study examined the effects of predictability on the onset or offset of an aversive stimulus. These researchers exposed subjects working on arithmetic problems to either predictable (regular intervals and length) or unpredictable noise burst. Subjects showed more signs of stress (racing hearts and headaches) when exposed to unpredictable noise. The researchers argued that this is because the unpredictable noise demands more attention and the subject becomes more aware of the aversive stimulus than does the predictable noise.

In addition, it is found that a temporary loss of control is stress-arousing whereas chronic feeling of no control is characterised by passivity and giving up in the face of failure.

So, strive for mastery and control over one's environment plays a central role in fostering psychological well-being. Many experimental findings confirm that increasing one's feeling of personal control will lead to an increase in positive effect. According to Seligman (1975), a person has control when a desired outcomes occurrence is dependent on the person's response.

Currently, several experiments have been conducted to test the psychological implication of perceived control. In a study the researchers of 92 patients with rheumatoid arthritis examined the role of appraisal of control and predictability in adapting to the disease. Perceiving greater personal control over one's medical care and treatment was associated with positive mood and psycho-social adjustment.

The result and analysis of studies in the area of control confirm perception of control as a major determinant of individual's sense of adequacy. It gives an individual a feeling of self-efficacy and thereby enhances his or her experience of well-being.

Social Support. There is abundant evidence linking social support with mental health. Feelings of being cared for and intimately tied to others have direct positive effects of health and well-being.

According to Moos (1985), social net-work, family support and supportive work environment are the criteria relevant for effective human adaptation which results in psychological well-being. Mental health programmes put emphasis on the topic of social support as it figures prominently as a key moderator of or "buffer to" effect of psychological stressors on health. Considerable research suggests social support is related to positive health outcomes and psychological well-being. It has been felt that social support has preventive role in resisting stress and acts as a general contributor to health and morale.

Social support neutralises psycho-social stressors in human milieu and also strengthens people's social competence and coping skill so as to improve their resilience in the face of stressors.

In the context of social support, authors emphasize direct effects on emotional well-being states. "Role" identities (positive evaluations from role partners) and comparatively successful role performances affect perceptions of belonging and security, esteem and efficacy respectively, which, in turn, have emotional consequences that are central indicators of psychological well-being or disturbance.

Working in a laboratory situation, Sarason, Sarason, Hacket and Basham (1985) compared social skills and physical appearance of men and women who were high or low in perceived availability of social support, as measured via the number scores of Social Support Questionnaire (SSQ: Sarason, Levine, Bashan, Sarason, 1983). They perceived that subject scoring high in perceived social support not only rated themselves as more socially skilled than those low in social support but were also similarly rated by their subject partners in a social interaction and also by trained raters who viewed a video tape of that interaction. They were also rated as more attractive by other raters who viewed a colour photo of each subject. In addition, the high support subjects showed more knowledge of social skills on story completion task than did low support subjects.

Many studies established a link between physiological mechanism with social support in health protection. A study by Jemmott and Locke (1984) indicated social support as a positive psychological state that enhances immunity to disease by affecting the neuro endocrine functioning. Jemmott and Magloire (1988) focusing on a different measure found that students with more adequate social support had superior immune functioning before, during and after examination period than those with less adequate social support as reflected by salivary measures of secretory immunoglobulin.

Persons with more social network encouraged self - care practices and thus were less vulnerable to disease and death than persons with less social ties.

A number of investigators have explored how interpersonal relationships influence people's responses to a variety of stressful events and the results of these studies clearly demonstrated a relationship between social support and effective adjustment. In a longitudinal study of reactions to job termination due to plant closing, Cobb and Kasl (1977) reported that social support from one's spouse, relatives and friends reduced much of the distress associated with the loss. Among the physically disabled, support from the family has been associated with rehabilitation success both in the hospital and in the community.

In the Indian culture, family support emerges as a positive and significant indicator of psychological well-being. Sahoo and Bidyadhar (1992) found family support was given high priority as a criterion of subjective psychological well-being by different professionals. Chakrapani (1996) has identified unemployment as a stressor. Social support system is a potential stress moderator. Family support and religion emerged as the two most important successful resources in altering the stressor character of unemployment. Banerjee and Gupta (1996) studied the moderating effect of social support in relation to occupational stresses and strains among 100 males and 100 females from four different occupations. Results indicated the moderating effects of social support in relation to stress and strain. Chandra and Sudha, (1995) examined mental health of mothers and found that husbands supportiveness was correlated positively with well-being in slum and urban subjects.

Moos (1985) gave social network and family support criteria of effective human adaptation. To him, family level composite indices are quality of conjugal relationship, family social activities, agreement on task sharing and agreement on household tasks. Indices of social functions and resources are given as social activities with friends, network contacts, number of close relationship, quality significant relationships etc.

Job Satisfaction. Since work has been given increasing importance in contemporary life, job satisfaction is considered as an indicator of psychological well-being. There has been substantial literature to support it. Occupational characteristics are related to various facets of self-evaluation such as self-confidence, self-esteem etc. Occupational control is associated with lower depression and anxiety. It gives an overall satisfaction to the individual concerned.

It is argued that more a member can understand how and why events happen, predict the frequency, timing and duration of events in the work environment and control the outcomes desired by effectively influencing the events, things or others in the work environment, less strain will result from the stressors existing in the work environment.

A substantial amount of literature exists in the relation between occupational characteristics and psychological well-being. Evidence suggests that employed men have higher well-being than do unemployed men (Cobb & Kasl, 1977) and paid employment has a positive relation to psychological well-being in women (Adelman, 1987). Higher income is associated with higher job satisfaction.

Adelman's (1987) study was to test whether three occupational characteristics (control, complexity, and personal income) are related to psychological well-being in employed men and women. The results of this study suggest that the job enrichment and job enlargement (increasing control) have the potential to influence not only productivity and job satisfaction, but the larger psychological life and well-being of employees as well. The variables are significantly related to well-being but the pattern of result varies somewhat from men compared with women. Narayan, Lakhmi, and Prabhakaran (1993) examined the mental health of 128 industrial employees and found that mental health was poor in case of employees who were not satisfied with their present job. Another study indicated that mental health has a moderating effect on the relationship between intrinsic job satisfaction and occupational stress.

An investigator conducted one interesting study to test whether the occupational characteristics of housewives bear a similar relation to the psychological well-being of full-time home-makers. Results indicate that full-time home-makers have generally lower psychological well-being than do employed men and women. It is argued that work in the home shares most of worst characteristics of dissatisfying paid employment, including monotony, repetitiveness and low social and monetary rewards. Similarly, using longitudinal data, researchers found that changes in occupational conditions can increase productivity and job satisfaction reduce psychosomatic complaints and lead to improvements in mental health

Competence. Competence has been widely discussed in the literature. For example Jahoda (1958) wrote in terms of "environmental mastery" viewing good mental health partly in terms of an acceptable degree of success in different spheres. Competence is the ability to bring expected outcome and hence always desirable. To be competent in any situation means to have the ability, power, skill, authority etc. to do what is needed in any situation.

People try to control their world. The more control a person has, the more is the self-efficacy. Self-esteem is to have a good opinion about oneself and it has a relationship with self-efficacy mechanism. Bandura (1977) finds that the level of induced self-efficacy is indirectly proportional to level of performance accomplishment and inversely proportional to emotional arousal.

Maton (1990) indicated that meaningful instrumental activity was positively related to life satisfaction. In addition, meaningful instrumental activity was positively related to self-esteem to a greater extent for adolescent male than for adolescent female college students. The findings emphasize, however, meaningful instrumental activity. It refers to task or skill related activity which has positive significance or value to the individual and contribute to well-being.

Autonomy. Autonomy has been widely postulated as a central criterion of mental health (Jahoda, 1958). Autonomy connotes an inner endorsement of one's action, the sense that they emanate from oneself and are one's own. Deci and Ryan (1985, 1987) describe this process as self-determination as it is characterized by the full endorsement of the behaviour by the self.

Deci, Schwartz, Sheinman and Ryan (1981) in one study created a measure that sampled teacher's attitude towards either supporting autonomy or controlling behaviour. In this research, students in classrooms of more autonomy supportive teachers were found to have greater confidence, more mastery, motivation and evidence of high self-esteem than children in classrooms with more controlling teachers.

Similar results were obtained in a study of worker supervisor relations in a corporate setting. Deci, Connell and Ryan (1989) showed that controlling managerial styles were associated with decreased satisfaction at work whereas supportive autonomy managerial styles were associated with improved satisfaction.

Beck (1983) proposed that two personality dimensions sociotrophy (social dependency) and autonomy may mediate vulnerability to depression. In highly socio-trophic individuals, depression occurs when there is perceived loss or rejection in social relationships. In highly autonomous individuals, depression occurs where there is perceived achievement failure or lack of control over the environment.

In sum, recent studies of psychological well-being have suggested multicriteria. It has also been suggested that different criteria may have differential relevance for varied subset of human population.

13
The Study: Androgyny and Well-Being

As reviewed earlier, androgyny represents a desirable mode expression of individuality. Its link with positive self-concept, job satisfaction, behavioural flexibility, and cross sex behaviour has been documented at least in western societies. The association between androgyny and mental health has also been shown. However, an adequate examination of the linkage between androgyny and well-being is required.

First, Indian socio-cultural system represents certain contrasting features compared with western societies. The societal standards and values are gradually changing in Indian society. Yet, the traditional rural sector forms a substantial part of Indian population. Industrialization has yet to take its roots in rural pockets. Although women have started to join in the workforce, their integration with working society has not been very smooth.

In such a context, androgynous individuals are not likely to gather social approval. Consequently, many of the findings relating to androgynous individuals of the west may not hold in India. Furthermore, the transformation taking place in Indian society requires periodic assessment of changing sex-roles. The empirical examination of androgyny would fulfill two important objectives. It would be possible to check the generality of the western findings in contemporary Indian society. Moreover, it would be possible to evaluate the changes with respect to sex-role behaviour in India.

Second, the examination of relationship between androgyny and well-being has not been adequately done in the past. Although the review of pertinent literature in the area presents some studies, the attempts are inadequate. Previously, mental health was defined in a narrow fashion. Dimensions such as depression and tension were considered as indicators of ill health. Accordingly studies of mental health were directed to examine the relationship between a criterion and androgyny.

However, recent changes in the conceptualization of well-being have suggested the significance of multi-factors. It has been shown that a large number of factors underlie psychological well-being

Apart from the absence of negative states such as depression, anxiety, and tension, the presence of positive conditions such as competence, control, and autonomy needs to be regarded as possible indicators.

More adequate studies of mental health need to involve both of these kinds of factors (negative and positive) as relevant dimensions of well-being. The empirical studies of androgyny need to be addressed to this comprehensive and contemporary view of well-being.

Furthermore, an important aspect is considered for the present investigation. It is asserted that persons may attach differential priorities to the criteria of mental health and the salient criteria are likely to have greater bearing on personal well-being. More specifically, the satisfaction of conditions considered salient by an individual is likely to have greater bearing on his or her well-being. With this rationale, the present investigation considers a number of criteria and evaluates the saliency of individual's own indicators. With the consideration of criterion saliency and multiple criteria, the present investigation is geared to examine the relationship between androgyny and psychological well-being.

Hypotheses

In view of the foregoings, a number of hypotheses are formulated for empirical examination.

1. Androgynous individuals would demonstrate higher scores on each of the criteria of psychological well-being than do sex-typed individuals. These criteria include achievement, social contact, control over the environment, feelings of happiness with family, good physical health, job satisfaction, values of spiritual quality, personal competence, social support, freedom from depression, autonomous activities, interpersonal trust, effective coping with stressful situations, integrated personality, and freedom from anxiety.

2. Androgynous individuals would show greater overall mental health compared with sex-typed individuals.
3. Androgynous individual would indicate higher score on salient criteria satisfaction than do the sex-typed person.
4. Males are likely to demonstrate greater well-being than do females.
5. Psychological well-being is significantly related to the satisfaction of salient criteria but it is unrelated with satisfaction of non-salient criteria.

Method of Study

The empirical examination of the hypotheses formulated requires a well-defined method of study. The following sequence of activities was undertaken to complete methodological requirements.

An Overview of the Design

The study adopted a 2x2 factorial design where males and females were categorized into sex-typed and androgynous individuals on the basis of their performance on sex-role inventory.

The participants of four quasi-experimental groups (male androgynous, female androgynous, male sex-typed, and female sex-typed) were individually administered a comprehensive measure of psychological well-being. This measure included sub-scales such as achievement, freedom from anxiety, social contact, feelings of happiness in the family, physical health, job satisfaction, values of spiritual quality, personal competence, social support, autonomous activity, freedom from depression, control over the environment, interpersonal trust, effective coping with stressful situation, and integrated personality.

Participants

Two hundred adults, 100 males and 100 females, from a semi-urban area of Cuttack district of Orissa were the participants. A large number of colleges affiliated to Utkal University were considered. A large number of schools managed by the State's Secondary Board of Education were also listed. From the very large pool of these schools and colleges, teacher participants were sampled on a random basis. While the case of teacher participants put some restriction on sampling frame, the randomisation process was adopted to expand the range of response variations.

Measures

The tools for the study involved two separate measures. These were administered on two different occasions.

The first session involved a measure of sex-role inventory, which was used to categorize participants into androgynous and sex-typed groups.

The second session concerned individual administration of a measure of psychological well-being.

The Measure of Androgyny. Although Bem's Sex-Role Inventory (BSRI) is an oft-used measure of androgyny, the scale is not considered suitable for the present investigation. It is argued that BSRI has masculine and feminine items whose relevance is restricted to western society. Accordingly, the masculinity and femininity scores (based on BSRI) obtained from Indian participants are not likely to be accurate expressions of sex-role orientation in India. With a view to effecting a meaningful operationalization, a culturally valid measure of androgyny was needed.

Sahoo (1990a) developed a culturally valid measure of androgyny (see Appendix A). For the development and validation of this scale, Sahoo's Sex-Role Inventory (SSRI) followed similar format of BSRI. Sahoo initially considered 200 characteristics in his original pool of items. While developing this preliminary list, he considered Bem's preliminary list; in addition, he also included items that are relevant in Indian socio-cultural system. As with Bem's scale development, this pool of 200 items was presented to males and females separately for judgement of their stereo-typic quality. Each participant (judge) was asked to indicate the trait which is considered desirable for male. A similar group of male and female participants was asked to indicate the desirability of each of these descriptors for women. The group difference analysis on desirability ratings for each of the descriptors identified traits that were significantly considered masculine. Similar analysis showed the traits that were significantly considered feminine. In addition, a number of traits that were not associated either with male or female characteristics were also identified.

On the basis of this empirical method, the SSRI was developed. It comprised of 20 masculine items, 20 feminine items and 10 neutral items. It is interesting to note that Bem's masculine items, such as masculine, has leadership ability, strong personality, aggressive and willing to take a stand etc., were retained in the SSRI. Similarly, Bem's feminine items like tender, affectionate, compassionate, loves children, flatterable were also found in the SSRI. However, masculinity items like progressive, realistic, energetic and femininity items like mild, charming, and soft-hearted, were new entrants in the SSRI. This change is conceivable in terms of cultural differences. The administration and scoring of SSRI is also similar to that of BSRI. The SSRI presents 50 items in a random order. Participants are asked to indicate on a 7-point scale the extent to which each descriptor is characteristic of himself or herself. At the time of scoring, masculinity, femininity, and neutral items are considered separately. The sum of endorsement ratings of an individual across masculinity traits indicates his or her masculinity score. Similarly, the sum of endorsement ratings across femininity items indicates femininity scores. The sum of ratings across sex neutral items indicates social desirability score.

Gap between masculinity and femininity score is indicative of sex-role orientation of an individual. Greater is the gap, more sex-typed is the individual. The lower is the gap, higher is the androgynous characteristics. It is important to point out that SSRI was presented and validated prior to its use in the present investigation. The satisfactory level of its reliability and validity is reported elsewhere (Sahoo, 1990). The test-retest reliability of the SSRI ranged from .75 to .81. The Cronbach's alpha for the SSRI was .78. The test scores were also moderately correlated with BSRI scores of participants.

Measure of Well-Being. While measures of mental health are available in the literature, most of these measures are heavily loaded on one or two specific dimensions such as anxiety, depression, and tension. There are only a few measures that employ multicriteria format. Furthermore, the positive attributes such as competence, control, family relation do not find place in conventional measures of well-being. With a view to include a multicriteria measure, a new scale was considered.

Sahoo (1990b) has developed a Health Behaviour Questionnaire (HBQ) that includes both multicriteria feature and cultural relevance (see Appendix B). The scale consists of five part series.

The first part consists of perceived importance of health criteria. A list of 15 health criteria is given. The criteria include achievement, social contact, control over the environment, feelings of happiness with family, good physical health, job satisfaction, values of spiritual quality, personal competence, social support, freedom from depression, autonomous activities, interpersonal trust, effective coping with stressful situations, integrated personality, and freedom from anxiety. Participants are required to indicate priority ratings against each of these criteria.

The salient criteria are those that are rated first and second by the individual. The non-salient criteria are those that are rated 14th and 15th by the individual. It is important to point out that salient and non-salient criteria are specific to an individual. This part of the questionnaire is useful in identifying specific criteria that are considered significant and salient by the individual.

The second part of the questionnaire presents 120 statements. Each statement indicates the presence or absence of a health criterion in one's life. The individual is asked to read each statement and to indicate the extent it characterizes his or her life. In order to facilitate responding, a six-point-scale is presented where '1' represents "very uncharacteristic" and '6' represents "very characteristic" of an individual.

In this part, multiple number of items represent each of the health criteria indicated earlier. There are unequal number of statements for these criteria. The items representing these 15 criteria are randomized. The items are keyed in both the directions. Scores are computed for each of the criteria for an individual.

Apart from individual health criterion score, overall well-being score is computed by summing the scores of an individual across 15 criteria. In addition, salient criteria score of an individual is computed by summing the two scores across those criteria that an individual rates as the first and second in the first part of the questionnaire. Similarly, non-salient criteria score is computed by summing the scores of those criteria that an individual rates 14th (fourteenth) and 15th (fifteenth) in the first part of the questionnaire.

The third part of the questionnaire employs semantic differential technique to measure well-being. Bipolar adjectives are presented to denote each of 15 criteria. Numerals from 1 to 7 between each set of descriptions were used. The individual is asked to encircle a number for each set to depict his/her well-being. While scoring, the direction of keying is considered. The closer is an individual's rating to a desired criterion, higher is the score.

In this part, score for each criterion and overall well-being scores are computed. In addition, the salient criteria score and non-salient criteria score are computed following similar method as indicated for the second part of this questionnaire.

The fourth part is the graphic method of measurement of well-being. In this part, there are seven sets of diagrams. Each set contains a human figure and a circle. The human figure represents the respondent and the circle represents the condition of good living. It is indicated to the individual that the condition of good living means a state of complete physical, mental and social well-being. In each set, the distance between human figure and circle is systematically varied. Each set of figure is assigned a number. The distance between the figure and circle is systematically varied across seven sets. The distance between the two is minimum for the upper most set and the distance between two is maximum at the bottom.

The respondents are asked to examine each set of diagrams and identify the specific set that represents his order fulfillment with health condition. In other words, the participant is asked to choose the set that accurately reflects his or her psychological well-being. The respondent is instructed to encircle the number shown against the set for identifying the distance.

The identification of the set is scored on a 7-point scale. The set representating minimum distance is indicative of maximum score, whereas the diagram representating maximum distance between the human figure and circle is indicative of the lowest score. The score of an individual is indicative of overall well-being.

The psychometric efficacy of the HBQ was examined prior to its present use. The test-retest reliability of the measure ranged from .73 to .89. The Cronbach's alpha for various parts ranged from .79 to .83. The scores of well-being as measured by various parts were significantly correlated with Quality of Life Scales used in India.

The last part of the questionnaire seeks personal information such as sex, marital status, age and education.

Procedure

The study was carried out in two separate sessions. The participants as described earlier were randomly sampled. They were contacted at their work places. They were individually administered the SSRI (Sahoo's Sex-Role Inventory). Prior to the test administration, necessary rapport was established and each subject was given the test during his or her leisure hours. The administration of the measure of androgyny generated two separate scores (masculinity score and femininity score) for each individual.

The difference score for each individual (masculinity femininity) was computed. The low difference score was indicative of androgynous orientation. On the basis of androgyny score, males and females within each sex group were separately categorized into sex-typed and androgynous groups. The half of the males obtaining low difference score were classified as androgynous, whereas the other half of the males were classified as sex-typed. Similar categorization was carried out for females.

Two weeks after the administration of the measure of androgyny, participants of each of these quasi-experimental groups (four groups) were individually administered the measure of psychological well-being.

As outlined in the test description portion, scores for each of the health criteria, overall well-being, salient criteria scores were obtained for each individual. The statistical examination of interrelationship amongst variables was undertaken to test predicted pattern of association. Furthermore, statistical analyses were geared to compare responses of these four quasi-experimental groups of each of the variables to investigate the association between androgyny and parameters of psychological well-being.

It is important to point out that the measure of well-being is based on the multicriteria approach. It involves 15 separate, though related, dimensions. Prior to the computation of overall well-being, an examination of the interrelationship of dimensions is undertaken.

Results

The application of statistical analyses lead to several findings.

Congruency of Measures

The congruent validity (Davis, 1964) is examined in the form of correlations amongst 15 dimensions of the heath behaviour measure. It is found that the dimensions cohere together. As shown in Table 13.1, the positive associations between measures are indicated in a number of cases. Job satisfaction is positively correlated with achievement of the individual, r (198)=.31, p ∠0.01; freedom from depression is positively correlated with feelings of happiness in the family and personal competence, r(198)=0.53, p∠0.01 and r(198)=0.53, p∠0.01. Similarly, freedom from anxiety is positively correlated with personal competence, freedom from depression, and coping, r(198)=.39, p∠0.01, r(198)=0.35, p∠0.01 and r(198)=0.37, p∠0.01.

Table 13.1 : Inter-correlation of Health Criteria Variables Measured by Questionnaire (N=200)

	Measures	Variables														
		1	2	3	4	5	6	7	8	9	10	11	12	13	14	15
1.	Achievement															
2.	Social contact	.02														
3.	Control	.15	.26**													
4.	Feelings of Happiness in Family	.16	.26**	.38**												
5.	Physical Health	-.09	.04	-.20*	-.07											
6.	Job Involvement	.31**	.09	.24**	.24**	-.10										
7.	Spiritual Quality	.14	.13	.07	.33**	-.02	.11									
8.	Personal Competence	.12	.30**	.56**	.39**	-.05	.30**	.25**								
9.	Social Support	.13	.27**	.11	.21*	.10	.05	.17	.13							
10.	Freedom from Depression	.31**	.23*	.42**	.53**	-.09	.36**	.25**	.53**	.27**						

(Contd...)

11. Autonomy	-.08	.25**	.26**	.28**	.04	.05	.17	.39**	.15	.22*					
12. Trust	.13	.09	.16	.22*	.05	.01	.08	.15	.15	21*	.05				
13. Coping	.10	.34**	.47**	.30**	.08	.19*	.22*	.56**	.11	.44**	.21*	.17			
14. Person Morale	.09	.30**	.45**	.44**	-.05	.29**	.17	.52**	.15	.46**	.37**	.19*	.31**		
15. Freedom from Anxiety	.22**	.14	.26**	.26**	-.05	.16	.07	.39**	.0	.35**	.11	.14	.37**	.24**	
16. Overall Mental Health	.33**	.51**	.65**	.67**	-.03	.42**	.38**	.73**	.38**	.72**	.46**	.32**	.64**	.67**	.47**

* p∠.05
** p∠.01

Note: While computing correlation between overall mental health and a variable, scores on that variable have been deducted from total mental health scores.

Although negative correlation coefficients are shown in some cases, all of these coefficients are of near-zero value. The solitary exception is the association between physical health and control, $r\,(198) = -0.20$, $p \angle 0.05$. In view of this single exception, it is shown that there is no contradiction to the predicted pattern of relationship.

A similar pattern is shown with respect to semantic differential technique. In this method, physical health is positively correlated with personal competence, $(198) = 0.38$, $P < 0.01$, and freedom from depression is positively correlated with person morale, $r(198) = 0.41$, $P < 0.01$.

There are some cases of negative relationship. But they show almost near-zero correlations with the solitary exception that feelings of happiness in family is negatively correlated with control, $\underline{r}(198) = -0.29$, $p \angle 0.01$. Considering correlation coefficients obtained on both the measures (questionnaire and semantic differential), the congruency of measures is evinced. Although the results do not yield positive associations in all possible cases, there is no contradictory evidence in the form of negative association with exception of only two cases. Most of the variables are positively related to each other, except the negative relationship between physical health and control when measured by questionnaire technique, and the negative association between feelings of happiness in family and control when measured by semantic differential technique.

However, the relationship between physical health and control is positive and it is in the predicted direction, when semantic differential technique is used, $r(198) = 0.19$, $p \angle 0.05$. Similarly, the association between feelings of happiness in family and control is positive and it is in the expected direction, when questionnaire technique is used, $r(198) = 0.38$, $P < 0.01$.

Furthermore, the examination of relationship between overall mental health and each of the variables provides support towards the predicted pattern of relationship. Its relationship with most of the variables is positive as expected. However, near-zero correlations are obtained only in a few cases. This pattern of predicted relationship is revealed in both the measures of the questionnaire and semantic differential technique. Thus, congruency of measures is largely supported.

Saliency Hypotheses

A basic hypothesis of the present investigation concerns the saliency of criteria. It was hypothesized that mental health is positively related to the satisfaction of criteria that are considered important by an individual. The correlational analysis supports the main hypothesis,

Table 13.2 : Inter-correlation of Health Criteria Variables Measured by Questionnaire (N=200)

	Measures	Variables														
		1	2	3	4	5	6	7	8	9	10	11	12	13	14	15
1.	Personal Competence															
2.	Physical Health	.38**														
3.	Freedom from Anxiety	-.07	-.09													
4.	Person Morale	.21*	.22*	.06												
5.	Freedom frcm Depression	.27**	.10	.02	.41**											
6.	Autonomy	.20*	.02	-.10	.11	.15										
7.	Trust	.25**	.14	.02	.08	.26**	.23**									
8.	Social Support	.08	-.08	.12	.11	.26**	.20*	.15								
9.	Control	.22*	.19*	-.02	.24**	.39**	.14	.10	.24**							
10.	Feeling of Happiness in Family	.12	.14	.08	.16	.28**	.05	.17	-.03	-.29**						
11.	Coping	.07	.13	.23*	.19*	.23*	-.05	.11	.22*	.20*	.31**					
12.	Job Involvement	.01	.08	.09	.01	.19*	-.05	.21*	.0	.20*	.27**	.12				
13.	Social Contact	.21*	.05	-.03	.19*	.27**	.26**	.29**	.43**	.28**	.13	.02	.03			

(Contd...)

Measures	Variables														
	1	2	3	4	5	6	7	8	9	10	11	12	13	14	15
14. Achievement	.22*	.05	-.03	.19*	.30**	.12	.18*	.06	.19*	.25**	.01	.25**	.30**		
15. Spiritual Quality	.16	.08	.15	.05	.11	.06	.11	.18*	.11	.10	.08	.16	.08	.12	
16. Overall Mental Health	.46**	.35**	.20*	.41**	.59**	.36**	.48**	.45**	.54	.48	.43**	.38**	.49**	.44**	.42**

* p∠.05
** p∠.01

Note: While computing correlation between overall mental health and a variable, scores on that variable have been deducted from total mental health scores.

although no support is found pertaining to the lack of relationship between well-being and nonsalient criteria.

Table 13.3

Correlation Coefficients Between Salient Health Criteria Satisfaction and Overall Mental Health Measures

Method Measuring Overall Well-being	*Salient Criteria Satisfaction*	
	Questionnaire	*Semantic Differential*
Questionnaire	.56**	.28**
Semantic Differential	.28**	.54**
Graphic	.17*	.27**

* p∠.05
** p∠.01

Table 13.4

Correlation Coefficients of Non-Salient Health Criteria Satisfaction and Overall Mental health Measures

Method Measuring Overall Well-being	*Non-Salient Criteria Satisfaction*	
	Questionnaire	*SemanticDifferential*
Questionnaire	.62*	.25*
Semantic Differential	.36*	.44*
Graphic	.27*	.06

* p∠.01.

It is important to point out that salient criteria are specific to the specific individuals. Salient criteria in this present study include those conditions that are considered the most important as rated by an individual. Following Part 1 of HBQ identification of each individual's salient criteria (criteria ranked first and second), the extent of satisfaction of these conditions as reported by the individual is determined. The examination of correlation between salient criteria satisfaction and well-being is found to be positive and significant. Similarly, criteria rated fourteenth and fifteenth were considered nonsalient; satisfaction scores on these nonsalient criteria were correlated with overall mental health scores.

Table 13.5
Salient and Nonsalient Criteria Identified by Androgynous and Sex Typed Groups

Groups	*Salient Criteria*	*Non-salient Criteria*
Androgynous Males	Feeling of happiness in family	Coping
	Spiritual quality	Freedom from anxiety
	Achievement	Control
Androgynous Females	Feeling of happiness in family	Coping
	Spiritual quality	Freedom from anxiety
	Achievement	Control
Sex-typed Males	Achievement	Coping
	Job involvement	Control
	Happiness in family	Freedom from anxiety
Sex-typed Females	Achievement	Coping
	Job involvement	Control
	Happiness in family	Freedom from anxiety

The identification of salient and nonsalient criteria of four quasi-experimental groups indicated some interesting features. It is found that androgynous individuals regard feeling of happiness in the family, spiritual quality, and achievement as three most important health criteria. This pattern is observed in the case of both androgynous males and females. However, the sex-typed males and females differ with respect to their priority ratings.

While sex-typed males regard achievement as their topmost health criterion followed by job involvement and feeling of happiness within the family, sex-typed females regard feeling of happiness within the family as their most salient criterion followed by job involvement and achievement. It is interesting to point out that there is uniformity across groups, with respect to nonsalient criteria. All the groups (androgynous males, androgynous females, sex-typed males, and sex-typed females) consider coping, control, and freedom from anxiety as the least important health criteria.

Criteria of Well-Being

The present investigation has employed a number of dimensions as criteria of well-being. The criteria include achievement, social contact, control, feelings of happiness with family, physical health, job involvement, spiritual quality, personal competence, social contact, freedom from depression, autonomy, trust, coping, personal morale, and freedom from anxiety. Accordingly, a Multivariate Analysis of Variance (MANOVA) was performed on well-being criteria ratings obtained from questionnaires. The results indicate a significant effect of sex [Wilks' Lambda (Λ) = 0.88, $F(15, 182) = 1.70, p \angle 0.01$]. However, the result does not show significant effect for orientation [Wilks' Lambda (Λ) = 0.94, $F(15, 182) = 0.84$, n.s.].

Table 13.6

Mean Well-Being Criteria Ratings Obtained from Questionnaire Measure

	Well-Being Criteria	*Groups*			
		AM	*AF*	*STM*	*STF*
1.	Achievement	21.2	20.3	20.9	21.4
2.	Social Contact	31.6	30.7	31.9	30.7
3.	Control	41.9	39.8	43.0	40.7
4.	Feelings of happiness with family	43.7	43.3	43.0	43.1
5.	Physical health	19.8	20.5	20.2	20.4
6.	Job involvement	32.2	33.0	31.1	31.2
7.	Spiritual quality	32.3	32.3	32.0	31.5
8.	Personal competence	42.2	42.2	42.5	39.3
9.	Social support	31.4	31.3	30.9	31.8
10.	Freedom from depression	32.6	32.7	34.3	32.7
11.	Autonomy	33.1	32.1	32.3	32.4
12.	Trust	22.1	22.0	21.2	22.4
13.	Coping	33.2	32.5	33.2	31.2
14.	Person morale	42.4	40.4	41.1	41.0
15.	Freedom from anxiety	20.5	19.5	20.5	19.3
16.	Overall mental health	479.0	469.6	477.5	467.9

AM = Androgynous males   AF = Androgynous females
STM = Sex-typed males   STF = Sex-typed females

Similar pattern of result is shown with respect to ratings obtained on semantic differential measure. The MANOVA performed on such rating shows significant effect of sex [Wilks' Lambda (Λ) = 0.87, $\underline{F}(15, 182) = 1.95, p<0.05$]. But the result does not show significant effect of orientation [Wilks' Lambda (Λ) = 0.93, $F(15, 182) = 1.03$, n.s.]. Similarly, the result also indicates nonsignificant Sex X Orientation effect [Wilks' Lambda (Λ) = 0.89, $F(15, 182) = 1.58$, n.s.].

Table 13.7
Mean Well-Being Criteria Ratings Obtained from Semantic Differential Measure

	Well-Being Criteria	*Groups*			
		AM	*AF*	*STM*	*STF*
1.	Achievement	4.4	4.8	4.7	4.4
2.	Social Contact	4.9	5.1	4.8	5.0
3.	Control	5.0	5.0	5.2	5.5
4.	Feelings of happiness with family	5.5	5.6	5.5	6.0
5.	Physical health	5.2	4.3	5.0	4.9
6.	Job involvement	5.1	4.8	4.8	5.5
7.	Spiritual quality	5.0	5.4	4.8	5.0
8.	Personal competence	5.8	5.6	5.5	5.2
9.	Social support	4.5	4.8	4.8	4.6
10.	Freedom from depression	5.0	5.1	4.9	5.0
11.	Autonomy	4.7	3.9	4.8	4.5
12.	Trust	5.0	5.2	5.1	5.3
13.	Coping	4.3	4.1	4.1	4.7
14.	Person morale	5.3	4.9	5.2	5.0
15.	Freedom from anxiety	3.8	2.9	3.5	3.3
16.	Overall mental health	72.7	71.1	72.5	74.0

AM = Androgynous males AF = Androgynous females STM= Sex-typed males
STF = Sex-typed females.

Thus on the both measures, significant sex difference was indicated, though the effects of orientation and Sex X Orientation were found to be nonsignificant. Specific analyses of variance were considered necessary to identify the domains of sex difference.

Achievement. The analysis of variance (ANOVA) computed on achievement strivings as measured by questionnaire indicates nonsignificant effect for orientation, $\underline{F}(1,196) = 1.19$, n.s.. As shown by Table 13.8, androgynous individuals indicate as much achievement as do sex-typed persons ($M = 20.75$ and 21.15 respectively). With respect to achievement measure obtained from semantic differentials (SD technique), result also does not show significant effect for orientation, $F(1,196) = .04$, n.s. The examination of mean scores shows that androgynous and sex-typed individuals experience same level of achievement ($M = 4.61$ and 4.57 respectively).

Table 13.8
Mean Ratings and Standard Deviations of Androgynous and Sex-Typed Individuals on Achievement

Method	*Groups*	*Androgynous*		*Sex-Typed*		*Combined*
		Mean	*SD*	*Mean*	*SD*	*Mean*
Questionnaire	Male	21.2	3.2	20.9	4.5	21.04
	Female	20.3	3.8	21.4	3.9	20.86
	Combined	20.75	3.45	21.5	4.19	
Semantic Differential	Male	4.4	1.6	4.7	1.5	4.54
	Female	4.8	1.3	4.4	1.4	4.64
	Combined	4.61	1.46	4.57	1.42	

The result does not show significant sex effect for achievement measures obtained from both the techniques, $F(1,196) = 2.22$, n.s., $F(1,196) = 0.23$, n.s.. Males and females report same level of achievement ($M = 21.04$ & 20.86 respectively) on SD measure.

The ANOVA also does not show Sex X Orientation effect for achievement as measured by questionnaire and SD technique, $F(1,196) = .26$, n.s. and $F(1,196) = 3.04$, n.s.

Social Contact. The analysis of variance (ANOVA) computed on social contact of androgynous and sex-typed individuals on questionnaire and SD technique indicates nonsignificant effect for orientation, $F(1,196) = 0.04$, n.s. and $F(1,196) = 0.43$, n.s., respectively.

Table 13.9
Mean Ratings and Standard Deviations of Androgynous and Sex-Typed Individuals on Social Contact

Method	*Groups*	*Androgynous*		*Sex-Typed*		*Combined*
		Mean	*SD*	*Mean*	*SD*	*Mean*
Questionnaire	Male	31.6	4.7	31.9	4.9	31.78
	Female	30.7	5.4	30.7	4.8	30.66
	Combined	31.15	5.03	31.79	4.85	

(Contd...)

(Contd...)

Semantic Differential	Male	4.9	1.7	4.8	1.8	4.85
	Female	5.1	1.5	5.0	1.5	5.04
	Combined	5.02	1.55	4.87	1.64	

So far as the mean scores of androgynous and sex-typed individuals are concerned, these are of undifferentiated levels (*M* = 31.15 & 31.79 respectively) in questionnaire method and (*M* = 5.02 & 4.87 respectively) in semantic differential technique (see Table 13.9).

The result does not show significant sex effect for social contact obtained on both the techniques. $F(1,196) = 2.51$, n.s., $F(1,196) = 0.69$, n.s. Males and females show same level of social contact in questionnaire (*M* = 31.78 & 30.66 respectively) and in SD technique (*M* = 4.85 & 5.04 respectively).

The ANOVA does not show Sex X Orientation effect for social contacts on the measurement by questionnaire and SD technique, $F(1,196) = 0.04$, n.s. and $F(1,196) = 0.02$, n.s., respectively.

Control. The analysis of variance (ANOVA) computed on control (measured by questionnaire) of androgynous and sex-typed individuals indicate nonsignificant effect for orientation, $F(1,196) = 1.12$, n.s. (see Table 11). As shown by Table 13.10, the androgynous individuals indicate as much control as do sex-typed persons (*M* = 40.86 & 41.83 respectively).

On semantic differential technique the ANOVA has shown nonsignificant effect on control for orientation, $F(1,196) = 2.31$, n.s. The androgynous and sex-typed individuals show the same level of control (*M* = 5.03 & 5.36 respectively).

The result of ANOVA computed for control for males and females has shown highly significant sex effect on questionnaire technique, $F(1,196) = 6.01$, P0.<01. The mean scores show that males experience greater control than females (*M* = 42.47 & 40.22). But it is nonsignificant when measured by SD technique, $F(1,196) = 0.36$, n.s.

The examination of mean also show same level of control on SD technique (M = 5.13 & 5.26 respectively).

The ANOVA also does not show sex X orientation effect on questionnaire method, $F(1,196) = 0.00$ and it is also nonsignificant on SD technique, $F(1,196) = 0.48$, n.s.

Table 13.10
Mean Ratings and Standard Deviations of Androgynous and Sex-Typed Individuals on Control

Method	*Groups*	*Androgynous*		*Sex-Typed*		*Combined*
		Mean	*SD*	*Mean*	*SD*	*Mean*
Questionnaire	Male	41.9	6.7	43.0	7.1	42.47
	Female	39.8	5.9	40.7	5.9	40.22
	Combined	40.86	6.32	41.83	6.49	
Semantic Differential	Male	5.0	1.5	5.2	1.4	5.13
	Female	5.0	1.7	5.5	1.5	5.26
	Combined	5.03	1.58	5.36	1.45	

Feelings of Happiness with Family. The analysis of variance (ANOVA) computed on feelings of happiness with family of androgynous and sex-typed individuals shows nonsignificant orientation effect on questionnaire measure, $F(1,196) = 0.05$, n.s., and also nonsignificant effect on SD technique, $F(1,196) = 0.49$, n.s. The androgynous and sex-typed persons show same level of feelings of happiness with family on both the techniques ($M = 43.53$ & 43.31 respectively) (see Table 13.11) and ($M = 5.59$ & 5.75 respectively).

Table 13.11
Mean Ratings and Standard Deviations of Androgynous and Sex-Typed Individuals on Feelings of Happiness in Family

Method	*Groups*	*Androgynous*		*Sex-Typed*		*Combined*
		Mean	*SD*	*Mean*	*SD*	*Mean*
Questionnaire	Male	43.7	6.2	43.0	6.5	43.40
	Female	43.3	6.8	43.1	7.2	43.60
	Combined	43.53	6.47	43.31	6.81	
Semantic Differential	Male	5.5	1.8	5.5	1.7	5.54
	Female	5.6	1.7	6.0	1.2	5.8
	Combined	5.59	1.74	5.75	1.43	

The ANOVA also does not show significant sex effect for the feelings of happiness with family on the above two measures, $F(1,196) = 0.00$, n.s. and $F(1,196) = 1.29$, n.s. The males and females show generally the same level of feelings on both the techniques, ($M = 43.40$ & 43.60, respectively) and ($M = 5.54$ & 5.8 respectively). The analysis of variance computed for sex X orientation has also shown nonsignificant effect for androgynous and sex-typed individuals on questionnaire and SD method, $F(1,196) = 0.28$, n.s. and $F(1,196) = 0.49$, n.s., respectively.

Physical Health. The analysis of variance (ANOVA) computed for physical health in questionnaire method indicates nonsignificant effect for orientation, $F(1, 196) = 0.11$, n.s. and on semantic differential method, it is also nonsignificant, $F(1, 196) = 1.15$, n.s. As shown by Table 13.12, the androgynous and sex-typed individuals also report same magnitude of physical health on both the techniques ($M = 20.16$ & 20.31 respectively) on questionnaire and ($M = 4.72$ & 4.98 respectively) on SD technique.

Table 13.12

Mean Rating and Standard Deviations of Androgynous and Sex-Typed Individuals on Physical Health

Method	*Groups*	*Androgynous*		*Sex-Typed*	*Combined*	
		Mean	*SD*	*Mean*	*SD*	*Mean*
Questionnaire	Male	19.8	2.3	20.2	3.3	20.02
Female	20.5	3.2	20.4	3.7	20.45	
	Combined	20.16	2.73	20.31	3.45	
Semantic	Male	5.2	1.6	5.0	1.6	5.1
Differential	Female	4.3	1.8	4.9	1.8	4.6
Combined	4.72	1.71	4.98	1.67		

The result does not show significant sex effect on physical health on questionnaire method, $F(1, 196) = 0.92$, n.s. However, it is significant on semantic differential technique, $F(1, 196) = 4.25$, $P<0.05$. As shown by Table 13.12, males score higher than do females (M = 5.1 & 4.6 respectively).

The ANOVA does not show sex X orientation effect for physical health on the questionnaire as well as on SD technique, $F(1, 196) = 0.22$, n.s., and $F(1, 196) = 2.45$, n.s., respectively.

Job Involvement. The analysis of variance (ANOVA) computed for job involvement shows a nonsignificant orientation effect on SD technique, $F(1, 196) = 0.43$, n.s. The androgynous and sex-typed individuals indicate same level of job involvement on SD technique (M = 4.97 & 5.14 respectively) (see Table 13.13). The result also indicates nonsignificant effect for orientation, when job involvement is measured by questionnaire method $F(1, 196) = 3.08$, n.s. The examination of mean scores shows that androgynous and sex-typed persons indicate similar levels of involvement (M = 33.03 & 31.15 respectively).

Table 13.13
Mean Rating and Standard Deviations of Androgynous and Sex-Typed Individuals on Job Involvement

Method	*Groups*	*Androgynous*		*Sex-Typed*		*Combined*
		Mean	*SD*	*Mean*	*SD*	*Mean*
Questionnaire	Male	32.0	5.0	31.1	6.1	31.57
	Female	33.0	4.8	31.2	6.0	32.11
	Combined	33.03	4.87	31.15	6.07	
Semantic Differential	Male	5.1	1.8	4.8	1.9	4.96
	Female	4.8	2.0	5.5	1.5	5.15
	Combined	4.97	1.90	5.14	1.70	

The result does not show a significant sex-effect on questionnaire and SDD techniques respectively. $F(1, 196) = 0.47$, n.s. and $F(1, 196) = 0.54$, n.s. The mean score for both males and females on both the techniques show the same level of job involvement (M = 31.57 & 32.11 respectively) (M = 4.96 & 5.15 respectively).

In the computation of ANOVA, it indicates a nonsignificant sex X orientation effect on questionnaire method and it is significant on SD technique. $F(1, 196) = 0.31$, n.s. and $F(1, 196) = 4.16$, $p \angle 0.05$. As depicted by Figure 13.1, with increasing sex-typings of individuals, the job involvement ratings of males decline whereas ratings of females rise.

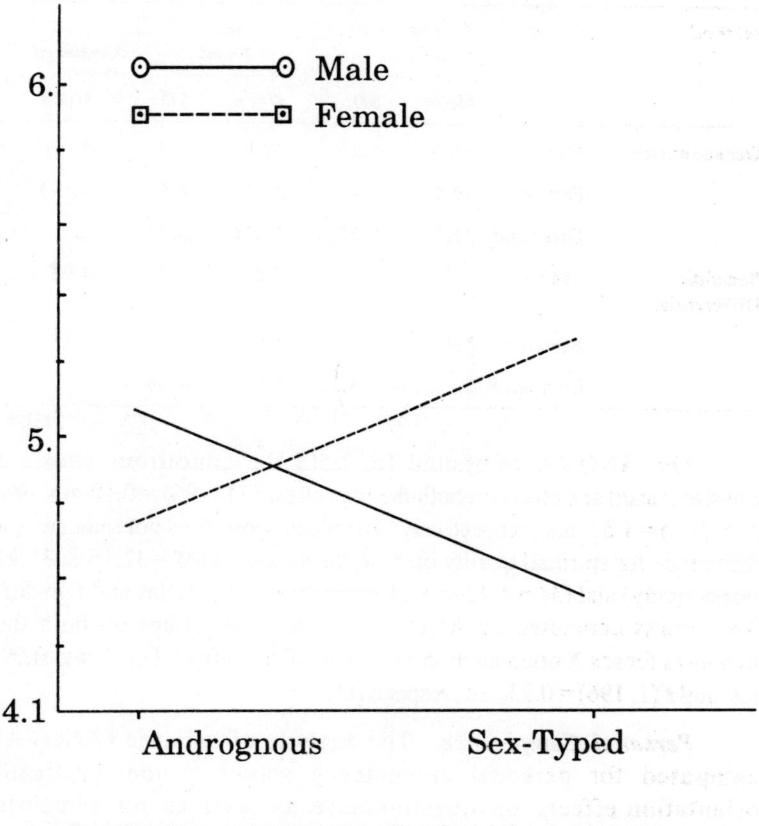

Fig. 13.1. The sex X orientation effect for job-involvement scores.

Spiritual Quality. The analysis of variance (ANOVA) computed on spiritual quality shows a nonsignificant orientation effect on questionnaire and semantic differential technique, $F(1, 196) = 0.64$, n.s. and $F(1,196) = 1.36$, n.s. respectively. The androgynous and sex-typed individual's mean scores show a similar intensity for spiritual quality on both the measures (M = 32.33 & 31.76 respectively) (M = 5.2 & 4.93 respectively) (see Table 13.14).

Table 13.14
Mean Ratings and Standard Deviation of Androgynous and Sex-Typed Individuals on Spiritual Quality

Method	*Groups*	*Androgynous*		*Sex-Typed*		*Combined*
		Mean	*SD*	*Mean*	*SD*	*Mean*
Questionnaire	Male	32.3	5.2	32.0	5.0	32.16
	Female	32.3	4.8	31.5	4.8	31.93
	Combined	32.33	5.05	31.76	4.91	
Semantic Differential	Male	5.0	1.7	4.8	1.8	4.92
	Female	5.4	1.3	5.0	1.5	5.21
	Combined	5.2	1.52	4.93	1.68	

The ANOVA computed for both the conditions shows a nonsignificant sex effect on both the measures, $F(1, 196) = 0.10$, n.s. and $F(1, 196) = 1.57$, n.s., respectively. The mean score does not indicate sex difference for spiritual quality on both the measures (M = 32.16 & 31.93 respectively) and (M = 4.92 & 5.21 respectively) for males and females. The results computed on ANOVA for both the groups on both the measures for sex X orientation show nonsignificant effect, $F(1, 196)= 0.09$, n.s. and $F(1, 196) = 0.23$, n.s., respectively.

Personal Competence. The analysis of variance (ANOVA) computed for personal competence shows a nonsignificant orientation effects on questionnaire as well as on semantic differential technique, $F(1, 196) = 0.13$, n.s. and $F(1, 196) = 2.34$, n.s. The examination of mean scores indicate that androgynous and sex-typed persons show the same magnitude of personal competence on both the techniques (M = 42.21 & 40.91 respectively; M = 5.67 & 5.37 respectively) (see table 13.15).

Table 13.15

Mean Ratings and Standard Deviations of Androgynous and Sex-Typed Individuals on Personal Competence

Method	*Groups*	*Androgynous*		*Sex-Typed*		*Combined*
		Mean	*SD*	*Mean*	*SD*	*Mean*
Questionnaire	Male	42.2	4.8	42.5	6.5	42.37
	Female	42.2	5.7	39.3	5.7	40.75
	Combined	42.21	5.21	40.91	6.09	
Semantic Differential	Male	5.8	1.2	5.5	1.7	5.63
	Female	5.6	1.1	5.2	1.5	5.41
	Combined	5.67	1.15	5.37	1.55	

The result shows a significant sex effect when ANOVA is computed on questionnaire measure. Males show greater personal competence than do females ($M = 42.37$ & 40.75 respectively). But it does not show significant sex effect on SD technique, $F(1, 196) = 1.26$, n.s. The mean scores indicate that males and females show same magnitude for personal competence on SD measure ($M = 5.63$ & 5.41 respectively). As indicated by ANOVA, sex X orientation effect is nonsignificant on both the techniques, $F(1, 196) = 0.57$, n.s., and $F(1, 196) = 0.04$, n.s.

Social Support. The analysis of variance (ANOVA) computed on social support has shown a nonsignificant orientation effect on questionnaire as well as on semantic differential technique, $F(1, 196) = 0.00$, n.s. and $F(1, 196) = 0.02$, n.s.

Table 13.16

Mean Ratings and Standard Deviation of Androgynous and Sex-Typed Individuals on Social Support

Method	*Groups*	*Androgynous*		*Sex-Typed*		*Combined*
		Mean	*SD*	*Mean*	*SD*	*Mean*
Questionnaire	Male	31.4	5.1	30.9	6.0	31.1
	Female	31.3	5.3	31.8	5.4	31.53
	Combined	31.33	5.2	31.36	5.71	
Semantic Differential	Male	4.5	1.7	4.8	1.8	4.65
	Female	4.8	1.9	4.6	1.8	4.69
	Combined	4.65	1.80	4.69	1.76	

Table 13.16 shows that androgynous and sex-typed individuals indicate same amount of social support on both the techniques (M = 31.33 & 31.36 respectively; M = 4.65 & 4.69 respectively).

The result does not show significant sex effect on both the techniques, $F(1, 196) = 0.22$, n.s. and $F(1, 196) = 0.02$, n.s. The mean scores indicate that both the males and females show same magnitude of social support on both the techniques (M = 31.16 & 31.53 respectively) and (M = 4.65 & 4.69 respectively). The ANOVA does not show a significant effect on both techniques when computed for sex X orientation component, $F(1, 196) = 0.43$, n.s. and $F(1, 196) = 0.75$, n.s.

Freedom from Depression. The ANOVA computed on freedom from depression shows a nonsignificant orientation effect on questionnaire and semantic differential techniques, $F(1,196) = 1.08$, n.s. and $F(1, 196) = 0.15$, n.s. The androgynous and sex-typed individuals show the same intensity of the freedom from depression (see Table 13.17) on both the techniques (M = 32.65 & 33.48 respectively; M = 5.03 & 4.94 respectively).

Table 13.17
Mean Ratings and Standard Deviation of Androgynous and Sex-Typed Individuals on Freedom from Depression

Method	*Groups*	*Androgynous*		*Sex-Typed*		*Combined*
		Mean	*SD*	*Mean*	*SD*	*Mean*
Questionnaire	Male	32.6	5.2	34.3	6.1	33.46
	Female	32.7	5.2	32.7	5.8	32.67
	Combined	32.65	5.21	33.48	5.95	
Semantic Differential	Male	5.0	1.4	4.9	1.8	4.94
	Female	5.1	1.6	5.0	1.7	5.03
	Combined	5.03	1.49	4.94	1.74	

The result does not show a significant sex effect on questionnaire and semantic differential techniques (see Table 13.17), $F(1, 196) = 0.98$, n.s. and $F(1, 196) = 0.15$, n.s. The males and females show same level of the freedom from depressive tendency on both the techniques (M = 33.46 & 32.67 respectively; and M = 4.94 & 5.03 respectively). The ANOVA does not show Sex X Orientation effect on freedom from depression as measured by questionnaire and semantic differential technique, $F(1, 196) = 1.03$, n.s. and $F(1, 196) = 0.02$, n.s.

Autonomy. The analysis of variance performed on the effect of autonomy shows a nonsignificant orientation effect on questionnaire and semantic differential technique, $F(1, 196) = 0.10$, n.s. and $F(1, 196) = 1.58$, n.s. As shown by Table 13.18, the androgynous individuals and sex-typed individuals indicate same level of autonomy on both the techniques (M = 32.57 & 32.38 respectively; M = 4.33 & 4.64 respectively).

Table 13.18

Mean Ratings and Standard Deviation of Androgynous and Sex-Typed Individuals on Autonomy

Method	*Groups*	*Androgynous*		*Sex-Typed*		*Combined*
		Mean	*SD*	*Mean*	*SD*	*Mean*
Questionnaire	Male	33.1	4.6	32.3	4.8	32.71
	Female	32.1	3.6	32.4	4.2	32.24
	Combined	32.57	4.1	32.38	4.9	
Semantic Differential	Male	4.7	1.8	4.8	1.8	4.76
	Female	3.9	1.6	4.5	1.7	4.21
	Combined	4.33	1.69	4.64	1.45	

The result does not show a significant sex effect on questionnaire method, $F(1, 196) = 0.58$, n.s., but it is significant when measured by SD technique, $F(1, 196) = 4.96$, $p \angle 0.05$.

The examination of mean scores indicates that males and females show same level of autonomous activities when measured by questionnaire method ($M = 32.71$ & 32.24 respectively). However, males report greater autonomous activity than females when the measurement involves SD technique ($M = 4.76$ & 4.21 respectively). The ANOVA does not show Sex X Orientation effect on both the techniques, $F(1,196) = 0.79$, n.s. and $F(1, 196) = 0.87$, n.s.

Trust. The analysis of variance computed on trust as measured by questionnaire and semantic differential technique indicate a nonsignificant effect for orientation, $F(1, 196) = 0.20$, n.s., and $F(1, 196) = 0.11$, n.s. The examination of mean indicates that the androgynous individuals as well as sex-typed individuals show same amount of trust on both the techniques (see Table 13.19) ($M = 22.03$ & 21.8 respectively; $M = 5.11$ & 5.19 respectively). The result does not show a significant sex effect on questionnaire as well as on semantic differential technique, $F(1, 196) = 1.20$, n.s., and $F(1,196) = 0.54$, n.s. The mean scores indicate same amount of trust on both the methods ($M = 21.63$ & 22.2; $M = 5.06$ & 5.24 respectively). The ANOVA does not show a significant Sex X Orientation effect on both the techniques, $F(1,196) = 1.66$, n.s. and $F(1, 196) = 0.00$, n.s.

Table 13.19

Mean Ratings and Standard Deviations of Androgynous and Sex-Typed Individuals on Trust

Method	*Groups*	*Androgynous*		*Sex-Typed*		*Combined*
		Mean	*SD*	*Mean*	*SD*	*Mean*
Questionnaire	Male	22.1	3.7	21.2	4.0	21.63
	Female	22.0	3.4	22.4	3.5	22.2
	Combined	22.03	3.53	21.8	3.74	
Semantic Differential	Male	5.0	1.9	5.1	1.6	5.06
	Female	5.2	1.8	5.3	1.5	5.24
	Combined	5.11	1.83	5.19	1.59	

Coping. Analysis of variance performed on coping effectiveness has shown a nonsignificant orientation effect on questionnaire and semantic differential technique, $F(1, 196) = 0.19$, n.s., and $F(1, 196) = 0.37$, n.s.. As shown by Table 13.20, the androgynous individuals indicate as much effective coping as do sex-typed persons (M = 31.87 & 32.19 respectively; M = 4.22 & 4.37 respectively).

Table 13.20

Mean Ratings and Standard Deviations of Androgynous and Sex-Typed Individuals on Coping

Method	*Groups*	*Androgynous*		*Sex-Typed*		*Combined*
		Mean	*SD*	*Mean*	*SD*	*Mean*
Questionnaire	Male	33.2	4.7	33.2	5.7	33.2
	Female	30.5	4.6	31.2	5.4	30.86
	Combined	31.87	4.67	32.19	5.55	
Semantic Differential	Male	4.3	1.7	4.1	1.9	4.19
	Female	4.1	1.7	4.7	1.5	4.4
	Combined	4.22	1.73	4.37	1.7	

When measured by questionnaire technique, the result shows highly significant sex effect, $F(1, 196) = 10.20$, $p \angle .01$. The males show greater effective coping than females, (M = 33.2 & 30.86 respectively). It is nonsignificant on SD technique $F(1, 196) = 0.73$, n.s.. Males and females indicate same level of coping effectiveness (M=4.19 & 4.4 respectively). The ANOVA does not show the significant Sex X Orientation effect on both the technique, $F(1, 196) = 0.30$, n.s. and $F(1, 196) = 2.26$, n.s.

Person Morale. The analysis on variance (ANOVA) computed for person morale indicates a non-significant orientation effect on both the techniques, $F(1,196) = 0.25$, n.s., and $F(1,196) = 0.05$, n.s. As shown by Table 13.21, the androgynous individuals show as much person morale as do sex-typed individuals (M=41.43 & 41.03 respectively; M=5.06 & 5.10 respectively.)

Table 13.21

Mean Ratings and Standard Deviations of Androgynous and Sex-Typed Individuals on Person Morale

Method	*Groups*	*Androgynous*		*Sex-Typed*		*Combined*
		Mean	*SD*	*Mean*	*SD*	*Mean*
Questionnaire	Male	42.4	5.3	41.1	5.9	41.74
	Female	40.4	5.2	41.0	6.0	40.72
	Combined	41.43	5.24	41.03	5.97	
Semantic Differential	Male	5.3	1.4	5.2	1.8	5.26
	Female	4.8	1.7	5.0	1.5	4.90
	Combined	5.06	1.56	5.10	1.65	

The result does not show a significant sex effect for person morale on questionnaire and semantic differential technique, $F(1, 196) = 1.62$, n.s. and $F(1, 196) = 2.31$, n.s. The examination of mean score indicates that the males and females show same amount of person morale on both the techniques (M = 41.24 & 40.72 respectively; M = 5.26 & 4.90 respectively). The ANOVA does not show a significant Sex X Orientation effect as measured by questionnaire and semantic differential technique, $F(1, 196) = 1.43$, n.s. and $F(1, 196) = 0.42$, n.s.

Freedom from Anxiety. The analysis of variance (ANOVA) computed has shown a nonsignificant orientation effect for freedom from anxiety, $F(1, 196) = 0.02$, n.s. and $F(1, 196) = 0.00$, n.s. The examination of mean scores indicates that androgynous as well as sex-typed individuals show the same level of the freedom from anxiety on both the techniques, ($M = 20.00$ & 19.91 respectively; $M = 3.35$ & 3.37 respectively).

Table 13.22

Mean Ratings and Standard Deviations of Androgynous and Sex-Typed Individuals on Person Morale

Method	*Groups*	*Androgynous*		*Sex-Typed*		*Combined*
		Mean	*SD*	*Mean*	*SD*	*Mean*
Questionnaire	Male	20.5	3.5	20.5	4.8	20.52
Female	19.5	4.6	19.3	4.7	19.39	
	Combined	20.0	4.07	19.91	4.74	
Semantic Differential	Male	3.8	1.7	3.5	1.9	3.62
	Female	2.9	1.8	3.3	1.7	3.1
	Combined	3.35	1.71	3.37	1.8	

The result shows a significant sex effect on the questionnaire technique, $F(1, 196) = 3.18$, n.s. The mean scores indicate that same level of freedom from anxiety are reported by males and females ($M = 20.52$ & 19.39 respectively). It is significant on SD technique, $F(1,196) = 4.28$, $p \angle 0.01$. The mean score indicates that males experience more freedom from anxiety than females ($M = 3.62$ & 3.1 respectively). The ANOVA does not show a significant Sex X Orientation effect on both the methods, $F(1, 196) = 0.00$, n.s. and $F(1, 196) = 1.83$, n.s.

Overall Mental Health. The analysis of variance computed on overall mental health as measured by questionnaire method and semantic differential technique do not show a significant orientation effect, $F(1, 196) = .08$, n.s., and $F(1, 196) = 0.73$, n.s. The androgynous as well as sex-typed individuals show same level of overall mental health on both the methods (M = 474.32 & 472.68 respectively; M = 71.89 & 73.25 respectively).

Table 13.23

Mean Ratings and Standard Deviation of Androgynous and Sex-Typed Individuals on Overall Mental Health

Method	*Groups*	*Androgynous*		*Sex-Typed*		*Combined*
		Mean	*SD*	*Mean*	*SD*	*Mean*
Questionnaire	Male	479.0	36.6	477.5	41.9	478.23
	Female	469.6	35.8	467.9	45.5	468.77
	Combined	474.32	36.21	472.68	43.72	
Semantic Differential	Male	72.7	11.2	72.5	11.8	72.59
	Female	71.1	10.1	74.0	11.4	72.55
	Combined	71.89	10.64	73.25	11.60	

The ANOVA computed (questionnaire method) shows a trend for sex effect although the value does not reach the level of significance ($p \angle 0.10$). Males tend to experience greater well-being than do females (M = 478.23 & 468.77 respectively). Yet the ANOVA does not show significant sex effect on semantic differential technique, $F(1, 196) = 0.00$, n.s. The examination of mean scores shown on SD technique indicates similar magnitude of well-being for male and females (M = 72.59 & 72.55 respectively). The ANOVA shows a nonsignificant Sex X Orientation effect on both the techniques, $F(1, 196) = 0.00$, n.s., and $F(1, 196) = 0.99$, n.s.

The analysis of variance computed on graphic ratings of overall mental health indicates a nonsignificant orientation effect, $F(1, 196) = 0.37$, n.s. As shown by Table 13.24, the androgynous as well as the sex-typed individuals report same level of overall mental health (M = 4.68 & 4.8 respectively).

Table 13.24

Mean Ratings and Standard Deviations of Androgynous and Sex-Typed Individuals on Mental Health (Graphic)

Method	*Groups*	*Androgynous*		*Sex-Typed*		*Combined*
		Mean	*SD*	*Mean*	*SD*	*Mean*
Questionnaire	Male	4.5	1.4	4.8	1.4	4.65
	Female	4.8	1.4	4.8	1.4	4.85
	Combined	4.68	1.37	4.8	1.38	

The ANOVA does not show a significant sex effect, $F(1, 196) = 0.84$, n.s.. The mean scores indicate that both males and females show same amount of overall mental health ($M = 4.65$ & 4.85, respectively). The result reveals a nonsignificant Sex X Orientation effect, $F(1,196) = 0.26$, n.s. No significant main effect is shown for overall mental health measured by graphic method. The Sex X Orientation effect is also nonsignificant.

Group Difference on Criteria Saliency

The study employs a multi-criteria approach. Since the criteria have been ranked by respondents, it is possible to identify salient health criteria of an individual. For the present study, salient criteria have been identified as those two criteria that have been ranked first and second by an individual. On the contrary, nonsalient criteria have been identified as those criteria that have been ranked 14th and 15th by an individual. In other words, salient health criteria score is the sum of satisfaction scores across two salient criteria of an individual. Similarly, nonsalient criteria scores is the sum of scores across two nonsalient criteria of an individual.

Salient Health Criteria. The analysis of variance computed for salient health criteria shows a nonsignificant effect for orientation on questionnaire technique $F(1,196) = 0.72$, n.s. As shown in Table 13.25, the androgynous and sex-typed individuals show same level of salient health criteria on the questionnaire technique ($M = 134.44$ & 132.04, respectively).

Table 13.25

Mean Ratings and Standard Deviations of Androgynous and Sex-Typed Individuals on Salient Health Criteria

Method	*Groups*	*Androgynous*		*Sex-Typed*		*Combined*
		Mean	*SD*	*Mean*	*SD*	*Mean*
Questionnaire	Male	134.3	21.3	133.1	20.6	133.71
	Female	134.5	15.3	131.0	21.5	132.77
	Combined	134.44	18.25	132.04	21.02	

The computation of ANOVA indicates nonsignificant sex effect on questionnaire technique, $F(1, 196) = 0.11$, n.s. The examination of mean scores shows that males and females report same level of salient criteria ($M = 133.71$ & 132.77 respectively). The ANOVA does not show a significant sex x orientation effect, $F(1, 196) = 0.16$, n.s.

Nonsalient Health Criteria. The analysis of variance computed on nonsalient health criteria as measured by questionnaire technique indicates a significant orientation effect, $F(1, 196) = 4.49$. $P \angle 0.05$. As shown by Table 13.26, the sex-typed individuals show greater satisfaction of non-salient health criteria than androgynous persons ($M = 126.03$ & 131.10 respectively).

Table 13.26
Mean Ratings and Standard Deviations of Androgynous and Sex-Typed Individuals on Nonsalient Health Criteria

Method	*Groups*	*Androgynous*		*Sex-Typed*		*Combined*
		Mean	*SD*	*Mean*	*SD*	*Mean*
Questionnaire	Male	127.5	15.2	132.4	18.9	129.94
	Female	124.6	15.3	129.7	16.7	127.15
	Combined	126.03	14.24	131.10	17.82	

The result does not show a significant sex effect, $F(1, 196) = 1.38$, n.s. The examination of mean score shows that males and females report same amount of satisfaction of nonsalient health criteria (M = 129.94 & 127.15 respectively). The ANOVA does not show a Sex X Orientation effect, $F(1, 196) = 0.00$, n.s.

Socio-Demographic Variables

While androgyny constitutes the focal variable, attention is however directed to the investigation of the role of socio-demographic features. Two such features are considered: age and education (see Table 13.27 & 13.28).

Table 13.27

Correlation Between Age and Health Criteria Measures Obtained from All Participants

Health Criteria Measures		*Method of Measurement*	
		Questionnaire	*Semantic Differential*
1.	Achievement	.02	.11
2.	Social Contact	.05	-.04
3.	Control	.09	.08
4.	Feelings of Happiness in Family	.00	-.01
5.	Physical Health	-.26*	.06
6.	Job Involvement	.14	.14
7.	Spiritual Quality	.06	.00
8.	Personal Competence	.04	.08
9.	Social Support	-.03	.02
10.	Freedom from Depression	.08	-.04
11.	Autonomy	-.03	.07
12.	Trust	.00	.00
13.	Coping	.15	.03
14.	Person Morale	.08	-.07
15.	Freedom from Anxiety	.05	.16
16.	Overall Mental Health	.08	.10

*p∠.05.

Age. The results indicate that age tends to the positively related with job involvement and coping, when measured by questionnaire technique. Age also tends to be related with job involvement, when semantic differential technique is used. With semantic differential technique, trend for positive association between age and achievement and between age and freedom from anxiety are shown. Only with semantic differential technique age tends to be positively related to overall mental health. Thus, with increasing age, people tend to indicate increasing level of achievement, job involvement, coping effectiveness, and freedom from anxiety. As expected, the negative relationship between age and physical health is shown. However, age is found to be unrelated to most other variables.

Table 13.28

Correlation Between Education and Health Criteria Measures Obtained from All Participants

Health Criteria Measures	*Method of Measurement*	
	Questionnaire	*Semantic Differential*
Achievement	- 0.01	0.17
Social Contact	0.16	0.03
Control	0.00	0.06
Feelings of Happiness in Family	0.07	0.00
Physical Health	- 0.17	0.05
Job Involvement	0.04	0.10
Spiritual Quality	0.17	0.11
Personal Competence	0.09	0.22
Social Support	-0.03	0.09
Freedom from Depression	0.05	0.05
Autonomy	-0.02	-0.03
Trust	0.06	0.03
Coping	0.11	-0.07
Person Morale	0.10	0.04
Freedom from Anxiety	0.09	0.09
Overall Mental Health	0.11	0.13

Education. The examination of relationship between education and health criteria measure yields trend for the positive relationship between spiritual quality and education when spiritual quality is measured by both the techniques. With questionnaire technique, trend for positive association of education with social contact, coping effectiveness, and person morale is shown. With semantic differential technique, trend for positive association of education with achievement, job involvement, and personal competence is shown. However, the trend for negative relationship between physical health and education is indicated on questionnaire technique. This implies that increasing level of education tends to be associated with greater achievement, job involvement, spiritual quality, personal competence, coping effectiveness and person morale. In addition, education also tends to be positively related with overall mental health.

Summary of Result

The health behaviour questionnaire employed in the study involves a number of sub-scales for various criteria. It is observed that when all participants are taken into consideration, a positive relationship is found amongst various sub-scales. Two exceptional cases include the negative association between physical health and control as measured by questionnaire and the negative relationship between feelings of happiness in family and control as measured by SD technique. All the criteria are positively intercorrelated excepting these two cases. Moreover the criteria are also positively associated with the overall psychological well-being. Thus, the congruency of measures is shown with respect to the efficacy of the health behaviour questionnaire.

The examination of group differences indicates a number of features when measured by questionnaire technique. Males score higher on control, coping, and personal competence. Males also show greater autonomy, freedom from anxiety, and physical health than females when criteria are measured by semantic differential.

On overall mental health measurement, males tend to show greater well-being than females on questionnaire technique although the difference was not statistically significant. There is no significant sex difference when overall mental health is measured by SD technique as well as by graphic design.

The group variation across androgynous and sex-typed individuals indicate that the androgynous individuals and the sex-typed individuals do not differ significantly with respect to well-being criteria. This is shown on both types of measures.

With respect to socio-demographic variables, the role of two important dimensions namely education and age is analysed. The relationship between educational level and health criteria has been examined for the entire group. The pattern of correlational data shows trends for positive relationship of education with achievement, social contact, job involvement, spiritual quality, personal competence, coping effectiveness and person morale. However, negative trend for relationship between physical health and education is shown. Moreover, the trend for positive association between education and overall health is indicated.

Furthermore, the examination of relationship between age and health criteria shows trends for positive relationship of age with achievement, job involvement, coping effectiveness, and freedom from anxiety. It has negative relationship with physical health. Its trends for positive association with overall mental health is indicated when SD technique is used.

14
Findings and Implications

The empirical findings generated from this study offer a number of salient features. These features are explainable in terms of the current status of the construct of androgyny. The role of Indian socio-cultural context is also manifest in these findings. Prior to discussion of the conceptual explanations, significant aspects of the measuring instrument and the hypotheses relating to criterion saliency need detailed exposition.

Congruency of Measures

The instrument of health behaviour is based on the premise that psychological well-being has a number of indicators. Since all these indicators have been expressed in positive terms, significant associations amongst these indicators are predicted. The pattern of data supports such expectation. When all participants are taken into consideration, the correlation coefficients between each of the pairs of the indicators is significant. However, there are a few cases of near-zero correlations. The exception involves negative relationship between physical health and control as measured by questionnaire and negative association between feelings of happiness in family and control as measured by semantic differential technique. A similar pattern emerges when coefficients of correlation are carried out for different groups.

On the whole, similar measures cohere or cluster together. Overall mental health is positively related with most of the health criteria variables.

While the psychometric efficacy of the health behaviour questionnaire has been reported elsewhere (Sahoo, 1990b), the present investigation offers further support regarding its robustness. It is shown that different criteria not only cohere positively amongst themselves, these indicators are also positively related to overall mental health. Furthermore, the techniques of questionnaire and semantic differentials interrelate significantly. The exceptional case of physical health may be explained in terms of the worldview of Indians. Although the programmes of physical fitness are entering into the day-to-day life events of Indians, it has not yet crystallized as a stable indicator of psychological health.

Criterion Saliency

The hypothesis of criterion saliency is partly supported. Although people regard several indicators of mental health, it is likely that salient criteria have greater bearing on their well-being. While satisfaction of all the indicators is ideal for the maintenance of complete well-being, it may not be feasible to attain all indicators. The constraint of resources and conditions may help to moderate people's ambition. With such perception and consideration, individuals may try to feel well when salient criteria are satisfied.

The hypotheses relating to nonsalient criteria predicted the absence of relationship between nonsalient criteria satisfaction and well-being. However, contrary to our expectation, positive association is shown between nonsalient criteria satisfaction and well-being. This discrepancy between hypotheses and finding can be explained. Although respondents have been asked to rate different indicators using serial numbers from 1 to 15, the gap between ratings may be too small to be perceived psychologically different. It can be conjectured that the nonsalient needs are nevertheless not unimportant needs. Considered from this angle, a positive relationship between nonsalient need satisfaction and well-being is not unlikely.

The Sex Differences

The result indicates that males and females differ on several aspects. It is seen from this result that males are better than females on control, autonomy, coping, person morale, personal competence, freedom from anxiety and overall mental health. Males also score higher on physical health.

Coping refers to cognitive and behavioural efforts to master, reduce or tolerate the internal and external demands that are created by stressful transaction (Folkman & Lazarus, 1980). That is, coping refers to the efforts to manage demands regardless of the success of those efforts. Coping is viewed in this formulation as having two major functions; the regulation of emotions or distress (emotion-focused coping) and the management of the problem that is causing distress (problem-focused coping). These two functions of coping have been recognized by numerous investigators (e.g., Kahn, Wolfe, Quinn & Snock, 1964) and have long been implicitly recognized by clinicians (Folkman & Lazarus, 1980).

Coping (and by implication stress) is determined by a secondary appraisal process in which people attempt to determine whether or not they have at their disposal the resources necessary to deal with the threat successfully.

The pertinent literature on coping has indicated that males employ direct forms of coping such as confrontation and problem-solving, whereas women use indirect and avoidant forms of coping such as denial and sleeping and it has also been shown that direct forms of coping are more efficacious than avoidant forms of coping (Folkman & Lazarus, 1980).

In nutshell, the literature pertaining to coping styles clearly indicates sex-difference at least in general population. The sex-difference may be narrowed in college population. In general, as pointed out by Lazarous and Folkman, men use direct forms of coping and women use indirect forms. This observation is consistent with the findings of the present study.

The finding that males experience greater freedom from anxiety compared with females is consistent with contemporary literature relating to sex-related clinical symptoms. The clinical psychologists using MMPI (Minnessota Multiphasic Personality Inventory) have largely documented that women more often than men report anxiety attacks and depressive symptoms. Some investigators have attempted to explain this difference in terms of neurophysiological terms as indicated in the context of competence. Apart from neurophysiological explanations, a few other factors appear relevant for this sex-difference. In the present study, women participants are working females. It is plausible that these women encounter role conflict and role-related stress while performing dual functions at home and work. The role conflict and role-related stress are likely to induce anxiety in women.

Similarly, working women are likely to find it difficult to register satisfaction in both the domains of work and family. The increasing gap between achievement and aspiration seems to generate depression in women. Thus, socio-cultural and sociological factors offer some explanations for an understanding of anxiety of women.

A number of studies within the framework of sex-role literature provide implicit assumption that males demonstrate greater job competence than females. Bakan's (1966) concept of agentic nature of males and communal features of women point towards such assumption. Similarly, Parson and Bales's (1955) view of affective/expressive domain in women and instrumentality of men provide further support to such contention. The recent neurophysiological studies have shown that when men and women experience similar brain injury, men take it longer to get back to earlier level of functioning. This has an implication that men have higher specialization and this specialization has representation in the brain, so that any damage makes it difficult for the association area to take over the function. Considered from this angle, greater professional competence of men compared to women is a likely phenomenon. This has also been supported by male's greater perception of their own competence.

Overall Mental Health

Thus, superiority of males over females with respect to psychological well-being is not without research evidence. Although the advantage of males over females has not been indicated on each of the criterion, it has been shown on a number of dimensions such as control and coping. However, this should not be interpreted as an irreversible process. This could be explained in terms of the disadvantaged conditions in which women have been placed for centuries. Furthermore, the difference has implicated the role of several variables that would be discussed later.

The group differences are also examined with respect to orientation. No significant difference is indicated with respect to any other criterion, although western studies predict superiority of androgynous individuals over sex-typed persons.

As an expression of balanced individuality, androgyny represents a willingness to abandon traditional sex-role ideals to accept role prescriptions for a more flexible, situation-appropriate mode of behaving which can incorporate either or both masculine and feminine attributes. Such individuals can be independent and capable of leading others (masculine) yet nurturant (feminine) and sensitive to others. The androgynous individuals emphasize adaptive behaviour pattern, as they are free from rigid behaviour standards for their sex and rely upon what is appropriate for the specific situation. According to Bem (1974, 1975), androgynous persons are conceptually interesting, because they are not constrained by sex-role stereotypes about what kinds of behaviours are differentially more appropriate for men and women. These persons seem less constrained by sex-role stereotypes in their preferences for task activities. These results have implication for behaviour in natural work settings, especially where jobs that have traditionally been associated with only one sex are or might become occupied by persons of either sex. Because androgynous persons are presumably less constrained by sex-role stereotypes, their attitudes and reactions towards persons in jobs unusual for their sex are likely to be different from those persons who are not androgynous.

Motowidlo (1982) examined the relationship between sex-role orientation and behaviour in a work setting. The study indicated that highly androgynous persons showed more acceptance of non-traditional job change and supported persons in non-traditional jobs.

The pertaining literature on work motivation suggests that the work involved persons have generally high self-esteem and better self-concept (Hosek, 1976; Vroom, 1964), and they enjoy more satisfaction out of their work. Since androgynous individuals experience high self-esteem and better self-concept, it is quite plausible to expect androgynous persons to be more work involved and satisfied in comparison to the sex-typed individuals. In the present study, the androgynous individuals indicate as much job involvement as do the sex-typed individuals. In Indian context, Sahoo and Rout conducted a study (1990). They investigated employees (males/ females) of various public sector enterprises and educational institutions of State of Orissa. The fact that a greater degree of adaptation to the demands of work setting helps androgynous individuals to experience satisfaction was indicated. It implied that with a combination of instrumental and expressive orientation, and high self-esteem, behavioural flexibility and cross-sex behaviour, androgynous individuals experience greater motivation towards work situations, and finally, they are more involved in their work life. Despite such expectation of greater job involvement in androgynous individuals, no significant difference was found in the present study.

It is generally recognised that the developing status of Indian society implies more and more flexibility of the social system. However, the flexibility has not yet been so pronounced that sex-typed individuals would lose their relative advantages over androgynous persons. In other words, sex-typed individuals continue to have certain benefits in Indian society as they were having in the past.

An important objective of the study concerns sex role orientation. Studies carried out in Euro-American context suggested greater well-being of androgynous individuals compared with sex-typed persons. Although similar prediction was hypothesized in the present study, the analysis of data did not support such a prediction. There are several socio-cultural conditions that may account for such lack of difference between androgynous and sex-typed groups.

First, the social change in modern India is not even across several parts of India (Srinivas, 1992). There are regions in India where urbanization and industrialization have taken deep roots. Yet, there are regions where traditional forms of living are prevalent. The other contexts are transitional where traditional pattern is changing into new ways.

The changing socio-cultural profile of Orissa represents a transitional setting (Ray, 1989). Except a few industrialized pockets, it exhibits a transitional pattern where pace of change is very slow. In such a sociocultural system, the androgynous individuals are unlikely to experience greater advantage than sex-typed individuals because of the lack of fit between their orientation and societal change. Perhaps the social climate of Orissa has not been modernized to the extent of placing androgynous individuals in certain advantageous positions. Dutta Das and Basu (1995) found that androgynous individuals themselves did not indicate more modern attitude towards sex roles than other persons.

Second, India is basically a plural society. The diversity of languages, religions and ethnicity has created a complex mosaic. Dube (1990) notes the plural features of Indian society and concludes that change of sex role attitudes has taken different pace in various parts of India.

Although the present study does not indicate difference between androgynous and sex-typed groups in Orissan context, different findings may emerge in other subcultural setting. An adequate generalization can be drawn only when the study is carried out in several subcultural contexts of India. The examination of the hypothesis in a number of contexts that vary in industrialization and urbanization would be very helpful in these respects.

The observation that males indicate greater well-being than females is consistent with our expectation. Women's dual involvement in work and family has been recognised as a complicating factor. Asha (1994) has cited evidence in Indian context. It has been recognized that expectations and demands placed on women are greater owing to their role multiplicity. More specifically working women in India encounter rigid norms with respect to their family obligations. Deviations from such obligations are not tolerated.

At the same time, coping mechanisms used by women are not efficacious. Dang and Gupta (1994) have reported greater role-stress in women in India. The analysis of coping mechanisms reveals that women use emotional forms of coping whereas men use problem-solving styles of coping (Jai Prakash & Bhogle, 1994). Jai Prakash and Bhogle (1994) have also documented the positive relationship between emotional (avoidant) coping and psychological distress and negative association between problem-solving coping and distress. Considered from this angle, women are expected to experience more distress and less well-being in comparison with males. The present finding has supported this generalization.

Thus, the main findings are conceivable in light of the social structure of Orissa and socialization practices adopted in this subcultural system.

Implications

The present study has offered a number of implications. The examination of interrelationship of different criteria has shown that the criteria are interrelated. The solitary exception involves the case of physical health. In India, the programmes for physical fitness have started to gain momentum. Although it has not yet stabilized itself as an important criterion, it is likely to be considered as a significant dimension in the coming years. Consequently, the change agents should not exclude this from the health inducing programmes.

The study has further supported criterion saliency hypothesis. It implies that the satisfaction of health criteria which are regarded important by individuals is related to overall well-being. However, it goes without saying that the satisfaction of all the criteria of health presents the ideal conditions. Yet, this is difficult to attain owing to the lack of resources. In view of resource constraints, the policy-maker may identify the salient health criteria in a given sub-set of human population and can mobilize their resources for the attainment of these criteria.

While superiority of androgynous individuals over sex-typed persons has been documented in several domains in the context of the western settings, no such overall advantage in the favour of androgynous individuals has been shown in the present study.

The observation that males indicate a greater degree of control, autonomy, personal competence, coping effectiveness and freedom from anxiety than females is significant from an applied point of view. More recently, the concepts of control and autonomy have been regarded as important elements in contemporary life. A feedback is necessary to enhance the perception of control. Through various control-enhancing programmes (for example, women should be placed in more responsible jobs) women will develop decision-making ability. Different care-giving activities should be given to them for the enhancement of control. Responsibilities in various spheres besides their home boundaries will make them independent and thereby they will develop stable self-concept that can incorporate both masculine and feminine characteristics. Moreover, they can choose and adopt personally satisfying behaviour without relying upon sex-based prescriptions. This will enable them to make life decisions. although females indicate less control and autonomy by various intervention programmes. A number of responsibility-inducing programmes can be suggested for women's training.

Similarly, the difficulties with respect to coping with anxiety and undesirable life events by women can be reduced. Research evidence in the area of coping has shown that females more often than males use avoidant forms of coping which are less efficacious. These coping forms are indirect such as denial, sleeping, and social support. On the contrary, males use direct and efficacious forms of coping such as confrontation, planned problem-solving, and analysis of alternatives. Since the present study has indicated difficulties of women in the areas of coping effectiveness and freedom from anxiety, suitable training programmes in the form of stimulating direct coping strategies need to be directed for women.

The evidence of overall mental health in favour of males also has some implication for women's training programmes. It is possible that women in our society are placed in several conflicting roles. The learning and educational material used in our socio-cultural system need to be adapted to train women and to reduce the severity of their problems. In other words, the educational policy requires a reformulation with a view to providing adjustment skills for women.

Directions for Future Research

The highlights of the present study offer a number of insights. The empirical associations have been shown in an important area of social inquiry. While such inquiry provides conceptual and applied leads in this area, the possibilities of exploration in several key issues lie in the future lines of investigation.

The participating individuals for this investigation are taken from educational institutions. This study is confined to limited settings. While restrictions on the sampling frame is admitted, the findings derived serve useful purposes. It is useful in formulating a few hunches and hypotheses for the future. Future study may be conducted including the participants from varied locations. It is very likely that the relationship between sex role orientation and well-being is influenced by the social context in which individuals find themselves. It is also a social fact that the context shows great variation in India along the dimensions of urban-rural differences, tribal-nontribal dimensions, and educated-uneducated dimensions. Consequently, it would be more scientific to expand the sampling frame. The sampling frame should be expanded to include various criteria such as castes and other population-related factors. Furthermore, because of limited number of studies in this particular field in Indian context, varied locations of setting would have been a hindrance to formulate a hypothesis.

Therefore, the conditions of setting were made uniform so that exact hypothesis could be examined properly.

The participating individuals have been asked to provide self-descriptions, and accordingly data are collected. There are various problems like social desirability and response set. In general, no supremacy of androgynous individual vis-à-vis sex-typed persons has been shown. The lack of difference between androgynous and sex-typed individuals with respect to health criteria is explainable in terms of the prevailing traditional pattern of India society; more fine-grained studies are needed to examine the hypotheses.

In this study, a number of criteria are employed and two techniques (questionnaire and semantic differential technique) are used. The varied number of criteria and two different techniques of measurement are likely to eliminate some of the problems of self-report method. However, an inclusion of other methods such as observation would improve methodological rigour in future.

While examining the relationship between androgyny and well-being, a number of critical factors may be considered in the future. It is important to recognize that India is a plural society. It has also several levels of transformations. Broadly, one can encounter three levels of transformations, traditional, transitional and modern. It is plausible that androgyny may have different patterns of relationship with well-being in these different settings. The investigation of such relationship in traditional, transitional and modern sectors of India is a potential area for future research.

15

Retrospect and Prospect

Research is a continuing process. Empirical research in the area of sex roles has answered a number of questions; it has predicted certain outcomes in the areas of personal and societal change. It has also suggested appropriate social technology in the form of sex-independent socialization practices to bring about human growth. Despite such developments, a broader view demands greater amount of research in some areas and rethinking on certain matters of crucial importance. A few such concerns can be identified.

Dimensionality of Sex-Role Constructs

Many theorists have agreed that gender role stereotypes are not unidimensional and that single measures do not tap into their complexity. Despite the usefulness of monolithic concepts such as gender-role identification or gender schema, the multi-factorial nature is explicit. For instance, it is important for researchers to determine whether they are interested to assess individual's beliefs about others or about the self. Infact, there are different forms of sex-typing measures.

While assessing sex-typing of others, an important element is the language in which the question is phrased. Such measures include questions such as "Who should be a……?" "Who can be a ….?", and "Who likes to…?". Response outcomes also vary from measure to measure. These characteristics (question, phrase options) influence responses. A critical examination of measures reveals that two aspects are measured: (a) the individual's *knowledge* about societal stereotype and (b) *personal belief* about stereotype. It is also found that knowledge of societal stereotypes can be assessed when individuals are (a) asked "who usually………?" performs various occupations or activities, or possess various traits, and/or

(b) forced to respond by choosing one or the other sex. It is argued that gender role attitudes are assessed when individuals asked "who can....?" or " who should.....?" performs various occupations or activities or possess various traits and are given the option of assigning items to both sexes.

Similarly a wide variety of measures exists for the measurement of sex typing of the self. Some measures require individual to pick from between two items- one "sex appropriate" and one "sex inappropriate". Others require individuals to rank-order items in terms of their preference. Still others require individuals to rate the degree to which items are self-descriptive (Bem, 1981, Sahoo, 1990a). In this context, it can be argued that the form of question is likely to bring about differences in response. Some form of questioning may seek information regarding individual's performances for occupations or activities. In contrast, other forms of questions may seek information regarding the activity taken up. For example, a question may involve "cleaning dishes". Males and females are likely to give similar answer (unfavourable) if preference is sought. But females would outnumber males if the question seeks information about actual performance because women do it more frequently than men.

In order to get around this problem, it is possible to ask individuals to rate a number of occupations, activities or traits as appropriate for "only men", "only women", "both men and women". In the case of traits, "neither men nor women" should also be included. The addition of the option "both men and women" would be useful. It is also important to recognize that the question "who should be ..?", (who should be a librarian) is a preferable pattern. The question " who usually is....?" is indicative of knowledge of societal stereotype.

In sum, it is asserted that a great deal of care is to be taken to frame appropriate questions for specific objectives. In other words, the language and format of measurement may tap quite different contexts.

Apart from the consideration of methodological aspects, another possibility demands research attention. The concepts such as sex role stereotypes and androgyny provide some understanding of social and cultural change. However, a comprehensive understanding of social change requires research based knowledge in behavioural domains as well.

Some researchers have recognized such broad prospectives. For instance, King and King (1997) have developed and recommended the use of *Sex-Role Egalitarian Scale* to measure attitude towards *men and women* (the equality of men and women across content domains). The construct of sex-role egalitarian was inferred to reflect the "bidirectional" movement from traditional to nontraditional gender roles. The construct assumes both beliefs or judgements about the role behaviour of women and beliefs or judgements about the behaviours of men. A true egalitarian would neither disapprove of a woman assuming the stereotypically male role of business executive nor disapprove of a man assuming the stereotypically female roles of child care provider. This bi-directional definition was intended to provide a more contemporary perspective on gender role equality.

The authors (King & Kings, 1997) identified five content categories reflecting what they believed to be relevant domains of adult life: marital roles, parental roles, employment roles, social interpersonal-hetrosexual roles, and educational roles. The authors recognized that these content categories were not exhaustive of all gender-related issues that might have been considered, but felt that role statements developed within these categories would be broadly shared and meaningful to most adults.

The Sex Role Egalitarian Scale (SRES) exists in four versions: two 95-item alternate full forms and two 25-item abbreviated forms. Instructions begin with a neutral declaration that the instrument contains "statements about men and women". Respondents are simply asked to judge the extent of agreement or disagreement with each, and they are cautioned to express their own personal views and not necessarily those that may be prevalent in the society. The items are accompanied by a 5-point Likert-type response scale, with options labelled as *strongly agree, agree, neutral or undecided or no opinion, disagree,* and strongly disagree. Items are scored such that higher values are indicative of a more egalitarian belief system.

The scale of this nature has tremendous implication to understand social change. It has also immense applicability in plural societies to examine changes in various sub-cultural populations. The SRES has been used to examine changes in gender-related behaviours in European-Americans, Africa-Americans, Asian-Americans, Hispanic-Americans and Native Americans (King & King, 1997). In addition, the SRES can also be applied for other categories of population such as college students.

It is also important to recognize that the SRES could be used to understand gender-based discrimination and sexual harassment. There has been some attention to how scores on the instrument account for judgements of women and men in job selection and placement decisions. It might be beneficial to incorporate the scale into studies of performance appraisal, especially when the job incumbent occupies a gender incongruent position. The authors also recommend continuing use of the SRES in inquiries related to domestic violence and intimate relationship. The predictive role of the SRES scores in precipitating domestic discord/ harmony is a research question. Similarly, its role in predicting egalitarian parenting and egalitarian attitude of their offspring is a possible candidate for research.

Cross-Cultural I.

While some studies have compared sex role changes internationally and cross-culturally (Williams & Best, 1990), few researchers have attended to cross-cultural equivalence of concepts, measures and response forms. In cross-cultural psychology, a conceptual distinction between *etics* and emics has been made. The etics refer to the universal aspects whereas emics refer to culture-specific aspects, Etics are phenomena, concepts or constructs that are universal or that are used as if they were universal. For example, the division of labour based on gender may be cross-cultural etics. When a phenomenon is assumed to be a universal without evidence, it is referred to as an imposed etics or pseudoetic (with negative connotation). When a phenomenon emerges from widespread studies, it is termed as a derived etic (with positive connotation). Emics are culturally specific phenomena, although these may serve as culturally specific indicators of etics. For example, among the indigenous Mayans in Gautamala, the persons who use the back-strap looms are almost exclusively females, whereas footlooms are operated mostly by men. This is specific phenomenon (emic) that represents the etic (all cultures assign tasks by gender). One of the questions that might be asked about instruments used internationally is whether they reflect emic perspective of the culture of origin or whether they reflect etics (either imposed or derived etics).

The most common procedure in cross-cultural research is to select an instrument that has been shown to be reliable and valid in one cultural setting and to use it (sometimes with slight modification) in another cultural setting. Most often instruments developed in the United States are used. For example, in one cross-cultural study the most widely used scale of attitude towards women's roles, the Attitude Towards Women Scale (Spence & Helmreich, 1972) was used in India and Great Britain. The authors acknowledged that use of a western research instrument in the Indian setting was problematic. Yet, they argued that they tried to overcome the obstacle by making sure that participants understood the questions and the concepts behind the questions. This is not a solitary example. Instruments are typically used in this manner.

However, there are also attempts to develop a scale emically and than extend it to other cultural systems. Suzuki (1991) has developed a scale of gender role beliefs in Japan, the scale of egalitinan sex role attitude and then used her scale to examine the beliefs of Japanese and U.S. women.

Suzuki took the precaution of demonstrating similar coefficient alpha reliability, and similar factor structure for the English version among U.S. participants as she had previously demonstrated for the Japanese version.

Sometimes researchers delete items before using an instrument because some items do not apply to the culture in question. For example, Williams and Best (1990) and their collaborators administered the 30-item Sex Role Ideology Scale (SRIS) in 14 countries. Prior to administration, local collaborators deleted questions that they felt were inappropriate. Specifically the cooperating researchers in Singapore and Malaysia deleted questions pertaining to women taking their husband's name at marriage and men offering seats to women on the bus. Three items about sexuality and sexual advances were deleted from the version used in Pakistan.

It may be noted that Sahoo and Rout (1990) in their preliminary study on androgyny and work involvement deleted some of the items from Bem sex role inventory for its use in India. However, they identified in appropriate items on the basis of empirical investigations and then deleted the unsuitable items. Subsequently, Sahoo (1990a) developed Sahoo Sex Role Inventory on the basis of empirical investigation so that etics constructs would be emically represented.

Infrequently, researchers have validated instruments from foreign countries against indigenously developed scales. For example Gupta and Murthy (1984) validated a sex role instrument against an instrument developed and validated in the Indian context (Bhadra & Gupta, 1976). They concluded that the western instrument was potentially a research tool in India.

Another approach is to add some items that may specifically address the culture-specific aspect of the construct being studied. For example, some researchers have added items to the Spence and Helmreich's. Attitude Towards Women Scale so that the scale would contain some culture-specific items relevant in China.

Finally, it may be pointed out that the administration of sex role inventories may function to influence people's sensitivity towards gender-related issues. In some cultures, it may have negative outcomes in the sense that attitudes may get polarized to the sex-typed end. In other cultural systems, such encounters with scales may produce positive impact of generating liberal thoughts. However, it is also possible that men and women may respond differentially to such effects. This, in combination with other issues, demands research attention of cross-cultural psychologists.

Of course, while discussing cross-cultural issues, the significance of subcultural studies is not to be overlooked. In plural societies, the subcultural differences may be greater than inter-cultural differences. India represents such a plural society. It appears that subcultural studies involving different linguistic groups religious groups, tribal-nontribal populations, and rural-urban sectors would provide substantial information both in theoretical and applied terms. Such a possibility is a fascinating research venture.

APPENDIX A

Sahoo Sex-Role Inventory (SSRI)

Name...age...........Sex...........................

Address..

....

ccupation..

Date...............................

On the opposite side of this sheet, you would find listed a number of characteristics. We would like you to use these *Characteristics to describe yourself.* More specifically, we would like you to indicate, on a scale from 1 to 7, how true of you each of these characteristics is. Please do not leave any characteristic unmarked. Your response would be kept confidential, and would be used only for research.

Thank you for your cooperation.

Example: Clever

Write 1, if it is never or almost never true that you are clever.

Write 2, if it is not usually true that your are clever.

Write 3, if it is sometimes but infrequently true that you are clever.

Write 4, if it is occasionally true that you are clever.

Write 5 if it is often true that you are clever.

Write 6, if it is usually true that you are clever.

Write 7, if it is always or almost true that you are clever.

Thus, if you feel it is often true that you are clever, always or almost always true that you are competent, it is never true that you are silly, and occasionally true that you are hardworking, then you would rate these characteristics are follows:

Clever	5
Competent	7

Silly	1
Hardworking	4

Never or almost never true	Usually not true	Sometimes but infrequently true	Occasionally true	Often true	Usually true	Always or almost always true

Clear-thinking
Innocent
Playful
Attractive
Calculating
Masculine
Productive
Tender
Inventive
Progressive
Takes Initiative
Mild
Optimistic
Likes Security
Realistic
Fashionable
Kind
Imaginative
Frank
Expressive
Affectionate
Energetic
Fair-minded
Charming
Courageous

Active
Daring
Insightful
Has Leadership Ability
Methodical
Loves Children
Modest
Loving
Industrious
Concerned About Group Harmony
Strong Personality
Competetive
Eager To Sooth Hurt Feelings
Dependent
Ambitious
Emotional
Individualistic
Aggressive
Willing To Take A Stand
Courtious
Feminine
Independent
Intellectual
Flatterable
Soft Hearted

Scoring Note: The list contains 20 masculinity items, 20 femininity items, and 10 filler items. The masculinity items are shown in Table 11.2 and femininity items are shown in Table 11.3. The sum of self-endorsement ratings across 20 masculinity items generates masculinity or 'M' score. The sum of self-endorsement ratings across all 20 femininity items yields femininity score or 'F'score. Androgyny, score is the difference between M score and F score. Lower the score, greater the androgyny.

APPENDIX B
Health Behaviour Questionnaire

Dear Friend/Sir

All of us are interest to improve the quality of life. Although research in the past has identified a number of criteria of healthful living, there have been recent changes in our notion of good living. We are seeking your cooperation in carrying out a project on good living. Kindly indicate your candid opinion. You may not mention your name. Your responses will be kept confidential and would be used for research only. Thank you for your support and cooperation.

Part-I

Instructions

Below is a list of things people look for in their lives. Please read all the items from top to bottom before making any choice. First, decide which one you think is the most important to you in maintaining and enhancing the quality of life and place 1 in the blank provided for the item. Do the same for your choice 2, 3, 4, 5 and so on. Since there are 15 items in the list given below, your choice 15 should represent the thing that is least important to your good living (a state of complete physical, mental and social well-being). Please be sure you have placed a number opposite each item.

- Achievement as expected
- Adequate social contacts
- Control (mastery) over the environment
- Feelings of happiness with family

- Good physical health
- Job satisfaction
- Values of spiritual quality (such as being part of mankind, having moments of ecstasy of bliss)
- Personal competence (ability to do works better)
- Social support (from friends, relations and neighbours)
- Freedom from depression
- Autonomous activities (activities that can be undertaken with choice)
- Interpersonal trust (Conditions that foster trust among people)
- Effective coping with stressful situations (such as loss of a job, etc)
- Integrated personality
- Freedom from anxiety

Part-II

Instructions

In this part are listed some characteristics or conditions people look for in their lives. We would like you to know the degree of characteristics as they relate to your life. Please indicate the extent to which each of the following items is characteristic of you by specifying a number that corresponds to your feeling. The numbers 6 to 1 represent categories in the following way:

6 = Very characteristic of me

5 = Characteristic of me

4 = Slightly characteristic of me

3 = Slightly uncharacteristic of me

2 = Uncharacteristic of me

1 = Very uncharacteristic of me

1. I have accomplished what I want to.
2. When I face challenging tasks, I do not easily give up.
3. If I know I was going to take an important assignment, I would feel confident and relaxed, before hand.
4. I sometimes worry that there is nobody who would really help my children if I were unable to do so or if I would be no more.

5. I feel attached to my job.
6. Matters of spiritual nature have no place in my scheme of life.
7. I feel confident that I will be helped out adequately by some one in case I loose my job or my property.
8. I feel depressed/dejected.
9. I believe that most people can be trusted.
10. I am happy with the things I have been doing in recent years.
11. I feel I have most of the things I need.
12. I feel that I can run my life much the way I want to.
13. I am free of anxiety most of the times.
14. I worry about my family life.
15. I find pleasure in living, eating and breathing my job.
16. I consider that I am alone in what I am aiming for.
17. I feel confident that relatives and/or friends will look after me if I am seriously ill or meet with an accident.
18. I worry about things that have had happened to me.
19. I find most people are so reasonable that it is pleasant to talk to them.
20. I have the ability to care for and about others.
21. I feel adequate about the education I have received.
22. If I decide to sit myself and learn something hard, I am sure I can learn it.
23. I have no trouble getting to sleep or staying asleep.
24. I sometimes worry about the relationship I have with my children.
25. I consider my job to be very central to my existence.
26. I believe in things tangible.
27. I feel a part of a group of a people who are mutually friendly and supportive.
28. I feel my life is boring.
29. I like to befriend a stranger.
30. I have the capacity for creative, productive work.

31. I sometimes worry about accomplishing so little of what I want to accomplish.
32. I control the pace and scheduling of my work.
33. I sometimes feel my heart beating very first during testing (challenging) situations.
34. I think my family is a burden on me.
35. I feel satisfied with my job.
36. I have worked hard for my career pursuits.
37. I have no one to whom I can talk freely.
38. I often blame myself and feel bad over things I have done.
39. I find it difficult to come across a dependable person.
40. I do my duty even in adverse circumstances.
41. I worry about having less success in life than I think I deserve.
42. I can stop bad things happening in my life.
43. Even when I am well prepared for an important work, I feel anxious about it.
44. In my family, there is disagreement on how family income should be spent.
45. My deteriorating job conditions bother me.
46. I exert greater efforts to master the challenges.
47. I can count on some people to help me out in a crisis situation, even though they would have to go out of their way to do so.
48. I engage in things of my own choice.
49. Considering the good things I have done for others, I have received very little.
50. I feel happy and contented.
51. Considering all the efforts I have made, I think I should have accomplished more in life.
52. When I make plans ahead, things generally come up to make change my plans.
53. I do not enjoy eating before an important test/task.
54. I feel adequate about my general health and physical fitness

55. I have no influence over the things that effect me on the job.
56. I consider myself useful of society.
57. I have no one who would comfort me when I need it by holding me in their arms.
58. I feel that I can do much to make my future what I want it to be.
59. I am puzzled by people's lack of reciprocation.
60. I feel like smashing things for no good reasons.
61. I feel adequate about the relationship I have with my friends.
62. Compared with most other people, bad things happen to me more often.
63. I consider my marriage to be successful.
64. I go to watch sports events.
65. I have other activities which are more satisfying than my job.
66. I feel full enthusiasm that I will certainly achieve my objectives.
67. I have no one to support me on the major decisions I make.
68. When I achieve a goal, I get more satisfaction from reaching the goal than from any praise I might get.
69. I am able to concentrate well on things I am doing.
70. No one cares much what happens to me.
71. I play an important role in social harmony (such as marriage ceremony)
72. I am dissatisfied with my present job.
73. I feel confident in getting things done.
74. I manage to get time to do things that suit my preferences.
75. I feel I can manage situations even when they do not turn out as expected.
76. I feel that my intimacy with my community is increasing gradually.
77. I have the feeling that I am a good father (mother).
78. I usually like to be by myself rather than with other people.
79. When I feel worried, tense or nervous, I feel like drinking alcoholic beverages to help me handle things.
80. I do not feel about the religious fulfillment in my life.

81. I sometimes experience moments of intense happiness almost like a kind of ecstasy or bliss.
82. I often feel restless wanting to be on the move doing something but not knowing what.
83. I get satisfactions from things I do in my leisure time.
84. When beset with difficulties, I entertain serious doubts about my capabilities.
85. I have to forgo my intentions quite often.
86. I feel physically disturbed when I encounter a stressful situation.
87. I enjoy participation in organizations (such as clubs, teams, etc).
88. I feel confident that in case of crisis (anything which substantially upsets my life situations) I will be able to cope with it/ face it boldly.
89. For the most part, I feel healthy enough to carry out the things I would like to do.
90. I wish to have more friends than I actually have.
91. I am bothered by nervousness.
92. When bad things happen, they tend to affect my whole life.
93. I feel that I miss a real close friend.
94. I feel that others are running my life for me.
95. I feel hopeful about the future.
96. I am perplexed by my contradictory thoughts
97. I find it difficult to go wherever I want.
98. It is a source of preoccupation for me that people around me do not like me.
99. I consider my family as a source of help to me in finding solutions to most of the problems I have.
100. I go to see medical doctor for slight illness like headaches, stomach upsets, etc.
101. I feel that I am loosing interest.
102. I feel my life is enjoyable.
103. I find less freedom in pursuing the things I like.
104. I worry much about things that might happen to me.

105. I feel irritation.
106. I feel whether or not I am successful is just a matter of luck and chance, rather than my own doing.
107. Most of the members of my family feel closely attached to each other.
108. I find it very difficult to attend to several responsibilities.
109. I get excited very easily.
110. I feel happy about the relationship I have with elders in my family.
111. I consider that various things in my life have led me to the most important values in my life.
112. I feel in good spirits almost all the times.
113. I feel that I have found the meaning in my life.
114. I sometimes worry about my physical health.
115. I sometimes experience a joyful feeling of being part of mankind as one large family.
116. I feel that I am not able to fully utilize my abilities in performing different duties.
117. When I look around, I find few people who would help me feel more relaxed when I am under pressure of tension.
118. I am not able to take such decisions as I want to take.
119. I am able to remain calm in critical situations.
120. I spend more of my free time doing things to help please other people.

Part-III

Instructions

Please think of your present life conditions/characteristics and evaluate it using each of the seven point scales presented below:

(i) With respect to my life, I feel

(a) Competent	1	2	3	4	5	6	7	Incompetent
(b) Physically healthy	1	2	3	4	5	6	7	Physically unhealthy
(c) Anxious	1	2	3	4	5	6	7	Clam
(d) Nonintegrated	1	2	3	4	5	6	7	Integrated
(e) Depressed	1	2	3	4	5	6	7	Joyful
(f) Autonomous	1	2	3	4	5	6	7	Bonded
(g) Trustful of others	1	2	3	4	5	6	7	Suspicious of others

(ii) My life presents conditions that indicate

(h) Lack of social support	1	2	3	4	5	6	7	Abundance of social support
(i) Uncontrollable situations	1	2	3	4	5	6	7	Controllable situations
(j) Happy family	1	2	3	4	5	6	7	Unhappy family
(k) Strainful	1	2	3	4	5	6	7	Relaxed
(l) Dissatisfying job	1	2	3	4	5	6	7	Satisfying job
(m) Abundance social contact	1	2	3	4	5	6	7	Lack of social contacts
(n) Full of achievement	1	2	3	4	5	6	7	Lack of achievement
(o) Spiritually barren	1	2	3	4	5	6	7	Spiritually fulfilling

Part-IV

Instructions

Below are seven diagrams. In each diagram there is a person representing yourself and a circle representing the good living (a state of complete physical, mental and social well-being). The figures are placed at different distances from one's cherished condition of good living. Distance in the diagram does not represent physical distances from the cherished condition of good living. Instead, being a close to the cherished status implied that you have approached to secure the conditions and characteristics you consider important for good living. In your judgement, how close are you to the conditions of good living. Circle the appropriate number.

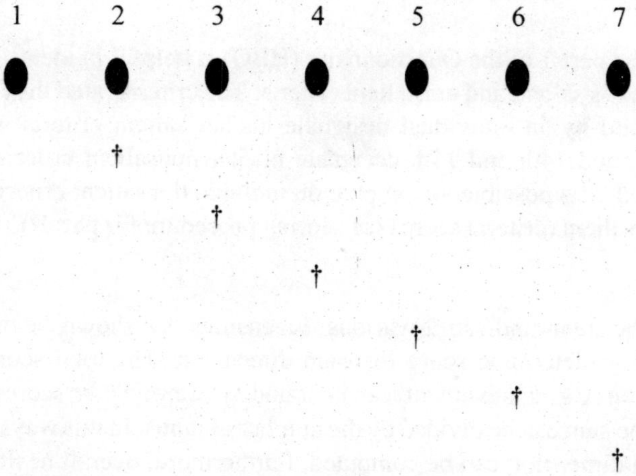

Part V

Instruction

Please provide the following information:

Sex-Male/Female	Marital Status-
Age-	Occupation-
Education	Residence: Urban/Rural

Thank You

Scoring (HBQ)

Part I

The part-1 of the Questionnaire (HBQ) is helpful in identifying an individual's salient and nonsalient criteria. The criteria rated the first and the second by an individual designate his/her salient criteria whereas criteria rated 14th and 15th designate his/her nonsalient criteria. Once identified, it is possible to compute on individual's salient criteria score and nonsalient (criteria score (see scoring procedure for part II).

Part II

The items indicating various dimensions are shown below. It is possible to determine score for each dimension. The total score for a dimension (e.g. achievement) can be found by summing the scores across items; the sum can be divided by the number of items. In this ways, scores for each dimension can be computed. Furthermore, overall health score can be found by summing the scores across all dimensions. It is also possible to determine salient criteria scores by summing scores across those two salient criteria identified by that individual in Part II. Similarly, nonsalient criteria scores can be computed by summing scores across two nonsalient criteria identified by the individual.

Achievement (AC)	:	1, 11, 21, 31*, 41*, 51*.
Social Contacts (SC)	:	61, 71, 76, 78, 87, 90*, 93*, 106*.
Control (C)	:	2, 12, 22, 32, 42, 52*, 62*, 92*, 94*, 106*.
Feelings of Happiness with Family	:	4*, 14*, 24*, 34*, 44*, 63, 77, 99, 107, 110.
Physical Health (PH)	:	54, 64, 79*, 89, 100*, 114*.
Job Involvement (J)	:	5, 15, 25, 35, 45*, 55*, 65*, 72*.
Spiritual Quality (S)	:	6*, 16*, 26*, 80*, 81, 111, 113, 115.
Personal Competence (PC)	:	36, 46, 56, 66, 73, 82*, 84*, 101*, 108*, 116*.
Social Support (SS)	:	7, 17, 27, 37*, 47, 57*, 67*, 117*.
Freedom from Depression (D)	:	8*, 18*, 28*, 38*, 83, 95, 102, 112.
Autonomy (AN)	:	48, 58, 68, 74, 85*, 97*, 103*, 118*.
Interpersonal Trust (T)	:	9, 19, 29, 39*, 49*, 59*.

Coping (CP) : 69, 75, 86*, 88, 91*, 104*, 109*, 119.
Person Morale (PM) : 10, 20, 30, 40, 50, 60*, 70*, 96*, 98*, 105*.
Freedom from Anxiety (AN) : 3, 13, 23, 33*, 43*, 53*.

Note: Items marked with * are negatively keyed. Scorings of these items are to be reversed.

Part III

It is to be noted that scoring for pairs a, b, f, g, j, m and n are to be reversed. For this part, scope for each item-pair represents specific dimension sure. The overall scope can be obtained by summing scores across all pairs. As with part-II, salient criteria score and nonsalient criteria of an individual can be computed by summing his/her scores across two salient and two nonsalient items separately.

Part IV

In this part of graphic design, the choice number of an individual is to be reversed. If an individual encircles 1, his/her score would be 7. Similarly, if he/she encircles 2, his/her score would be 6 and so on.

Bibliography

Abramson, L.Y., Selligman, M.E.P., & Teasdale, J.D (1978). Learned helplessness in humans: Critique and reformulation. *Journal of Abnormal Psychology,* 87, 49-74.

Adelman, P.K. (1987). Occupational complexity, control and personal income: Their relation to psychological well-being in men and women. *Journal of Applied Psychology,* 72, 529-537.

Agarwal, S. & Agarwal, S. (1999). Creativity and intelligence: Explanation with sex difference. *Psycho-lingua,* 29(2), 127-132.

Agrawal, T.D. & Upadhayay, S.N. (1983). Sex and age differences in affiliation behaviour. *Psychological Studies,* 28, 25-29.

Allen, M.G. (1976). Twin studies of affective illness. *Archieves of General Psychology,* 33, 1476-1478.

Andrews, F.M., Frank, M., & Whithley, S.B. (1976). *Social indicators of well-being: American's perceptions of life quality.* New York: Plenum Press.

Andrews, F.M., & McKennell, A.C. (1980). Measures of self reported well-being: Their affective cognitive and other components. *Social Indicators Research,* 8, 127-155.

Angarist, S.S. (1978). Masculinity and femininity: T*heir psychological dimensions, correlates and antecedents,* Austin: University of Texas Press.

Asha, C.S. (1994). Job satisfaction among women in relation to their family environment. *Journal of Community Guidance and Research,* 11(3), 43-50.

Ashmore, R.D., & DelBoca, F.K. (1979). Sex-stereotypes, one implicit personality theory: Towards a cognitive-social psychological conceptualization. *Sex-Roles,* 5, 219-248.

Asthana, H.S. & Handal, M.K. (1998). Hemfacial a symmetry in emotion expressions. *Behaviour Modification,* 22(2), 177-183.

Bagley, C., Evan-Wang, L. (1975), Neuroticism and entroversion in response to Coopersmith's self-esteem inventory. *Psychological Reports,* 36, 253-254.

Bakan, D. (1966). *The Duality of Human Existence.* Chicago: Rand McNally.

Bandura, A. (1969). Social learning theory of identification process. In D.A. Goslin (Ed). *Handbook of socialization theory and research.* Chicago: Rand McNally.

Bandura, A. (1997). *Self-efficacy: The Exercise of Control.* New York: Freeman.

Banerjee, U., & Gupta, H.N. (1996). Moderating effect of social support in occupational stress strain relationship. *Journal of Indian Academy of Applied Psychology,* 22(1&2), 27-34

Barnett, P.A. & Gotlib, J.H. (1988). Psychological functioning and depression: Distinguishing among antecedents, concomitants and consequences. *Psychological Bulletin,* 104, 97-128.

Barry, H. III., Bacon, M.K. & Child, I.L. (1957). A cross-cultural survey of some sex differences in socialization. *Journal of Abnormal and Social Psychology,* 55, 327-332.

Barry, H.III., Josephson, I. Lauer, E., & Marshall, C. (1976). Traits incalculated in childhood: Cross-cultural codes. *Ethnology*, 13, 88-114.

Bassof, E.S., & Glass, G.V. (1982). The relationship between sex-roles and mental health: A meta-analysis of twenty-six studies. *Counselling Psychologist,* 10, 105-112.

Baucom, D.H. (1976). Independent masculinity and femininity scales on the California Psychological Inventory. *Journal of Consulting and Clinical Psychology*, 44, 876.

Baucom, D.H. (1980). Sex role identity and the decision to regain control among women : A learned helplessness investigation. *Journal of Personality and Social Psychology,* 44, 334-343.

Baucom. D.H., & Danker-Brown, P. (1979). Influence of sex-roles on the development of learned helplessness. *Journal of Consulting and Clinical Psychology,* 47, 928-936.

Beck, A.T. (1967). *Depression: Clinical Experimental and Theoretical Perspectives.* New York: Harper & Row.

Beck, A.T. (1976). Cognitive theory and the emotional disorders. New York: International University Press.

Beck, A.T. (1983). Cognitive therapy of depression: New perspectives. In P.J. Clayton & J.E. Burett (Eds.). *Treatment of depression: Old Controversies and New Approaches* (pp. 265-290). New York: Raven

Bem, S.L. (1974). The measurement of psychological androgyny. *Journal of Consulting and Clinical Psychology,* 31, 634-643.

Bem, S.L. (1975). Sex-role adaptability: One consequence of psychological androgyny. *Journal of Personality and Social Psychology,* 31, 634-643.

Bem, S.L. (1977). On the utility of alternative procedures for assessing psychological androgyny. *Journal of Consulting and Clinical Psychology,* 45, 196-205.

Bem, S.L. (1979). Theory and measurement of androgyny: A reply to the Pedhazur-Tetenbaum and Locksley-Colten critiques. *Journal of Personality and Social Psychology,* 37, 1047-1054.

Bem. S.L. (1981a). Gender schema theory: A cognitive account of sex-typing. *Psychological Review,* 88, 354-364.

Bem, S.L. (1981b). The BSRI and gender schema theory: A reply to Spence and Helmreich. *Psychological Review,* 88, 369-371.

Bem, S.L. (1981c). *Bem Sex Role Inventory.* Palo Alto California: Consulting Psychologists Press.

Bem, S.L. (1982). Gender Schema Theory and self-schema theory compared: A comment on Markus, Crane, Bernstein and Siladi's "self-schema and gender". *Journal of Personality and Social Psychology,* 43, 1192-1194.

Bem, S.L. (1985). Androgyny and gender schema theory: A conceptual and empirical integration. In T.B. Sonderegger (Ed.). *Nebraska Symposium on Motivation: Psychology and Gender.* (pp. 179-222). Lincoln: University of Nebraska Press.

Bem, S.L., & Lenney, E. (1976). Sex typing and avoidance of cross-sex behaviour. *Journal of Personality and Social Psychology,* 33, 48-54.

Bem, S.L., Martyna, W., & Watson, C. (1976). Sex-typing and androgyny: Further explorations of the expressive domain. *Journal of Personality and Social Psychology,* 34, 1016-1023.

Benbow, C.E. & Stanley, J.C (1980). Sex difference in mathematical ability: Fact or artifact? *Science,* 210, 1262-1264.

Berger, E.M. (1952). The relationship between expressed acceptance of self and expressed acceptance of others. *Journal of Abnormal and Social Psychology,* 47, 778-782.

Berland, J.C. (1977). *Psychological differentiation among Khanbadesh of Pakistan.* Unpublished doctoral dissertation, University of Hawaii, Honolulu, Hawaii, USA.

Berry, J.W. (1971). Ecology and cultural factors in spatial perceptual development. *Canadian Journal of Behavioural Science,* 3, 324-336.

Berzins, J.I., Welling, M.A., & Wetter, R.E. (1978). A new measure of psychological androgyny based on the personality research form. *Journal of Consulting and Clinical Psychology,* 46, 126-138.

Billings, A.G. & Moos, R.H. (1984). Coping stress and social resources among adults with unipolar depression. *Journal of Personality and Social Psychology,* 46, 877-891.

Bhadra, B.R., & Gupta, G.R., (1976). A scale for the measurement of attitudes towards women. *Asian Journal of Psychology and Education,* 1', 41-44

Block, J.H. (1973). Conceptions of sex-roles: Some cross-cultural and longitudinal perspectives. *American Psychologist,* 28, 515-526.

Block, J., Vonder Lippe, A., & Block, J.H. (1973). Sex-role and socialization patterns: Some personality concomitants and environmental antecedents. *Journal of Consulting and Clinical Psychology,* 41, 332-341.

Bogley, C., Evan-Wang, L. (1975). Neuroticism and extroversion in response to Coopersmith's self-esteem inventory. *Psychological Reports,* 36, 253-254.

Bradburn, N. (1969). *The structure of psychological well-being.* Chicago: Aldine.

Broverman, I.K., Broverman, D.M., Clarkson, F.E. Rosenkrantz, P.S., & Vogel, S.R. (1970). Sex-role stereotypes and clinical judgements of mental health. *Journal of Consulting and Clinical Psychology,* 34, 1-7.

Broverman, I.K., Vogel, S.R., Broverman, D.M., Clarkson, F.E., Rosenkrantz, P.S. (1972). Sex-role stereotypes – A current appraisal. *Journal of Social Issues,* 28, 59-78.

Bryant, F.B., & Veroff, J. (1982). The structure of well-being: A socio-historical analysis : *Journal of Personality and Social Psychology,* 43, 653-673.

Bryant, F.B., & Veroff, J. (1984). Dimensions of subjective mental health in American men and women. *Journal of Health and Social Behaviour,* 25, 116-135.

Buffery, A.W.H. & Gray, J.A. (1972). Sex differences in the development of spatial and linguistic skills. In C. Ounsted & D.C. Taylor (Eds.). *Gender Differences*: Their category and significance, (pp.125-157). Edinburh: Churchill Livingstone.

Burt, R.S., Wiley, J.A., Minor, M.J., & Murrays, J.R. (1978). Structure of well-being. *Sociological Methods of Research,* 6, 365-407.

Buss, D.M. (1995). *Psychological Sex Difference*: Origin through sexual selection.

American Psychologist, 50, 164-168.

Carli, L.L. (1989). Gender differences in interaction style and influence. *Journal of Personality and Social psychology*, 56, 565-576.

Carli, L. (1982). Are women more social and men more task oriented: *A meta-analytic review of sex differences in group interaction, reward allocation, coalition formation, Prasoners' Dilemma Games.* Unpublished manuscripts, University of Massachusetts, Amherts, Massachusetts, USA.

Cambell, A. (1980). *The sense of well-being in America.* New York: McGraw Mill.

Chakrapani, C. (1996). Unemployment as a stressor: Role of socio-psychological factors. *The Indian Journal of Social Work*, 57 (4), 578-590.

Chandra, P.S., Sudha, M.B., Subbarathana, A.R., & Rao, S. (1995). Mental Health in mothers from a transitional society. The role of spouse supportiveness. *Family Therapy*, 49-59.

Chapman, S.F., Bush, L.R. Wilson, D.M. (Eds.) (1985). *Women and Mathematics: Balancing the equation.* Hillside, New Jersey: Erlbaum.

Cherlin, A., & Reader, L.G. (1975). The dimension of psychological well-being. *Sociological Methods and Research*, 4, 189-214.

Chodorow, N. (1978). *The Reproduction of Mothering: Psychoanalysis and the sociology of gender.* Berkeley, California, University of California Press.

Chodorow, N. (1979). Feminism and difference: Gender relation and difference in psychoanalytic therapy perspective. *Socialist Review,* 9(4), 51-70.

Cobb, S. & Kasl, S. (1977). *Termination: The consequences of job loss* (DHEM rep.) Washington, D.C: U.S. Government Printing Office.

Cohn, L.D. (1991). Sex differences in the course of personality development: A meta-analysis. *Psychological Bulletin,* 109, 252-262.

Constantinople, A. (1973). Masculinity-femininity: An exception of famous dictum. *Psychological Bulletin,* 80, 380-407.

Cook, E.P. (1985). *Psychological Androgyny.* New York: Elmford.

Coopersmith, S. (1967). *The antecedents of self-esteem.* San-Francisco: Freeman.

Cossentino, P., & Heilburn, A.B. (1964). Anxiety correlates of sex-role identity in college students. *Psychological Reports,* 14, 729-730.

Crane, M., & Markus, H. (1982). Gender identity: The benefits of self-schema approach. *Journal of Personality and Social Psychology,* 43, 1195-1197.

Dang, R. & Gupta, R. (1994). A study of role stress, behaviour patterns and gender among teachers. *Journal of the Indian Academy of Applied Psychology*, 20(2), 183-188.

Davak, B.V. (1999). Mental health of Indian Women: A feminist agenela. New Delhi: Sage.

Davis, F.B. 1964. Basic characteristics of test scores. In F.B. Davis, *Educational Measurements and their Interpretations,* Belmont, California: Wadworth Publishing Company.

Dawson, J.L.M. (1972). Effects of sex hormones on cognitive style in rats and men. *Behaviour Genetics,* 2, 21-42.

Deci, E.L., Connel, J.P., & Ryan, R.N. (1989). Self-determination in a work organization. *Journal of Applied Psychology,* 74, 580-590.

Deci, E.L., & Ryan, R.N. (1985). *Intrinsic motivation and self-determination in human behaviour.* New York: Plenum press.

Deci, E.L., Ryan, R.N. (1987). The support of autonomy and control of behaviour. *Journal of Personality and Social Psychology,* 53, 1024-1037

Deci, E.L., Schwardz, A.J., Sheinman, L., & Ryan, R.M. (1981). An instrument to assess adults orientation. *Journal of Educational Psychology,* 73, 642-650.

Diggory, J.C. (1966). *Self-evaluation Concepts and Studies.* New York: Wiley.

Donnell, S.M.& Hall, J. (1980). Men and women as managers: A significant case of no significant difference. *Organizational Dynamics,* 8, 60-77.

Dube, S.C. (1990). *Indian Society.* New Delhi: National Book Trust.

Dutta, S., Das, S., & Basu, J. (1995). Effect of gender role identity and gender role attitudes in India. *Journal of Community Guidance Service.* 12(1), 55-62.

Dweck, C.S. & Reppucci, N.D. (1973). Learning helplessness and reinforcement responsibility in children. *Journals of Personality and Social Psychology,* 25, 109-116.

Eagly, A.H. (1983). Gender and social influence. A social psychological analysis. *American Psychologist,* 38, 971-981.

Eagly, A.H. (1987). Sex difference in social behaviour: *A Social Role Interpretation.* Hillside, New Jersey: Erlbaum.

Eagly, A.H. & Carli, L.L. (1981). Sex of researchers and sex-typed communications as determinants of sex differences in influencability: A meta-analysis of social influence studies. *Psychological Bulletin,* 90, 1-20.

Eagly, A.H., & Crowley, M. (1986). Gender and helping behaviour. A meta-analytic review of the social psychological literature. *Psychological Bulletin,* 100, 283-308.

Eagly, A.H. & Steffen, V.J.C (1986). Gender and aggressive behaviour: A meta-analytic review of the social psychological literature. *Psychological Bulletin,* 100, 309-330.

Eaton, W.O. & Enns, L.R. (1986). Sex differences in human motor activity. *Psychological Bulletin,* 100, 19-28.

Eccles, J. (1983). Sex differences in mathematics participation. In M. Steinkamp & M. Machr (Eds.). *Women in Science* (pp. 80-110). Connecticut: JAI Press.

Eccles, J.S. (1987). Gender roles and Women's achievement-related decisions. *Psychology of Women Quarterly, 1*1, 135-172.

Eccles, J. Adler, T. & Meece, J.L. (1984). Sex differences in achievement: A test of alternate theories. *Journal of Personality and Social Psychology,* 40, 26-43.

Edelbrock, C., & Sugawara, A.I. (1978). Acquisition of sex-typed performances in pre-school aged children. *Developmental Psychology,* 14, 268-276.

Ellis, A., & Greiger, R. (1977). *Handbook of Rational Emotive Therapy.* New York: Springer.

Ember, C.R. (1977). Cross-cultural cognitive studies. *Annual Review of Anthropology,* 6, 33-56.

Erikson, E. (1964). Inner and outerspace reflections on womanhood, In R.J. Lifton (Ed). *The women in America,* (pp. 1-26), Houghton: Mifflin.

Fagot. F. (1985). Changes in thinking about early sex-role development. *Developmental Review,* 5, 83-98.

Fennema, E. (1974). Mathematics learning and the sexes. *Journal of Research in Mathematics Education,* 5, 126-129.

Fennema, E. & Peterson, P. (1985). Autonomous learning behaviour: A possible explanation of gender-related difference in mathematics. In L.S. Wilkinson & C.B. Marret (Eds.). *Gender Difference in Class-room Instruction* (pp.17-36). New-York: Academic.

Fennema, E. & Sherman, J.A. (1976). Fennema-Sherman mathematics attitude scale. Instrument designed to measure attitude towards learning mathematics by males and females. *JSAS Catalog of Selected Documents in Psychology,* 6, 31. (Ms. No.1225). (Reprinted by Wisconsin Centre for Education Research, University of Wisconsin-Madison)

Fiengold, A. (1988). Cognitive gender differences are disappearing. *American Psychologist*, 43, 95-103.

Folkman, S., & Lazarus, R.S. (1980). An analysis of coping in a middle aged community sample. *Journal of Health and Social Behaviour,* 21, 219-239.

Frabel, D. (1986). *Sex-typing and the perception of gender roles*. A paper presented at 94th annual convention of the American Psychological Association, Washington, D.C.

French, J.W., Eustrom, R.B., & Prince, L.A. (1965). *Manual for Kit of Tests for Cognitive Factors (*rev. ed). Princeton, NJ: Educational Testing Service.

Freud, S. (1959a). Some psychological consequences of the anatomical distinction between the sexes (1925). In E. Johnes (Ed). *Collected Papers of Sigmund Freud* (Vol. 5). New York: Basic Books.

Freud, S. (1959b). The passing of the Oedipus complex (1924). In E. Johnes (Ed). *Collected papers of Sigmund Freud,* 5, New York: Basic Books.

Fujita, F., Diener, E. & Sandvik (1991). Gender difference in negative affect and well being: The case for emotional intensity. *Journal of Personality and Social Psychology,* 61, 427-434.

Gall, M.D. (1979). The relationship between masculinity-femininity and manifest anxiety. *Journal of Clinical Psychology,* 25, 277-295.

Garter,G., Tansella, M. Kokten, A.T., Bea, G., Venos, G. & Olatawurf, M.O. (1998). Sex difference in the prevalence and detection of depressive and anxiety disorders. *Archives of General Psychiatry,* 55(5), 405-413

Gilbert, L.A. (1981). Towards mental health. The benefits of psychological androgyny. *Professional Psychology,* 12, 29-38.

Glass, D.C., & Singer, J.E. (1972). *Urban stress:* Experiments on noise and social stressors. New York: Academic press.

Glick, P. & Fiske, S.T. (2001). An ambivalent alliance: Hostile and benevolent sexism as contemporary publication for gender inequality. *American Psychologist*, 56, 109-118.

Gough, H.G. (1967). *Manual for the California Personality Inventory*, Palo Alto, CA: Consulting Psychologists Press.

Gough, H.G. & Heilburn, A.B. (1965). *Manual for the Adjective Checklist and the need scales for the ACL.* Palo Alto, CA: Consulting Psychologists Press.

Grey, A. & Kalshed, D. (1971). Oedipus east and west: An explanation via manifest dream content. *Journal of Cross-Cultural Psychology*, 2, 337-352.

Grey, S.W. (1957). Masculinity-femininity in relation to anxiety and social acceptance. *Child Development,* 28, 203-214.

Golding, J.M., & Singer, J.L. (1983). Patterns of inner experiences: Day dreaming styles, depressive moods and sex-roles. *Journal of Personality and Social Psychology*, 45, 663-675.

Gualtieri, T. & Hicks, R.E. (1985). An immunoreactive theory of selective male affiliation. *The Behaviour and Brain Sciences*, 8, 427-441.

Gupta, G.R., & Murthy, V.N. (1984). Attitude towards the female role questionnaire- its usefulness for an Indian sample. *Psychological Studies,* 29, 189-191.

Gupta, N.L. (1995). Personality difference on moral judgement among male and female students of Himachal Pradesh. *Journal of Psychological Researches*, 39(1&2), 67-71.

Gupta, U., & Gupta, B.S. (1997). Sex difference in haptic perceptual judgement. *Psychological Studies*, 42(2&3), 72-74.

Haavio-Mannila, E. (1971). Satisfaction with family: work, leisure and life among men and women. *Human Relation*, 24, 585-601.

Hall, J.A. (1984). *Nonverbal sex differences*: Communication accuracy and expressive style. Baltimore, Maryland: John Hopkins University Press.

Hardfor, T.C., Willis, C.H., & Deabler, H.L. (1967). Personality correlates of masculinity-femininity. *Psychological Reports*, 21, 881-889.

Hare-Mustin, R.T. (1987). The problem of gender in family therapy/theory. *Family Process*, 26, 15-27.

Hare-Mustin, R.T. & Marecek, J. (1988). The meaning of difference: Gender, theory, postmodernism, and psychology. *American Psychologist*, 43, 455-460.

Hartley, R.E. (1960). Children's concepts of male and female roles. *Merrill-Palmer Quarterly of Behaviour and Development*, 6, 83-91.

Hartley, R.E., & Hardesty, R.P. (1964). Children's perceptions of sex-roles in childhood. *Journal of Genetic Psychology*, 105, 83-91.

Heisenberg, W. (1952). Philosophic problems of nuclear science (F.C. Hayes, trans). New York: Pantheon.

Heilburn, A.B. (1968). Sex-role instrumental expressive behaviour and psychology in females. *Journal of Consulting and Clinical Psychology*, 41, 1106-1108.

Heilburn, A.B. (1976). Measurement of masculine and feminine sex-role identities of independent dimensions. *Journal of Consulting and Clinical Psychology,* 44, 183-190.

Heilburn, A.B. (1978). An exploration of antecedents and attributes of androgynous and undifferentiated sex-roles. *Journal of Genetic Psychology,* 32, 97-107.

Heilburn, A.B. (1981). *Human sex-role behaviour,* New York: Pergaman.

Heilburn, A.B., & Pitman, D. (1979). Testing some basic assumptions about psychological androgyny. *Journal of Genetic Psychology*, 135, 175-188.

Hertzberg, F. (1966). *Work and nature of man*. Cleveland: World Publishers.

Hill, C.A. (1987). Affiliation motivation: People who used people, but in different ways. *Journal of Personality and Social Psychology*, 52, 1008-1018.

Hinrichsen, J.J., Follansbee, D.J., & Ganellen, R. (1981). Sex-roles related differences in self concept and mental health. *Journal of Personality Assessment*, 45, 554-599.

Hoffman, L.R. (1965). Group problem solving. In L. Berkowitz (Ed.). *Advanced in experimental psychology* (Vol.2, pp.99-132). New York: Academic Press.

Hoffmann, L.W. (1977). Change in family roles, socialization and sex differences. *American Psychologist,* 32, 644-657.

Hoffman, M.L. (1977). Sex differences in empathy and related behaviours. *Psychological Bulletin,* 84, 712-722.

Horner, M.S. (1973). Toward an understanding of achievement-related conflict in women. *Journal of Social Issues,* 28(2), 157-173.

Hosek, J. (1976). Job involvement concepts and measurements. *Academy of Management Journal,* 19, 213-214.

Huston, A.C. (1983). Sex-typing. In P.H. Mussen (Ed.). *Handbook of Child Psychology* (4th ed. Vol. 4). New York: John Wiley.

Hyde, J.S. (1981). How large are cognitive-gender differences? *American Psychologist*, 36, 892-901.

Hyde, J.S. (1984). How large are gender differences in aggression? A developmental meta-analysis. *Developmental Psychology,* 20, 722-736.

Hyde, J.S. (1986). Gender difference in aggression. In J.S. Hyde & M.C. Linn (Eds.). *The Psychology of gender: Advances through metaanalysis* (pp.51-66). Baltimer, Maryland: John Hopkins University Press.

Hyde, J.S., Fennea, E. & Lamon, S.J. (1990). Gender differences in mathematics performance. *Psychological Bulletin*, 107, 139-155.

Hyde, J.S., Fennema, E, E, Ryan, M., Frost, L.A & Hopp, C. (1990). Gender comparisons on mathematics attitudes and affects. *Psychology of Women*,

Quarterly, 14, 299-324.

Hyde, J.S. & Linn, M.C. (1988). Gender differences in verbal ability: A meta-analysis. *Psychological Bulletin,* 104, 53-69.

Ickes, W., & Banes, R.D. (1978). Boys and girls together and alienated: An enacting stereotyped sex-roles in mixed sex-dyads. *Journal of Personality and Social Psychology*, 36, 669-683.

Jackson, D.N. (1967). *Personality Research Form Manual*. Goshen, New York: Research Psychologists Press.

Jahoda, M. (1958). *Current Concepts of Positive Mental Health.* New York: Basic Books.

Jahan, A. (1996). Sex differences in modes of frustration. *Journal of Community Guidance and Research,* 13(3), 227-234.

Jain, M. & Bansal, M. (1996). Sex differences in feeling of inferiority and insecurity among female delinquents. *Prachi Journal of Psychocultural Dimensions*, 14(1), 55-58.

Jain, V.K., Arora, O.P. (1995). Effects of school level variables on achievement gap bet boys and girls. *Indian Educational Review, Special number*, 26-51.

Jai Prakash, I. & Bhogle, S. (1994). Coping strategies: Factor structure, sex differences and relationship with psychological distress. *Journal of the Indian Academy of Applied Psychology*, 20(1), 31-38.

Jamison, W. & Signurella, M.L. (1980). Sex typing and spatial ability: The association between masculinity and success on Piaget's water level task. *Sex Roles*, 6(3), 345-352.

Jemmott, J.B., III & Locks, S.E. (1984). Psychological factors, immunologic mediation, and human susceptibility to infections diseases: How much do we know? *Psychological Bulletin,* 95, 78-108.

Jemmott, J.B., III & Magtoire, K. (1988). Academic stress, social support, and secretory immunoglobulin. *Journal of Personality and Social Psychology,* 55, 803-810.

Kagan, J. (1964). Acquisition and significance of sex-typing and sex-role identity. In M.L. Hoffman & L.W. Hoffman (Eds.). *Review of Child Development Research*, 1, New York: Wiley.

Kagan, J. & Lemkin, J. (1960). The child's differential conception of parental attributes. *The Journal of Abnormal and Social Psychology*, 61, 440-447.

Kahn, R., Wolfe, D.M., Quinn, R.P., & Snock, J.D. (1964). *Organizational Stress. Studies on Role Conflict and Ambiguity*, New York: Wiley.

Kakar, S. (1981). *The inner world: A psychoanalytic study of childhood and society in India.* Delhi: Oxford University Press.

Kanter, R.M. (1977). *Men and women of the corporation.* New York: Basic Books.

Kaplan, A.G. (1976). Androgyny as a model of mental health for women: From theory to therapy. In A.G. Kaplan & J.P. Beans (Eds.). *Beyond sex-role stereotypes: Readings towards a psychology of androgyny.* Boston: Little, Brown and Company.

Kaplan, A.G., & Bean, J.P. (Eds.). (1976). *Beyond sex-role stereotypes: Readings towards a psychology of androgyny.* Boston: Little, Brown.

Kelly, J.A., O'Brien, G.G., Hosford, R. (1981). Sex-roles and social skills considerations for interpersonal adjustment, *Psychology of Women Quarterly*, 5, 758-765.

Kelly, J.A., & Worell, J. (1977). New formulations of sex roles and androgyny: A critical review. *Journal of Consulting and Clinical Psychology*, 45, 1101-1115.

Kelly, R.M. (1983). Sex and becoming eminent as a political organizational leader. *Sex Roles,* 9, 1073-1090.

Kessler, R.G. (1979). Stress, social-status and psychological distress. *Journal of Health and Social Behaviour*, 20, 259-272.

Khanan, M. & Sen, A.K. (1996). The influence of creativity, sex, and type of school on creative self perception. *Social Science Institutional Interdisciplinary,* 14(1&2), 60-70.

King, L.A. & King, D.W. (1997). Sex-Role Egalitarian Scale. *Psychology and Women Quarterly*, 4, 71-97.

Kohleberg, L. (1966). A cognitive developmental analysis of children's sex-role concepts and attitudes. In E.E. Maccoby (Ed.). *The development of sex differences*, Standford, U.S.A.: Standford University Press.

Kohlberg, L. (1984). *The psychology of moral development: The nature and variety of moral stages.* New York: Harper & Row.

Koteswaraiah, G. & Rani, M.V.U (1996). Impact of gender and gender role orientation on expression of aggression. *The Creative Psychologist*, 7(1&2), 47-53.

Kuhn, T. (1962). *The structure in scientific revolutions.* Chicago, Illinous: University of Chicago Press.

La France, M., & Carmen, B. (1980). The nonverbal display of psychological androgyny. *Journal of Personality and Social Psychology*, 38, 36-49.

Langer, E.J. (1983). Playing the middle against both ends: The usefulness of adult cognitive activity as a model for cognitive activity in childhood and old age. In S.R. Yussen (Ed.). The development of reflection. New York: Academic Press.

Langer, T.S. (1962). A twenty two items screening score of psychiatric symptoms indicating impairment. *Journal of Health and Social Behaviour,* 3, 269-276.

Larson, R. (1978). Thirty years of research on the subjective well-being of other *Americans. Journal of Gerontology,* 33, 109-125.

Lazarus, R.S. (1966). *Psychological Stress and Coping Process*. New York: McGraw-Hill.

Lazarus, R.S., & Folkman, S. (1984). *Stress Appraisal and Coping.* New York: Springer.

Leaderer, W. J., & Jackson D. (1968). *The Mirages of Marriage*. New York: Norman.

Lever, J. (1978). Sex differences in the complexity of children's play and games. *American Sociological Review,* 43, 471-483.

Levy, J. (1975). Cerebral lateralization and spatial ability. *Behaviour Genetics*, 6, 171-183.

Lewinsohn, P.M., Hoberman, H.M., Ter, L., & Hautzinger, M. (1985). An integrative theory of depression. In S. Reiss & R. Bootzin (Eds.). *The Theoretical Issues on Behaviour Therapy.* (pp. 331-359). New York. Academic Press.

Lewis, M. & Brooken-Gunn, J. (1979). *Social cognition and the acquisition of self.* New York: Plenum.

Linn, M.C. & Peterson, A.C. (1985). Emergence and characteristics of sex difference in spatial ability: A meta-analysis. *Child Development*, 56, 1479-1498.

Linton, R. (1936). *The study of man*. New York: Appleton century.

Loevinger, J. (1976). *Ego development: Conception and theories*. San Francisco: Jossey Bass.

Maccoby, E.E. (1966). Sex differences in intellectual functioning. In E.E. Maccoby (Ed.). *The development of sex differences.* Standford, California: Standford University Press.

Maccoby, E.E., & Jacklin, C.N. (1974). *The psychology of sex-differences.* Standford: Standford University Press.

Macmillan, A.M. (1957). The health opinion survey technique for estimating prevalence of psychoneurotic and related types of disorder in communities. *Psychological Reports.* 3, 325-329.

Marecek, J. (1979). Social change, positive mental health and psychological androgyny. *Psychological of Women Quarterly*, 3, 241-247.

Martocchio, J.J. & O Leary, A.M. (1989). Sex differences in occupations stress. *Journal of Applied Psychology,* 74, 459-501.

Maslow., A.H. (1970). *Motivation and Personality.* (2nd Ed.), New York: Harper & Row.

Mathur, C.N. (1997). Psychosexual disorders before and after menstruation. *Journal of Community Guidance and Research*, 14(2), 189-196.

Mathur, M. (1994). Spontaneous act of high and low achievers. *Indian Educational Review,* 29(1&2), 69-93.

McAdams, D.P. & Constantian, C.A. (1983). Intimacy and affiliation motive in daily living: An experience sampling analysis. *Journal of Personality and Social Psychology*, 45, 851-861.

McClleland, D.C. (1975). *Power: The inner experience*, New York: Irvington.

Mckee, J.P., & Sheriffs, A.C. (1959). Men's and women's beliefs, ideals and self-concepts. *American Journal of Sociology*, 64, 356-363.

Mckennell, A.C., & Andrews, F.M. (1980). Models of cognition and affects in perceptions of well-being. *Social Indicators Research*, 8, 257-298.

Meichenbaum, D. (1977). *Cognitive behaviour modifications.* An integrated approach, New York: Plenum.

Michalos, A.C. (1987). *Final Progress Report on Global Report on Student Well-being: Application of Multiple Discrepancies Theory.* Guelph, Onterio: University of Guelph.

Minton, H.L., & Schneider, F.W. (1980). *Differential Psychology*: Belmon, California: Brooks & Cole.

Mischel, W. (1966). A social family view of sex differences in behaviour. In E.E. Maccaby (Ed.). *The Psychology of sex difference* (pp. 56-81). Stinfird, California, Stanford University Press.

Mischel, W. (1970). Sex-typing and socialization. In P.E. Mussen (Ed.). *Carmichael's Manual of Child Psychology,* 2, (3rd Ed). New York: Wiley.

Mishra, G., & Mishra, P.C. (1991). Mental health as a moderator variable of intrinsic job satisfaction and occupational stress. *Psychological Studies,* 36 (3), 198-202.

Mishra, R.C., Sinha, D. & Berry, J.W. (1996). *Ecology acculturation and psychological adaptation: A study of Adivasis in Bihar.* New Delhi: Sage.

Mohan, B. (1972). *Social psychiatry in India: A treatise on the mentally ill.* Calcutta: The Minierva.

Mohaṇ, V. & Tandan, S. (1997). A study of aptitude of socially deprived and handicapped adolescents. *Journal of Personality and Clinical Studies*, 13 (1&2), 63-70.

Moos, R.H. (1985). Creating healthy human contents. In J.C. Rosen and L.J. Soloman (Eds.). *Prevention in the Health Psychology.* (PP. 336-389) Hanover University press of New England.

Motowidlo, S.J. (1982). Sex-role orientation and behaviour in work setting. *Journal of Personality and Social Psychology*, 42, 935-945.

Munroe, R.L. & Munroe, R.H. (1975). *Cross-cultural human development*, California, USA: Brookes/ Cole.

Murdock, G.P. & Provost, C. (1973). Factors in the sex division of labour. *Ethnology*, 12, 208-225.

Mussen, P.H. (1962). Long term consequent of masculinity of interest in adolescence. *Journal of Personality and Social Psychology*, 26, 435-440.

Mussen, P.H. (1969). Early sex-role development. In D.A. Goslin (Ed). *Handbook of socialization theory and research*, Chicago: Rand, McNally.

Myers, D.G. (2000). The funds, friends and faith of happy people. *American Psychologist*, 55, 56-67.

Nagartnamma, H. (1999). Organizational employees and their mental health status. *Journal of Community Guidance and Research*, 16(2), 101-109.

Nagpal, R., & Sell, H. (1985). *Subjective well-being.* World Health Organization. Regional Office for South-east Asia: New Delhi.

Nash, S.C. (1979). Sex role as a moderation of intellectual functions. In M.A. Wittig & A.C. Peterson. In M.A.Wittig & A.C. Peterson (Eds.), *Sex-related difference in Cognitive Functioning,* (pp. 263-302). New York: Academic.

Nayayan, T.R., Lakshmi & Prabhakaran, P. (1993). A study on mental health of industrial employees. *The Creative Psychologist*, 5, (1&2), 47-52.

Neisser, U. (1976). *Cognition and reality.* San Francisco: Freeman.

Nickerson, E.T. (1977). *Learned Helplessness and Depression in Women or how to Keep a Woman from being Depressing.* Boston: Boston University, (ERIC Document Reproduction Service, no. Ed., 146507).

Nolen-Hoeksema, S. (1986). *Unpublished data*. University of Pennsylvania, Philadelphia, Pennsylvania, USA.

Nolen-Hoeksema, S. (1987). Sex differences in unipolar depression: Evidence and theory. *Psychological Bulletin*, 101, 259-282.

Ojha, S.K. (1995). Gender difference in manifest needs. *Journal of Psychological Researches*, 39(1&2).

Orlofsky, J.L. (1981). Relationships between sex-roles attributes and personality traits and behaviours and interests. *Journal of Personality and Social Psychology*, 40, 927-940.

Orlofsky, J.L., Ransedan, M.W. & Cohen, R.G. (1982). Development of the revised sex-role behaviour scale. *Journal of Personality and Social Psychology*, 46, 632-638.

Olds, L. (1981). *Fully human*. Englewood cliffs, NJ: Prentice-Hall.

Parson, T., & Bales, R.F. (1955). *Family Socialization and Interaction Process*. New York: Free Press.

Parson, T. & Bales, R.F. (1955). *Family socialisation and interaction process*. New York: Free Press.

Pattnaik, T. (1996). Decision making behaviour in form sector: A study. *The Indian Journal of Social Work*, 67(2), 236-244.

Pattnayak, B., Panda, M. & Mohanty, S. (1997). Impact of family structure and gender bias on role stress and coping styles: An empirical study. *Social Science International,* 13 (1&2), 42-50.

Percell, L.P., Berwick, P.T. & Beigel, A. (1974). The effect of assertive training on self-concepts and anxiety. *Achieves of General Psychiatry,* 31, 502-504.

Peterson, C. & Seligman, M.E.P. (1984). Causal explanations as a risk factor in depression: Theory and evidence. *Psychological Review,* 91, 347-374.

Pradhan, M. & Mishra, N. (1996). Gender differences in type A behaviour pattern: Born out relationship in medical professionals. *Psychological Studies*, 41 (1&2), 4-9.

Pradhan, N. & Panda, A.K. (1996). More Judgement in tribal secondary school children in relation to their sex. *Indian Journal of Psychology and Education*, 97(1), 21-25.

Rao, A.Y. (1970). A study of depression as prevalent in south India. *Transcultural Psychiatric Research Review,* 7, 166-167.

Ray, B.C. (1989). *Tribals of Orissa*. New Delhi: Gian Publishing House.

Richardson, F.C. & Suinn, R.M. (1972). The Mathematics-Anxiety Rating Scale: Psychometric data. *Journal of Counselling Psychology*, 19, 551-554.

Rohner, R.D. (1976). Sex differences in aggression. *Ethos*, 4, 57-72.

Rosenkrantz, P.S., Vogel, S.R., Bee, H. Broverman, I.K., & Broverman, D.M. (1968). Sex-role stereotypes and self-concepts in college students. *Journal of Consulting and Clinical Psychology*, 32, 287-295.

Rotter, J.B. (1966). Generalized expectancies for internal versus external control of reinforcement. *Psychological Monographs*. 80 : 1, Whole number 609.

Sahoo, F.M. (1990a). *Sahoo's Sex-Role Inventory* (SSRI), unpublished report, Psychology Department, Utkal University, Bhubaneswar, India.

Sahoo, F.M. (1990b). *Health Behaviour Questionnaire*. Unpublished report, Psychology Department, Utkal University, Bhubaneswar, India.

Sahoo, F.M. & Bidyadhar, S. (1992). The subjective components of psychological well-being: An idiographic investigation using the lens model: *Psychological Studies*, 37, 151-160.

Sahoo, F.M., & Dash, P. (1984). *An adaptation of Bem's sex-role Inventory*. Unpublished report, Utkal University, Bhubaneswar, India.

Sahoo, F.M. & Rout, J. (1990). Androgyny and work involvement. *Indian Journal of Community Guidance Service,* 7, No. 3.

Sahoo, F.M., Rout, J., & Rout, A.K. (1985). *Androgyny and psychological rigidity*. Psychological Studies, 30(2), 111-115.

Sarason, J.G. (1978). The test of anxiety scale; concept and research in C.D. Soiellegar, & I.G Sarason (Eds.). *Stress and Anxiety*, 5, Washington D.C: Hemingtone Publishing Corporation.

Sarason, I.G., Levine, H.M., Basham, R.B., & Sarason, B. (1983). Assessing social support: The social support questionnaire. *Journal of Personality and Social Psychology*, 44, 127-139.

Sarason, B.R., Sarason, G., Hacket, T.A., & Bauham, R.B. (1985). Concomitants of social support: Social skills, physical attractiveness, and gender. *Journal of Personality and Social Psychology*, 44, 127-139.

Schopler, J. & Bateson, N. (1965). The power of dependence. *Journal of Personality and Social Psychology*, 2, 247-254.

Schopler, J. (1967). An investigation of sex differences on the influence by dependence. *Sociometry*, 30, 50-63.

Schroth, M.L. (1985). The effect of defining measuring method on the relationship of motives. *Journal of Psychology*, 119, 213-218.

Sears, R.R. (1970). Relation of early socialization experiences to self-concept and gender role in middle childhood. *Child Development*, 41, 267-289.

Seligman, M.E.P. (1975). *Helplessness: On depression, Development and Death*. San Francisco: Freeman.

Shaw, J.S. (1982). Psychological androgyny and stressful life events. *Journal of Personality and Social Psychology*, 43, 145-153.

Siegel, R.C., Galassi, J.F. & Ware, W.B. (1985). A comparison of two model for predicting mathematics performance: Social learning versus meta-aptitude-anxiety. *Journal of Consulting Psychology*, 33, 531-538.

Signurella, M.L. Jamison, W., & Krupa, M.H (in press). Predicting spatial performance from gender stereotyping in activity preference and self-concept. *Developmental Psychology*.

Signurella, M.L. & Jamison, W. (1990). Masculinity femininity, androgyny, and cognitive performance. *Psychological Bulletin*, 100, 207-228.

Sinha. R. (1972). Internal versus external locus of control of reinforcement as related to sex and achievement values among high school students in India. *Journal of the Indian Academy of Applied Psychology*, 9, 1-8.

Sinha, V. & Prabhat, R.K. (1993). Relationship between ego strength and job satisfaction. *Indian Journal of Psychology and Education*, 24(2), 99-102.

Spense, J. (1979). Traits, roles and concepts of androgyny. In J. Gullanhorn (Ed). *Psychology and Women in Transition*, Washington, D.C.: V.H. Kinston.

Spence, J.T. (1983). Comment on Lubinski, Tellegan and Butcher's "Masculinity, Femininity and androgyny viewed and assessed as distinct concepts: *Journal of Personality and Social Psychology*, 44, 440-446.

Spence, J.T., & Helmreich, R.L. (1972). The Attitudes Towards Women Scale: An objective instrument to measure attitudes towards the rights and roles of women in contemporary society. ISAS: *Catalog of Selected Documents in Psychology*, 2, 667-668.

Spence, J.T., & Helmreich, R.L. (1978). *The Psychological Dimensions of Masculinity and Femininity: Their Correlates and Antecedents*. Austin: University of Texas Press.

Spence, J.T., & Helmreich, R.L. (1979). The many faces of androgyny: A reply to Locksley and Colten. *Journal of Personality and Social Psychology*, 37, 1032-1046.

Spence, J.T., Helmreich, R.L, & Stapp, J. (1974). The Personal Attributes Questionnaire. A measure of sex-role stereotypes and masculinity-femininity. JSAS : *Catalogue of Selected Documents in Psychology*, 4, 43-44.

Spence, J.T., Helmreich, R.V, Stappe, J. (1975). Ratings of self and peers on sex-role attributes and their relation to self-esteem and conceptions of masculinity and femininity. *Journal of Personality and Social Psychology*, 32, 29-39.

Srinivas, M.N. (1992). *Social change in modern India*. Delhi: Orient Longman.

Stage, E.K., Kreinberg, N., Eccles, J.R., & Becker, J.R. (1985). Increasing the participation and achievement of girls and women in mathematics, science and engineering. In S.S. Klein (Ed.) *Handbook for achieving sex equality through education* (pp.237-269). Baltimore: John Hopkins, University Press.

Stewart, A.J. & Chester, N.E. (1982). Sex differences in human motives, achievement. Affiliation, and power. In A.J. Stewart (Eds.). *Motivation and Society* (pp.172-218). San-Francisco: Jossey-Bass

Suzuki, A. (1991). Egalitarian sex role attitudes: Scale development and comparison of American and Japanese women. *Sex Roles*, 24, 245-259.

Tauvab, M. (1999). Perceptual defense as a function of sex difference and social class. *Indian Journal of Psychological Issues*, 7(1), 52-54.

Taylor, M.C. & Hall, J.A. (1982). Psychological androgyny : Theories, methods and conclusions. *Psychological Bulletin*, 92, 347-366.

Terman, L.M. & Miles, C.C. (1936). *Sex and Personality*. New York: McGrow Hill.

Thomas, S.J. (1986). Examining sex difference in the comprehension and preferences of moral issues. *Developmental Review*, 6, 165-180.

Thurstone, L.L., and Thurstone, T.G. (1941). Factorial Studies of Intelligence. *Psychometric Monographs,* 2.

Tobias, P.V. (1966). The peoples of Africa south of the Sahara. In P.J. Backer & J.S. Weiner (Eds.). *The biology of human adaptability*, (pp.111-200). Oxford: Clavendor.

Upamanyu,V.V. & Upamanyu, S. (1994). Depression in relation to sex role identity and hopelessness among male and female Indian adolescents. *Journal of Social Psychology,* 134(4), 551-552.

Ushasree, S., Shesu Reddy, B.V. & Vinolya, P. (1995). Gender role and age effects on factors job stress and job satisfaction, *Psychological Studies*, 40(2), 72-76.

Vandenberg, S.G., & Kuse, A.R. (1978). Mental rotations: A group test of three-dimensional spatial visualisation. *Perceptual and Motor Skills,* 47, 599-604.

Vroom, V. (1964). *Work and motivation,* New York: Wiley.

Walker, L.J. (1984). Sex difference in a development of moral reasoning. *Child Development*, 55, 677-691.

Warr, P., Barter, J., & Browbridge, G. (1983). On the independence of positive and negative effect. *Journal of Personality and Social Psychology*, 44, 644-651.

Webb, F.P. (1963). Sex-role preferences and adjustment in early adolescents. *Child Development*, 34, 609-618.

Weiner, B. (1972). *Theories of Motivation. From Mechanism to Cognition*. Chicago, Illinous: Rand McNally.

Wesley, F., & Wesley, C. (1977). *Sex-role psychology*. New York: Human Science Press.

Witkins, H.A. & Berry, J.W. (1975). Psychological differentiation in cross-cultural perspective. *Journal of Cross-Cultural Psychology*, 6, 4-87.

Whiting, B.B. & Edwards, C.P. (1973). A cross-cultural analysis of sex differences in the behaviour of children aged three through 11. *Journal of Social Psychology*, 91, 171-188.

Whiting, B.B. & Edwards, C.P. (1988). *Children of different worlds: The formation of social behaviour*. Cambridge, Massachusetts: Harvard University Press.

Whiting, B.B. & Whiting, J.W.M. (1975). *Children of Six Cultures: A psycho-cultural analysis*. Cambridge, Massachusetts: Harvard University Press.

Whitley, B.E. (Jr.) (1980). Sex-role orientation and mental health. An annotated research bibliography. J & As, *Catalogue of selected documents in Psychology,* 10, 90 (Ms. No. 2114).

Whitley, B.E. (1983). Sex-role orientation and self-esteem. A critical meta-analytic review. *Journal of Personality and Social Psychology*, 44, 765-785.

Williams, J.B & Spitzer, R.L. (1983). The issue of sex bias to DSM-III. American Psychologist, 38, 793-798.

Williams, J.E., Bennett, S.M., & Best, D.L. (1975). Awareness and expression of sex-stereotypes in young children. *Developmental Psychology*, 11, 635-642.

Williams, J.E., & Best, D.L. (1982). Measuring sex-stereotypes: *A Thirty Nation Study*. London : Sage Publication.

Williams, L.E., & Best, D.I. (1990). *Sex and psyche: Gender and self viewed cross-culturally*. London: Sage Publication.

Williams, J.E., & Roberson, J.K. (1967). A method of assessing racial attitudes in preschool children. *Educational and Psychological Measurement*, 27, 671-689.

Wilson, E.O. (1975). *Sociobiology: The new synthesis,* Cambridge: Harvard University Press.

Wong, M.M. & Csikszentmihalyi, M. (1991). Affiliation motivation and daily experiences: some issues on gender differences. *Journal of Personality and Social Psychology,* 62, 154-164.

Wood, W. (1987). Meta-analytic review of sex differences in group performance. *Psychological Bulletin*, 102, 53-71.

Yagar, G.G., & Bakar, S. (1979). *Thoughts on androgyny for the counselling Psychologist*. A paper presented at annual meeting of American Psychological Association, New York.

Index